NOBODY

NOBODY

Casualties of America's War
on the Vulnerable, from
Ferguson to Flint and Beyond

Marc Lamont Hill

ATRIA BOOKS

NEW YORK LONDON TORONTO SYDNEY NEW DELHI

ATRIA BOOKS

An Imprint of Simon & Schuster, Inc.
1230 Avenue of the Americas
New York, NY 10020

First Atria Books hardcover edition August 2016

ATRIA BOOKS and colophon are trademarks of Simon & Schuster, Inc.

For information about special discounts for bulk purchases, please contact Simon & Schuster Special Sales at 1-866-506-1949 or business@simonandschuster.com.

The Simon & Schuster Speakers Bureau can bring authors to your live event. For more information or to book an event, contact the Simon & Schuster Speakers Bureau at 1-866-248-3049 or visit our website at www.simonspeakers.com.

Interior design by Renato Stanisic

Manufactured in the United States of America

10 9 8 7 6 5 4 3 2 1

Library of Congress Cataloging-in-Publication Data is available.

ISBN 978-1-5011-2494-5
ISBN 978-1-5011-2497-6 (ebook)

For the two Mikes who changed my life:

Michael Eric Dyson—mentor, teacher, and dear friend—
who placed before me an open door;
and
Michael Brown, who died on August 9, 2014, so that
a new generation of Freedom Fighters could live.

Contents

Foreword

The ghost of Ralph Ellison hovers over this book. Ellison, of course, was the gifted twentieth-century writer, an African-American, author of *Invisible Man*. When that novel was released in 1952—and "released" is the right verb, considering the out-of-the-gates energy it possessed—it was described by one reviewer as a work of "poetic intensity and immense narrative drive." Intensity and drive it certainly had. But it is the book's central, contradictory image that, even sixty years later, lingers in the mind. Ellison's protagonist-narrator is, as the title tells us, both a man and invisible, there but not there, "of substance, of flesh and bone, fiber and liquids" who "might even be said to possess a mind" and who is yet invisible "simply," as he says, "because people refuse to see me."

Ellison died in 1994, having never again equaled the artistic or commercial success of his one undeniable masterpiece, and *Invisible Man* has been taught in high school English classes for decades, tamed now by time and history in a way that has dampened the book's original incandescent rage—explained away, sadly, as not so much a great book as a great *black* book, and, at that, a relic of a time when segregation and bigotry were still firmly embedded in the social order. What a disarming thing it is, then, to think of Ellison's image reappearing to us now in what we tend to think of as a more enlightened era, and that it does so in conjunction with the deaths of so many African-Americans, victims of both State and what you might call "vigilante" violence. The names of the dead form a list that recites, especially in the black communities that lost them, like a rosary: Michael Brown, Jordan Davis, Eric Garner, Sandra Bland, Walter Scott, Freddie Gray, Tamir Rice, Trayvon Martin.

These were not the caricature criminals whom middle-class white Americans had been taught to fear, not the late twentieth century's image of the "superpredator" hatched in academic corridors where studies predicted—incorrectly, as it turned out—a coming wave of rampant juvenile violence, and which was then picked up by politicians who formulated crime-prevention and incarceration policies as bulwarks against the coming tide. No, they were people whose "crimes"—jaywalking, playing loud music, failing to signal a lane change, making eye contact with a police officer, selling loosies, fleeing a traffic citation, holding a realistic-looking toy gun, being a stranger—were surreally dissonant with their fates; "ordinary" people, for lack of a better term, more representative than exceptional, who were struggling through lives of quiet desperation, and they all are now dead.

In most of these cases, we know how and where they were killed, and even by whom they were killed. Why, we even have video. Cell phones and dashboard cameras have given us this strange artifact, part criminal evidence, part memorial evocation. You can go onto YouTube right now and watch the unarmed, fifty-year-old Walter Scott be shot eight times in the back as he lumbers away from North Charleston police officer Michael Slager, and you can watch it for as long as there is a YouTube. You can eavesdrop on Sandra Bland's degrading encounter with Texas trooper Brian Encinia, see the moments right before Freddie Gray gets loaded into a paddy wagon for his fateful ride to the station house, or take in Eric Garner's desperate cry—"I can't breathe"—as he is pinned to the ground by a Staten Island cop, even as we know that those will be Garner's last words on this earth.

One feels guilty for watching these short, crudely rendered films, like gazing through a peephole onto some private pain, and yet we should be grateful to have seen them nonetheless. Not only do they serve as nearly incontrovertible evidence to be considered at trial but they raise our awareness of what has been going on long before the video camera became miniature, personal, and ubiquitous. This is the other side of the emerging "surveillance society": now that everything we do is being watched, we can actually watch the things we do, and see them for what they are. For surely it is not that the fates of Sandra Bland and Walter Scott and Eric Garner are unusual or even exclusive to our time. It is, instead, that the cell phone has become social science's microscope, permitting us to see daily life in atomistic detail, and as we do, old assumptions and standing narratives fall by the wayside. Watch, for instance, Officer Slager check Scott's pulse before apparently running to get his Taser and dropping it by the victim's dead body—the better, one presumes, to illustrate the falsehood that he had been forced to kill him in a fight over his weapon. Had Feidin Santana, a young Dominican barber, not been strolling by on his way to work and raised his cell phone to record the scene, we would be primed to accept such a story. (Scott, after all, isn't here to contradict the officer.) But just think, now, about how many generations of Michael Slagers we have believed and how many Walter Scotts we have buried in the cold mist provided by such fictions.

Marc Lamont Hill's take on all of this goes beyond the easy or predictable analysis. Too often in response to these events we have heard the chagrin that 150 years after the Civil War, fifty years after the Civil Rights Act, eight years after the election of our first black president, racism still motivates too much of what we do. Of course that is true. Who among us is naïve enough to believe otherwise? But to see these events as nothing more than the vestiges of a persistent racial antagonism is to misunderstand them. Doing so would only confirm a simplistic remedy, one heard repetitively in political rhetoric—even, one might add, in the rhetoric of that first black president—that argues that while the nation has made great progress in race relations, *we still have a lot of work to do*. Okay, but precisely what is that "work," and how will it differ from the "work" we have already done?

Hill sees another, more complicated, message, one that defies such trite sloganeering. It is that these recent, very public killings of African-Americans fit a picture that is not as racist as it is intolerant, not as uncaring as it is unseeing, not as malevolent as it is indifferent, and not as much a continuation of America's original sin as the product of regressive policies and attitudes nurtured in the post–civil rights era: indeed, in the last thirty years. In describing the path from Ferguson to Flint—an artificial definition that nonetheless forms a narrative arc, expertly articulating his vision—Hill shows us how a creeping sense of "otherness" has descended on American society, dividing those who are "somewhere" from those who are, to recall another expression of Ellison's, "nowhere." ("In Harlem," Ellison wrote, "the reply to the greeting 'How are you?' is very often 'Oh man, I'm *nowhere*'—a phrase revealing an attitude so common that it has been reduced to a gesture.") The latter, of course, are the "vulnerable" people of the book's subtitle. Most of them are black, but all of them have been cut off from the emerging American future, left behind because they are expendable, disposable, "invisible."

By Hill's definition, the helpless form an eclectic community that contains the chronically (and perhaps permanently) unemployed, the hopelessly addicted, the fatherless, the motherless, the imprisoned, the accused seeking justice, and the convicted seeking mercy. It includes victims and, ironically, even some victimizers, for in many of the cases cited here those who perpetrated violence were as damaged as those who fell prey to it. Both Freddie Gray and one of the Baltimore officers who arrested him shared a history of childhood lead poisoning, a fate that compromises mental development and can lead to a propensity for aggression.

We made this happen, all of us—sometimes overtly, more often not—and the mistakes were the work of both liberal and conservative, Republican and Democrat, black and white, racist and humanist. Hill shows us that the error was in public housing that tore apart communities; in harsh drug laws that demonized addicts and social misfits; in crime prevention policies that put away fathers for decades for nonviolent offenses and, in the process, wreaked havoc on families, perpetuating the damage into the next generation; in social welfare programs that increased dependency; in police forces that adopted the tools and the mind-set of occupying armies; in a gun culture that embraced firearms as a private right and violence as a first means of protection; in courts that replaced the pursuit of justice with the art of the deal, a system of plea bargaining that shows more interest in clearing the docket than in discovering the truth; and in economic policies that increasingly marginalized unskilled labor. In the plight of the citizens (both white and black) of Flint, Michigan, there is a metaphor for all of this; there, where no one paid attention to the mother who first raised a question about the brown poison gushing from her faucets and the fiery rashes that she discovered on her children's skin until it was too late. She, too, as it turned out, was "invisible."

At least some of the blame can be cast on the harsh rhythms of our public conversation. In the 1960s, Americans became keenly aware of the plight of the poor and the black. High court decisions addressed fundamental inequities. Political muscle reinforced the State's responsibility to provide a safety net. When that approach largely failed, it led to a backlash that essentially reversed the dynamic, diminishing the spirit for collectivity while accentuating, even glorifying, the role of the individual in determining his or her own fate.

While we are still riding the crest of that wave, it is clear that this approach has also been unsuccessful. Or, to put it more precisely, it has failed for all but a precious few people who are buffered by birth and accumulated wealth in what has been described as a return of the Gilded Age. Indeed, if you had to choose the two most dramatic social differences between today and fifty years ago, they would be the stark income disparities between the few and the many and the unprecedented numbers in our nation's prisons, and therein lies this tale. With the signs of a new populism emerging on the Right and the Left, the public consensus may be shifting again—but if so, to what? Hill shows us that there can be no solution that does not reassert the primacy of the public sphere, of a shared understanding that we all occupy this moment in time and that a society that neglects the least of its people neglects the notion of a society itself.

This is why the book's evocative title, *Nobody*, is so important. Like Ellison's "invisible man," it has echoes of a long-standing racial slur. For generations, the term "spook" rendered the black man an apparition, a "shadow" lurking dangerously in the darkness, a savage beast in hiding. At the same time it reinforced the opposite—the frightened, dancing fool of the minstrel show, "spooked" by his ignorance into believing in spirits and voodoo. Either way, the black man was "nobody"'—seen not for who he was but for who he was told he was: not a body, *no*body living *no*where. Today the same can be said of a whole class of people, growing in size, desperate in circumstances, living on the edge. They too have been caricatured and, as such, resigned to oblivion.

—TODD BREWSTER

Preface

This is a book about what it means to be Nobody in twenty-first-century America.

To be Nobody is to be vulnerable. In the most basic sense, all of us are vulnerable; to be human is to be susceptible to misfortune, violence, illness, and death. The role of government, however, is to offer forms of protection that enhance our lives and shield our bodies from foreseeable and preventable dangers. Unfortunately, for many citizens—particularly those marked as poor, Black, Brown, immigrant, queer, or trans—State power has only increased their vulnerability, making their lives more rather than less unsafe.

To be Nobody is to be subject to State violence. In recent years, thousands of Americans have died at the hands of law enforcement, a reality made even more shameful when we consider how many of these victims were young, poor, mentally ill, Black, or unarmed. The cases of Michael Brown in Ferguson, Missouri; Eric Garner in New York City; Kathryn Johnston in Atlanta; Trayvon Martin in Sanford, Florida; Freddie Gray in Baltimore; and Sandra Bland in Hempstead, Texas, have forced a stubborn nation to come to terms with the realities of police corruption, brutality, and deeply entrenched racism. While media coverage and global activism have turned these individuals into household names, they are not, sadly, exceptional. Instead, they represent the countless Americans who die daily, and unnecessarily, at the hands of those who are paid to protect and serve them.

To be Nobody is to also confront systemic forms of State violence. Long before he was standing in front of the barrel of Darren Wilson's gun, Michael Brown was the victim of broken schools and evaporated labor markets. Prior to being choked to death by Daniel Pantaleo, Eric Garner lived in a community terrorized by policing practices that transform neighborhoods into occupied territories and citizens into enemy combatants. Sandra Bland's tragic death sequence did not begin with a negligent jailer or an unreasonable cop but with a criminal justice system that has consistently neglected the emotional, physical, and psychological well-being of Black women and girls. For the vulnerable, it is the violence of the ordinary, the terrorism of the quotidian, the injustice of the everyday, that produces the most profound and intractable social misery.

To be Nobody is to be abandoned by the State. For decades now, we have witnessed a radical transformation in the role and function of government in America. An obsession with free-market logic and culture has led the political class to craft policies that promote private interests over the public good. As a result, our schools, our criminal justice system, our military, our police departments, our public policy, and virtually every other entity engineered to protect life and enhance prosperity have been at least partially relocated to the private sector. At the same time, the private sector has kept its natural commitment to maximizing profits rather than investing in people. This arrangement has left the nation's vulnerable wedged between the Scylla of negligent government and the

Charybdis of corporate greed, trapped in a historically unprecedented state of precarity.

To be Nobody is to be considered disposable. In New Orleans, we saw the natural disaster of Hurricane Katrina followed by a grossly unnatural government response, one that killed thousands of vulnerable citizens and consigned many more to refugee status. In Flint, Michigan, we are witnessing this young century's most profound illustration of civic evil, an entire city collectively punished with lead-poisoned water for the crime of being poor, Black, and politically disempowered. Every day, the nation's homeless, mentally ill, drug addicted, and poor are pushed out of institutions of support and relocated to jails and prisons. These conditions reflect a prevailing belief that the vulnerable are unworthy of investment, protection, or even the most fundamental provisions of the social contract. As a result, they can be erased, abandoned, and even left to die.

Without question, Nobodyness is largely indebted to race, as White supremacy is foundational to the American democratic experiment. The belief that White lives are worth more than others—what Princeton University scholar Eddie Glaude calls the "value gap"—continues to color every aspect of our public and private lives.[1] This belief likewise compromises the lives of vulnerable White citizens, many of whom support political movements and policies that close ranks around Whiteness rather than ones that enhance their own social and economic interests.

While Nobodyness is strongly tethered to race, it cannot be divorced from other forms of social injustice. Instead, it must be understood through the lens of "intersectionality," the ways that multiple forms of oppression operate simultaneously against the vulnerable.[2] It would be impossible to examine the 2015 killing of Mya Hall by National Security Agency police without understanding how sexism and transphobia conspire with structural racism to endanger Black trans bodies. We cannot make sense of Sandra Bland's tragic death without recognizing the impact of gender and poverty in shaping the current carceral state. To understand the complexity of oppression, we must avoid simple solutions and singular answers.

Despite the centrality of race within American life, Nobodyness cannot be understood without an equally thorough analysis of class. Unlike other forms of difference, class creates the material conditions and relations through which racism, sexism, and other forms of oppression are produced, sustained, and lived. This does not mean that all forms of injustice are due to class antagonism, nor does it mean that all forms of domination can be automatically fixed through universal class struggle. Rather, it means that we cannot begin to address the various forms of oppression experienced by America's vulnerable without radically changing a system that defends class at all costs.

This book is my attempt to tell the stories of those marked as Nobody. Based on extensive research, as well as my time on the ground—in Ferguson, Baltimore, New York City, Atlanta, Hempstead, Flint, and Sanford—I want to show how the high-profile and controversial cases of State violence that we've witnessed over the past few years are but a symptom of a deeper American problem. Underneath each case is a more fundamental set of economic conditions, political arrangements, and power relations that transforms everyday citizens into casualties of an increasingly intense war on the vulnerable. It is my hope that this book offers an analysis that spotlights the humanity of these "Nobodies" and inspires principled action.

I.

Nobody

Forty years from now, we will still be talking about what happened in Ferguson. It will be mentioned in high school history textbooks. Hollywood studios will make movies about it, as they now make movies about Selma. Politicians will talk about "how far we have come since Ferguson" in the same way they talk today about how far we have come since Little Rock, Greensboro, or Birmingham.

Ferguson is that important.

But why?

After all, to some, Ferguson isn't as worthy as other markers on the historical timeline of social-justice struggle. And Ferguson's native son Michael Brown, whose tragic death in 2014 put the small Missouri town on the map, was certainly no traditional hero. He did not lead a march or give a stirring speech. He did not challenge racial apartheid by refusing to sit in the back of a bus, attempting to eat at a "Whites only" lunch counter, or breaking the color barrier in a major professional sport. He wrote no books, starred in no movies, occupied no endowed chair at a major university, and held no political office. He was no Jackie Robinson, no Rosa Parks, no

Bayard Rustin, no Fannie Lou Hamer, no Barack Obama. If he could see what has happened in reaction to his death, he would likely be stunned.

Brown was just eighteen years old on the morning of Saturday, August 9, 2014, when he decided to meet up with his friend Dorian Johnson—who would later become Witness 101 in the Department of Justice (DOJ) federal investigation report—and together they settled on a mission to get high. Johnson, who was twenty-two, had not known Brown very long but, being older, considered himself as somewhat of a role model to the teen. Although he was unemployed, Johnson worked whenever he could find available jobs, paid his rent on time, and consistently supported his girlfriend and their baby daughter.

Brown had just graduated, albeit with some difficulty, from Normandy High School, part of a 98 percent African-American school district where test scores are so low that it lost state accreditation in 2012.[1] In addition to low test scores, incidents of violence have become so common at Normandy that it is now considered one of the most dangerous schools in Missouri.[2] Conditions in the Normandy School District are so dire that it has become a talking point in the school-choice debate, with conservatives pointing to the schools' failures as evidence that privatized educational options are necessary.[3] Despite this troublesome academic environment, Brown, like many teenagers of color, had a positive and eclectic set of aspirations. He wanted to learn sound engineering, play college football, become a rap artist, and be a heating and cooling technician; he also wanted to "be famous."[4, 5] All of this was part of the conversation between Brown and Johnson that morning.

In need of cigarillos to empty out for rolling paper for their marijuana blunts, Brown and Johnson entered Ferguson Market and Liquor, a popular convenience store at 9101 West Florissant Avenue. As video footage shows, Brown swiped the cigarillos from the counter without paying. The store's owner, an immigrant from India[6] who did not speak English, came around to challenge him. Brown, whose nickname "Big Mike"[7] derived from his six-foot-four-inch and nearly three-hundred-pound frame, gave a final shove[8] to the shopkeeper before departing. While the surveillance camera captured the entire interaction, it did not show how badly the incident shocked Johnson. He had never seen Brown commit a crime, nor had Brown given him any reason to think he would. "Hey, I don't do stuff like that," he said to Brown as they walked home, knowing that the shopkeeper had promised to call the police. Quickly, Johnson's feelings shifted from shock and anxiety about being caught on camera to genuine concern for Brown. He turned to him and asked, "What's going on?"[9]

While interesting, all of this was mere overture to the main event that tragically awaited Brown and Johnson, one that would make both of them unlikely entries in the history books. Brown and Johnson were in the middle of residential Canfield Drive a few minutes later when twenty-eight-year-old police officer Darren Wilson saw the two jaywalking "along the double yellow line."[10] According to Johnson, Wilson told them to "get the fuck on the sidewalk," though Wilson denies using profanity.[11, 12] Regardless of the tone of their initial exchange, the interaction created room for Wilson to link Johnson and Brown to the robbery report and suspect description that had been given over the police radio. The next forty-five seconds—disputed, dissected, and debated ad nauseam throughout the ensuing months—would soon became the focus of international attention.

But how could such a random encounter, in the largely unknown St. Louis suburb of Ferguson, possibly mean so much?

Until the killing of Michael Brown, this city of twenty thousand people spread across six square miles was unknown to just about anyone outside of St. Louis. One of ninety incorporated municipalities that surround St. Louis,[13] located a few minutes from the famous Gateway Arch, Ferguson was established in 1855 as Ferguson Station, a train depot named for William B. Ferguson, the farmer who deeded the land to the North Missouri Railroad. Michael McDonald—the White baritone soul singer famous for his time performing with Steely Dan and the Doobie Brothers, as well as his albums paying tribute to the "Motown sound"—is from Ferguson;[14] so was the aviation pioneer Jimmy Doolittle, who received the Medal of Honor for the Doolittle Raid on Tokyo in 1942. In the late 1940s, while he was a member of the St. Louis Cardinals, baseball slugger Enos "Country" Slaughter lived in Ferguson as well. Slaughter is famous for scoring the winning run against the Boston Red Sox in Game 7 of the 1946 World Series, a "mad dash" from first to home that is still remembered fondly by old-timers in the town. He was also among the most vocal of the hundreds of racial catcallers who greeted Jackie Robinson from the opposing dugout when Robinson became the first African-American to play Major League baseball a year later. Robinson himself recalled in his autobiography that Slaughter purposely cleated him while running through first base, an incident which, ironically, unified Robinson's Brooklyn Dodgers in defiance.[15]

Ferguson was, for all intents and purposes, an exclusively White city in those days, as it had been since its establishment. Its demographic profile was well guarded by both custom and law. When municipally drawn racial zoning was made illegal in 1917 with the Supreme Court's decision in *Buchanan v. Warley*, the court invalidated ordinances like the one that designated certain areas of St. Louis as

"Negro Blocks" and forbade Blacks from housing elsewhere.[16] But privately drafted "restrictive racial covenants"—contractual obligations between two private parties requiring that a piece of real estate be sold only to White buyers in perpetuity[17]—still ensured that suburban neighborhoods like Ferguson and others around St. Louis remained exclusively White.[18]

In St. Louis—once described by civic leader Elwood Street as "northern in industrial development, but largely southern in its inter-racial attitude"[19]—racial covenants were used as a defense against the Great Migration that brought African-Americans north after World War I. While Blacks make up nearly 50 percent of St. Louis's population today, only 6 percent of St. Louis's population was Black in 1900.[20] But with the growth of manufacturing opportunities in the industrial north, as well as the continuing deterioration of conditions in the old Confederacy—the decline of the cotton industry due to boll weevil infestation, the harsh realities of Jim Crow, and the arrival of a new, second-era Ku Klux Klan, with all its attendant terrorism and lynchings—thousands of southern Blacks took the journey up the Mississippi River each year, resulting in the movement of roughly six million people from 1910 to 1970. Henry Louis Gates Jr. accurately called this odyssey "the largest movement of Black bodies since slavery."[21]

The transition was an uneasy one. In 1917, the same year that the Supreme Court found civil-government-instituted segregation illegal, the city of East St. Louis—just across the Mississippi River—erupted in one of the worst race riots in American history. Marauding gangs of White workers, angry that Blacks had been recruited to take their jobs and inspired by unfounded fears that Black migrants had brought smallpox and other diseases from the South, burned down whole blocks of the city's Black neighborhoods, killing at least forty people, though likely many more.[22, 23] Some police and National Guardsmen were complicit in the violence. More riots followed in the "Red Summer" of 1919, when Whites were once again the aggressors in Washington, DC, Charleston, South Carolina, and dozens of other American cities. Particularly deadly riots consumed Chicago that year, sparked by the killing of a Black sunbather who was stoned to death after crossing an invisible racial line and venturing into a "Whites only" area on Lake Michigan.[24]

Yet even after the violence subsided, what Blacks found in cities like St. Louis was merely a more subtle version of the structural and interpersonal racism to which they had been subjected in the South. While Black men did not have to tip their hats in deference to White men on the street or use separate public facilities, as was tradition in the South, Blacks arriving in northern cities were nonetheless greeted as a Du Boisian "problem" that needed to be contained, lest disease, vice, and even "Bolshevism" overtake the heartland. To White traditionalists, much was at stake. It was one thing for White Northerners to have fought for an end to slavery and speak glowingly about the principle of equality, so long as they could do it from afar. But when Blacks came north to live with them, to enter into their neighborhoods, their churches, their schools, their workplaces—what Black intellectual Harold Cruse called the "sacred spaces" of life—a line had been crossed that brought the Negro too close.

Real estate agents participated in the defense of their homogeneous neighborhoods. Protection from the encroaching tide of African-Americans was trumpeted in the same way as one might argue for protection from fire or burglary. To promote the 1916 segregation ordinance, for instance, one realty association produced pamphlets showing pictures of blighted areas of the city over captions declaring "An entire block ruined by Negro invasion" and pleading with people to "Save your home! Vote for segregation!"[25] Even when that ordinance was declared illegal, agents followed an unwritten edict: sell homes in White neighborhoods to Black buyers and you will lose your license.

Things got more complicated in 1948, with a case involving the sale of a house roughly eight miles from Ferguson in which the Supreme Court took down restrictive racial covenants as well. The justices' decision did not bar such private agreements per se, but said that courts could not uphold such contractual provisions, since it would involve the State acting in a discriminatory manner barred by the equal protection clause of the Fourteenth Amendment. To the surprise of almost no one, the high court's determination coincided with the sentiments that brought about "White flight," or the movement of White families (and necessary resources) out of the cities and into the suburbs. This trend largely animated the decline of urban America in the second half of the twentieth century. Over the next twenty years, nearly 60 percent of the White population of St. Louis left the city.[26]

To minimize the chance that Blacks would follow Whites there, many of these suburban communities adopted strict zoning regulations. While they did not overtly exclude Blacks, these rules eliminated the kinds of environments—such as multifamily housing or industrial districts with factory jobs—that Blacks would need and desire. Ferguson, as one of these first ring suburbs, used zoning to block Black access, creating dead-end streets where roads would naturally have met the incorporated Black town of Kinloch and even barricading through streets to prevent their use for passage. But since its establishment predated the mid-century migration of Whites out of the central cities, Ferguson did not have zoning laws prohibiting apartment buildings or factories.[27] As a result, places like the Canfield

Green apartments, where Michael Brown and Dorian Johnson lived, and factories like the now demolished seven-thousand-square-foot Emerson Electric Company plant on West Florissant Avenue provided the types of housing and employment opportunities that drew Black people to the city.[28]

Named for John Wesley Emerson, the Civil War commander for the Union Army and Missouri Circuit Court judge who helped found it, Emerson Electric Company was a major defense contractor and the largest producer of airplane gun turrets for the American effort in World War II. Like many American firms, it has since become much more diversified, focusing now on the manufacture of equipment for monitoring industrial processes and components for HVAC systems.[29] To do so, Emerson has taken advantage of the labor markets of the low-wage, low-regulation Far East, where most of its manufacturing is now done. The Ferguson factory first outsourced labor overseas in the late 1970s and began shutting down operations in the 1980s.[30] All that remains locally is the Emerson corporate headquarters, situated within minutes of where Michael Brown was killed. There, as much of the town lives in suburbanized poverty, Emerson's CEO, David Farr, guides the company while pulling in annual compensation worth as much as twenty-five million dollars.[31]

THERE WAS, AND IS, no disagreement as to the result of Darren Wilson's confrontation with Michael Brown. After a brief struggle at Wilson's car,[32] Brown fled the scene and was pursued by the officer in a chase that ended with the unarmed Brown struck dead by bullets fired from Wilson's Sig Sauer S&W .40-caliber semiautomatic pistol. What remains, however, is the dispute about whether the shooting was criminal. Both the St. Louis County grand jury, which

met for twenty-five days over a three-month period and heard a
total of sixty witnesses,[33] as well as a separate investigation done by
the USDOJ that investigated potential civil-rights violations, determined that there was no cause to indict Wilson for his actions. The
seven men and five women who made up that grand jury—three
Black and nine White, chosen to reflect the racial makeup of St.
Louis county, though not the overwhelmingly Black population of
Ferguson itself—and the FBI investigators working on the federal
study concluded that Brown had not been shot in the back, as some
had initially said. Assertions that Brown had put his hands in the air
and said "Don't shoot" in the moments before he was killed—an
image so disturbing, it became a rallying cry for protesters determined to see that Wilson was indicted—were also not supported
by witnesses who watched the encounter. Those conclusions, when
matched with Wilson's testimony that he feared for his life in the
confrontation with Brown and with Missouri's broad latitude for
police use of deadly force,[34] left little legal room to justify an indictment. But the law does not tell the full story.

The law is but a mere social construction, an artifact of our social,
economic, political, and cultural conditions. The law represents only
one kind of truth, often an unsatisfying truth, and ultimately not the
truest of truths. The rush of public emotion that spilled into the streets
after the killing of Michael Brown alerted the world to the existence
of a multitude of other, competing truths. Whatever the facts may
have shown in this instance—including the forensic evidence and
the parade of witnesses who recanted earlier statements—Michael
Brown's life was taken with disturbingly casual ease. This indifference
unmoored racial and class antagonisms long held in awkward restraint.

There was not only Brown's shooting to consider; there was
also the aftermath. There was Brown's body, left for hours on the

hot pavement, his crimson blood puddling next to his young head, staining the street, flowing in a crisscross pattern, a tributary running slowly to the gutter. Eventually, an officer produced a bedsheet and placed it over Brown's frame, a figure so large that the cover could not shield it all, the oversized teenager's legs left peeking out from the bottom. Though it was early August, a wintry stillness set in over the next four hours, as police officers stood stone-faced and crowds of passers-by gazed in astonishment. While this was happening, Michael Brown remained on the street, discarded like animal entrails behind a butcher shop. As Keisha, a local resident who I interviewed a week after the shooting, said to me, "They just left him there . . . Like he ain't belong to nobody."

Nobody.

No parents who loved him. No community that cared for him. No medical establishment morally compelled to save him. No State duty-bound to invest in him, before or after his death. Michael Brown was treated as if he was not entitled to the most basic elements of democratic citizenship, not to mention human decency. He was treated as if he was not a person, much less an American. He was disposable.

Despite the heated claims by many observers, Michael Brown was not "innocent," as either a moral or legal designation. To the contrary, it is virtually indisputable that Brown made bad choices, both in the convenience store and in his subsequent interactions with Darren Wilson. But the deeper issue is that one should not need to be innocent to avoid execution (particularly through extrajudicial means) by the State. After all, theft, even strong-arm theft, is not a capital offense in the United States.

It is also not clear that Wilson was acting with racist intentions—but, like debates about Mike Brown's "innocence," this is beyond the point. Even if Wilson operated with the best of conscious intentions, he was nonetheless following the logic of the current moment, one marked by what Princeton race scholar Imani Perry calls "post-intentional racism."[35] Perry argues that contemporary understandings of racism cannot be reduced to intentional acts of bigotry, beliefs in biological determinism, or even subconscious prejudices. Instead, we must rely on a thicker analysis, one that accounts for the structural, psychological, and cultural dimensions of racism. With regard to Darren Wilson, even if he held no personal racial animus, he nonetheless approached Michael Brown carrying a particular set of assumptions about the world. Like everyone else's, Wilson's assumptions included socially constructed narratives about Black men, Ferguson residents, and even what constituted a lethal threat.[36] Beyond the level of the personal, Wilson also obediently and uncritically followed the protocol of a system already engineered to target, exploit, and criminalize the poor, the Black, the Brown, the queer, the trans, the immigrant, and the young.

For many of the thousands who erupted in protest after Michael Brown's death, and again after the grand jury's subsequent decision not to indict Darren Wilson, the motivating factor for their anger was not shock.[37] To the contrary, the incident between Brown and Wilson was animated by a set of beliefs and conditions that were all too familiar: the assumptions that all people of color are violent criminals from birth; that petty crimes are the neon arrow pointing to someone already involved in, or destined to commit, more serious crimes; that there is money to be made in overpolicing minor offenses; and that poverty, race, and gender nonconformity are identifiers of moral failings so rich that there is no longer any reason to recognize the rights, the citizenship, or the humanity of those so identified.

This attitude—most visible in the conduct of law enforcement, but pervasive throughout the halls of power—is not a phenomenon limited to Ferguson or even St. Louis. In response to the grand jury's decision not to indict Darren Wilson, crowds of protesters appeared in Oakland, Los Angeles, Dallas, Denver, Washington, Minneapolis, Chicago, Atlanta, and New York to stand in solidarity. They wanted not only to see justice prevail in this particular instance but also to assert the deeper symbolic importance of the story. They wanted to express its clear resonance, to speak to their own sense of familiarity with the circumstances that in an instant left an unarmed eighteen-year-old Black boy holding a pack of stolen cigarillos dead in the street. "Enough," read placards raised by marchers in Atlanta. "We are all one bullet away from being a hashtag."[38]

The teenager and the police officer had become like characters in a national morality play with so many rich ironies and plot twists, so many double meanings in the language of its participants, that it was hard not to feel that we were witnessing the playing out of a civic parable. "As he is coming towards me, I . . . keep telling him to get on the ground," the sandy-haired Wilson told the grand jury, using phrases that made him sound like he was a game hunter confronting a wildebeest:

"He doesn't. I shoot a series of shots. I don't know how many I shot, I just know I shot it."

"It." Not "him," not "Brown," not "the teenager," not even "the perp." Wilson told the grand jury that he had shot "It."[39]

"I know I missed a couple, I don't know how many, but I know I hit him at least once because I saw his body kind of jerk."[40]

The aim was not mere incapacitation; it was execution.

"At this point I start backpedaling and again, I tell him get on the ground, get on the ground, he doesn't. I shoot another round of shots . . ."

An invader who had burst through the neighborhood barriers.

"It looked like he was almost bulking up to run through the shots, like it was making him mad that I'm shooting at him."

A Magical Negro with superhuman powers.

"And the face that he had was looking straight through me, like I wasn't even there, I wasn't even anything in his way."

In Wilson's account, it is the Magical Negro who dehumanizes the courageous officer. Ironically, this process humanizes the officer and dehumanizes the Magical Negro to the jury and the broader public.

"And then when [the bullet] went into him, the demeanor on his face went blank, the aggression was gone . . . the threat was stopped."

Nobody.

THERE ARE FEW MOMENTS in American history that can match the shimmering optimism of the 1950s. There was not only the sense of triumph that came with the winning of World War II and the revving of the engine of American prosperity; there was also the growing belief that all problems, even social problems, could be solved through an earnest application of American ingenuity. This was not the first time that technological determinism held the nation in its grip. Indeed, throughout American history, a kind of fetish for technology, joined to visions of the Utopian future that it would provide, had harmonized well with the traditional American trumpet flare for the "free" market. St. Louis was the setting for one of the most celebrated such displays of American confidence when it hosted the Louisiana Purchase Exposition of 1904, known to many as the St. Louis World's Fair, with its 1,240 acres of walkways and buildings[41] containing exhibits heralding the accomplishments of the "advanced" (read: White) peoples of the world.

Just to emphasize that this kind of prospect was only possible in White capitalist America, the fair featured anthropological displays of native peoples in their natural environments. When arrayed together, this "Congress of Races," as the fair's organizers called it,[42] demonstrated that "the white man can do more and better than the yellow, the yellow man more and better than the red or black."[43] The story of "human progress," the fair's literature continued, could be reduced to the passage from "the dark prime to the highest enlightenment, from savagery to civic organization, from egoism to altruism."[44]

By 1939, with the opening of another World's Fair—the New York World's Fair—much of that overt racial hubris had faded, but not the investment in science as an agent of social transformation. In what is now Flushing Meadows Corona Park, in Queens, the 1939 World's Fair was laid out on 62 miles of roads, inside 200 buildings, featuring the work of 1,354 exhibitors[45] from 58 nations and 33 states.[46] The future as seen in Queens in 1939 was the product of an emerging American religion, urban renewal, derived from a gospel written by strict modernists like Charles-Édouard Jeanneret-Gris, the Swiss-French architect who was more popularly known as Le Corbusier. "Revise the shelter and one improves the people," he had said, with an attitude that in its purest form can now be understood as equal parts optimistic and fascistic. In his time, though, the architect was revered by the academy, and while Le Corbusier's designs resulted in only a handful of actual buildings, he was hugely influential. Less-celebrated architects, sociologists, and postwar city planners happily followed Le Corbusier's lead as they endeavored to build postwar America.[47]

It can be challenging today to understand the passion with which a past generation embraced housing alone as a solution to urban blight, but this is precisely what happened. During the middle part of the twentieth century, interlocking highways were erected and gleaming suburban enclaves brought forth the city dweller with a few dollars to spend. At the same time, however, after the passage of the Housing Act of 1949, African-American neighborhoods were gutted en masse. In their place, monuments of glass and steel were built that were intended to house and reform the poor.

Among those who established the postwar plan for St. Louis, there were several impulses. White flight from the inner city had become so great that there was concern that downtown was losing its residential character. "We cannot have a city without people," wrote distinguished urban designer Harland Bartholomew in St. Louis's Comprehensive City Plan of 1947.[48] Yet Bartholomew's warning for St. Louis coincided with the country's need to accommodate the new automobile culture, even though those very automobiles tended to bring people both into the city and out of the city to its burgeoning suburbs. A 1948 study raised the issue of the unsightliness of the city's slums—not so much out of concern for those who lived in them as for those who had to witness this blight on their daily commutes and on visits to downtown attractions.[49] "[P]eople going and coming from work . . . are offended by the state of decay they witness on all sides."[50] The resulting plan for St. Louis was much as it was for New York City in the Robert Moses years: bulldoze the slums to make room for highways and then build gleaming new high-rise communities for those who were displaced by the construction. Like the model city at the 1939 World's Fair's Futurama exhibit, these were plans that favored the automobile and those who could afford it. "The city is doomed," Henry Ford once said. "The future of the city is to leave the city."[51]

Mill Creek Valley, a Black neighborhood that was once home to Scott Joplin and Josephine Baker, fell victim to the St. Louis Land Clearance for Redevelopment Authority.[52] White slums were cleared along with Black slums, and new public housing developments were designed with an intent to maintain segregation. Bartholomew was not shy about admitting this. Public housing, he acknowledged, would keep Blacks from venturing outside acceptable areas and "reduce their migration [to] other portions of the city that would not welcome them."[53] The St. Louis Housing Authority even operated two separate relocation offices, one for Whites, the other for Blacks. Still, under any circumstance, those being displaced by the dream of a new St. Louis—one modeled on a Utopian metropolis like those exhibited at the World's Fair—got little help. A federal audit of those moved out of Mill Creek Valley, for instance, found that more than half received no assistance at all and ended up in housing worse than that from which they had been "removed."[54]

Those who did make it to the new projects were likely to find themselves caught in the grip of a Le Corbusian nightmare. The most famous of the developments was Pruitt-Igoe, a multistructure complex containing 2,870 housing units on 56 acres that was commissioned in 1950 and completed in 1955. Built on the remains of the African-American neighborhood of DeSoto-Carr, which had once been home to 3,200 families, it was designed to house Black residents in the Pruitt homes—named for Wendell O. Pruitt, an African-American pilot who was one of the famed Tuskegee Airmen who fought in World War II—while White residents would live in the Igoe buildings, named for William L. Igoe, a White St. Louis politician.[55] Designed by Minoru Yamasaki, who would go on to crown his career with the design for the World Trade Center in New York, Pruitt-Igoe was part of Mayor Joseph Darst's attempt to erase St. Louis's "hick town" reputation by luring the nation's finest architectural and engineering minds to redesign his city.[56]

Yamasaki himself preferred low-density, low-rise residential planning. "If I had no economic or social limitations," he later wrote, "I'd solve all my problems with one-story buildings."[57] But, of course, he did have such limitations. The social ones were born of a deep-seated community prejudice that dictated that public housing should be sited downtown—certainly nowhere near the prosperous suburbs—and at high density, so as to leave the commercial core of the city intact. His economic limitations came from the federal government's lukewarm support. Many politicians, particularly Republican politicians, regarded public housing as a "socialist" idea,[58] and so they saddled the legislation with strict construction-cost guidelines and a policy that dictated that the buildings be maintained on rent monies alone. The latter regulation was based upon the professed immorality of "giveaways," with the "stench of Russian communism" attached to public housing then being felt so intensely that for a period of time tenants were even required to pledge their loyalty to America as a precondition of residency, lest the largess being granted them become the first step toward their being recruited into a communist cell.[59] Yet, ironically, all along subsidies in the form of Federal Housing Administration (FHA) loans—"giveaways" of a different sort—were assisting White homeowners as they moved to the suburbs, to sites from which Blacks were by definition excluded.[60] The agency even forbade loans to female-headed households[61] and pledged to avoid loan practices that might force together "inharmonious racial or nationality groups."[62]

Yamasaki's solution to the restraints that he faced was to build thirty-three eleven-story buildings at Pruitt-Igoe, packing thousands of lives onto a relatively modest parcel of urban real estate. To retain the feeling of "neighborhood" that the high-rise design sacrificed, Yamasaki then stole an idea from Le Corbusier's sketchbook: skip-stop elevators. The elevators at Pruitt-Igoe were designed to stop only on every third floor, where they would open upon a common space filled with sunlight, a room where children could play and families could gather. From there, residents would walk to their individual apartments by stairways, mimicking the feeling of a street-block neighborhood. It was all part of what Le Corbusier had once called his "White World," an architecture of clean lines and precise angles, of meticulous measurements and distinctive materials—"culture standing alone," as one critic dismissively described it—dictating not only how a building was to be constructed but how its inhabitants were to live within it. To Le Corbusier, the "White World" stood in contrast to the "Brown World" of "muddle, clutter, and compromise, the architecture of inattentive experience,"[63] where life unfolded at its own pace and according to its own terms.

Pruitt-Igoe opened in 1954 and was immediately hailed by architecture critics and urban planners as a demonstration of how design could drive social change. But their dreams of a shining new St. Louis, formed from a carefully rendered blueprint, quickly fell victim to some harsh realities. The Supreme Court ended racial segregation in public housing, opening up Igoe as well as Pruitt to Black families. Ultimately, this decision was immaterial, as few White residents had applied to live there anyway. With the slums cleared, even the poorer Whites had left the city, meaning that urban renewal in St. Louis had become essentially a "Negro Removal" operation, as some residents cynically called it, or, better yet, a "Negro Containment" operation.

To the surprise of Yamasaki and others, the skip-stop elevators did not create the feeling of a neighborhood. Instead, their isolation created pockets of shelter for thieves and violent criminals; residents described the feeling of moving from the elevators through the common areas to their apartments as like running a gantlet. Children preferred vacant lots to the "playgrounds" the planners had prescribed for them, especially since budget cuts had forced the architect to dramatically reduce the number of playgrounds. Finally, the construction-cost restrictions imposed upon Yamasaki by government policies meant that the architect had to choose the cheapest of materials, which naturally did not hold up very well. Doorknobs came off on first use; locks were quickly broken and windows shattered. Pipes froze and burst. Because occupancy levels were less than capacity,[64] the rent monies were not sufficient to fix these or other problems. When administrators, in response, tried to raise the rents, residents went on a rent strike, prompting a sympathetic Congress to pass the Brooke Amendment, which capped rent in public housing units at 25 percent of household income.[65] Noble as that may have seemed, it doomed most projects to permanent disrepair. At Pruitt-Igoe, light bulbs regularly went unreplaced, creating further hazardous conditions. With increased vacancy came even more crime, the pervasive mood of abandonment providing license to those who would operate in the shadows.

Recent scholarship attributes Pruitt-Igoe's failure to social and economic factors more than the architecture itself. That's probably right, but for a place described by one housing official as "a cancer within a cancer,"[66] there is plenty of blame to go around. From the distance of our day it appears as though public housing never had a chance, for the tragic flaw here was in the conception: an initiative born not out of compassion but out of a penitentiary mentality that sought to hide the city's struggling peoples, to punish them for getting in the way of progress, and to equate their poverty with little more than degeneracy.

In the process, authorities razed tight-knit slum communities that, while poor and confined to substandard housing, had still retained the kind of social cohesion that engenders dignity of space. They then replaced these neighborhoods with a high-minded social engineering project that was both untested and unrealistic. When this failed, they blamed the residents themselves, ignoring the fact that the deck had been stacked against them. Not only was there an official unwillingness to properly build and manage the public housing projects, but punitive rules like the one limiting public assistance to households absent an able-bodied male further undermined any chance for social cohesion. By all records, the dominant family unit at Pruitt-Igoe was one with a single mother on welfare. Yet was it? Former residents describe fathers and boyfriends hiding in closets to avoid detection when officials came to patrol the hallways in search of men whom they could evict.[67]

By 1970, St. Louis had closed more than half of the Pruitt-Igoe apartments. Before long, the entire community was emptied. The project was considered to be such a mistake, such an embarrassment, such a towering failure of urban planning, that it earned the nickname "the Monster." Then, on March 16, 1972, the first of the buildings was destroyed, in a magnificent scene of implosion as dramatic as anything Allied bombers visited upon Berlin. The destruction was over by July. In 1951, consumed with their enthusiasm for a new, rationally designed city, for a perfect urban society that would answer all social problems, planners had leveled the run-down African-American neighborhood of DeSoto-Carr. Roughly thirty years later, they leveled their new experiment too, and returned the land back to nature. Today, the site that once held Pruitt-Igoe is an urban forest, a dense thicket of greens and browns interrupted by the occasional non-natural relic, a decayed piece of what was once an asphalt curb or a broken streetlight rising incongruously from the trees,[68] shards proclaiming to anyone who knows the story that "the future once happened here."

And where did the people who lived at Pruitt-Igoe and in other projects go?

They moved to Ferguson.

. . . .

IN A MOCKERY OF the city's longstanding efforts to maintain segregation, St. Louis's inner ring of suburbs, once nearly exclusively
White, became home to thousands of poor and middle-class Blacks.
One reason for the shift was economic: there were simply too few
opportunities for employment in St. Louis. Another was the opportunity for better housing; as Whites moved out to shinier, newer
developments, housing in the older suburbs opened up. But while
the Black population in Ferguson had grown from just 1 percent
in 1970 to roughly 25 percent in 1990, the 2010 census revealed an
even more dramatic shift to 67 percent Black. Over the course of
forty years, Ferguson had become a majority-Black city, indicative
of a trend that extended beyond St. Louis. Amazing as it may seem,
there are now more poor people and more African-American people
living in American suburbs than in American cities.[69]

The problem in Ferguson, of course, was that the administration
of the city did not change with these demographic shifts. While the
city itself was becoming largely African-American, most positions of
authority—including the mayoralty, most of the city council, and all
but three police officers in a fifty-three-officer department—were held
by Whites.[70] But much more important than that, as the second part
of the DOJ investigation of the killing of Michael Brown revealed, the
social distance between those in positions of authority—particularly
the police, but others as well—and those who actually lived in Ferguson was now vast. As the city became African-American, the Ferguson Police Department (FPD) shifted from being the protector of the
people of Ferguson to their user and abuser.

How else to explain the DOJ's finding that Ferguson officers
"routinely conduct[ed] stops that [had] little relation to public safety

and a questionable basis in law," often issuing multiple citations for the same violation, and all in the interest of increasing revenue to the department?[71] How else to understand that in the FPD budgets, "fines and fees" accounted for nearly one quarter of the department's operating revenue ($3.09 million in 2015), and that it urged officers in performance reviews to help achieve this number, as if they were a sales team needing to make their fourth-quarter projection? What else are we to make of the fact that at the time of the DOJ investigation, more than sixteen thousand people—this out of a population of twenty thousand—had some form of outstanding arrest warrant, nearly all of them relating to a missed payment or court appearance on a traffic fine or a (usually minor) municipal code violation?[72] As a report in the *Washington Post* revealed, it was not unusual for towns in St. Louis County to cite residents for loud music, unkempt property, disruptive behavior, and even "saggy pants."[73] These penalties reflect a long history of public-nuisance laws being used in ways that further marginalize the vulnerable, and reinforce the idea that poverty, mental illness, and even Blackness are threats to the public good.[74]

In the course of their study, the DOJ investigators also discovered repeated instances of Ferguson police issuing arrest warrants without probable cause, in direct violation of the Fourth Amendment, and of police being unaware, in general, of the constitutional restrictions on their conduct. Confronted, for instance, about one situation in which Ferguson officials arrested a man without a warrant (and, as it turned out, on false conclusions), the officers explained away objections by asserting that the detainee was held in an "air-conditioned" environment. They also told investigators that the disproportionate arrest of African-Americans in Ferguson was indicative of the lack of "personal responsibility" among members of the Black race.

Finally, the DOJ investigation report, released only days before the commemoration of the fiftieth anniversary of the Selma voting rights march known as "Bloody Sunday," found despicable racial stereotypes in e-mails routinely sent within the department, including e-mails comparing President Obama to a chimpanzee and mocking Black citizens' use of language. Others repeated age-old stereotypes of Black people as lazy, ignorant, and "on the take." These Ferguson officials were merely reenacting the quintessentially American ritual of humiliating and dehumanizing Black bodies while at the same time exploiting them for economic gain.

A few months after the DOJ report was issued, another study of Ferguson[75] conducted by a Missouri state commission appointed by Governor Jay Nixon, issued a call for reforms, including an expansion of Medicare eligibility, an increase in the minimum wage, a reform of zoning laws, and a new scrutiny of police incidents requiring the use of force. "We know that talking about race makes a lot of people uncomfortable," asserted the authors of the report. "But make no mistake: This is about race."[76]

Yes, except that the story of Ferguson, Missouri—the epic tale that prompts us to keep talking about it—is not only about race. It is not only about the death of a Black teenager at the hands of a White policeman in a department that routinely abused and exploited the city's majority African-American population, not only about the virtual exoneration of Darren Wilson for acting in a manner that, if not criminal, was certainly reckless and avoidably deadly.

Despite the widespread outrage about the grand jury's failure to indict Darren Wilson, the deeper meanings of Ferguson have become more apparent in the aftermath of the non-indictment. If an indictment had been made, a trial convened, and perhaps even a conviction secured, the story of Ferguson would have been reduced to the story of a single act of injustice in a single place at a single time. Such an analysis would only have given comfort to those who would like see the error here as Wilson's (or even Brown's) alone, rather than a signpost of a much deeper and more intractable set of problems.

Michael Brown died at the hands of police in Ferguson, but his killing was preceded by the death of seventeen-year-old Trayvon Martin—armed only with a hoodie, an Arizona Iced Tea, and a bag of Skittles—who was shot dead not as a victim of the police, but of the vigilante George Zimmerman, who was then exonerated in a trial that played out in minute detail on CNN; and by the death of Jordan Davis, who was killed neither by the police nor a vigilante but by Michael Dunn, a White software developer who became irritated by the sound of "thug music" coming from Davis's car.

Michael Brown's death was succeeded by Cleveland, Ohio, police officer Timothy Loehmann's killing of twelve-year-old Tamir Rice in a playground when Rice's toy gun was mistaken for the real thing;[77] by the killing of Samuel DuBose after University of Cincinnati police officer Ray Tensing stopped DuBose for driving a car without a front license plate and then, when DuBose appeared to be getting ready to drive away, shot him in the head;[78, 79] by the killing of Walter Scott after North Charleston, South Carolina, police officer Michael Slager stopped him for a broken taillight. Scott was unarmed and sprinting from the scene when Slager shot him eight times in the back.[80, 81]

Michael Brown's death came after the death of Eric Garner, suffocated by New York City policeman Daniel Pantaleo as he arrested Garner for selling loose cigarettes; and before that of Sandra Bland, who allegedly hung herself in a jail cell after she had been arrested for refusing to cooperate with an aggressive Waller County, Texas, officer who had stopped her for changing lanes without signaling.[82] Finally, it came before the death of Freddie Gray from injuries suffered in a Baltimore police van while Gray was in custody for possession of a legal knife. It was this last death—suspicious as it was tragic—that led to weeks of rebellion in Baltimore. These incidents were not extraordinary circumstances, but representations of a chilling pattern of deadly encounters between Black bodies and State power.

Back in 2009, in the heady days of enthusiasm that accompanied the election of a Black man, Barack Obama, to the presidency, the nation was riveted by the "teachable moment" offered when a Cambridge, Massachusetts, police sergeant arrested Henry Louis Gates Jr., the eminent Harvard African-American studies professor, in front of his home. Gates had been dealing with a faulty door key when a passerby, mistaking the scene as a break-in, called the police. Gates verbally challenged Sergeant James Crowley for investigating the scene—the citation refers to "loud and tumultuous behavior"—and in turn, Crowley arrested Gates for disorderly conduct. Amid the ensuing public outcry, President Obama intervened, resulting in what became known as the "Beer Summit," with Crowley, Obama, and Gates engaging in "guy talk and trouser hitching"—Darryl Pinckney's wonderful image in the New York Review of Books[83]—over a few cold-and-frosties at the White House.

The unfortunate and dishonest conclusion of that incident—the first landmark episode of the Obama presidency—was a kind of twenty-first-century retort to Rodney King's 1994 plea for peace: "Yes, we can all get along." Maybe now, with a Black man in the White House, the American Empire was finally prepared to enter its much-desired post-racial era, in which race would no longer be a central organizing feature of our social world. As wrongheaded as the idea was then, it seems downright absurd today. In light of Ferguson, the Beer Summit is quite easily exposed for what it was:

a gross trivialization of the racial, cultural, and economic divides that continue to starkly define American life well into the twenty-first century.

Given that it occurred in an upper-middle-class town known for its conspicuously liberal allegiances, and with a protagonist in the form of the very distinguished and respected Gates, one could see how so many were deluded into thinking that the confrontation was all one big, unfortunate misunderstanding. Such an analysis, however, would be nothing short of delusional. The "presumption of guilt," as Harvard law professor Charles Ogletree described it,[84] that characterized Crowley's initial attitude toward Gates was no mere accident. Rather, it has always been the governing logic for White officers engaging Black men and women in America. As the ensuing years have demonstrated so vividly, the Gates-Crowley incident was only the most polite demonstration of this logic.

Indeed, thanks to the Beer Summit, the implicit understanding reached about this event was not that Black America should not be made to suffer such unfortunate and degrading indignities, but that Henry Louis Gates Jr.—prosperous, educated, friend of the president, a commingler with White society—should not be made to suffer such unfortunate and degrading indignities. And precisely why should he not? Because Gates was, in fact, "one of us" who had tragically been mistaken for "one of them."

It is this same dynamic that informed then-senator Joe Biden's 2007 comments about fellow presidential candidate Barack Obama when he said that Obama was the "first mainstream African-American who is articulate and bright and clean and a nice-looking guy."[85] In each case, the inference is that Black men who fit in deserve respect—but what about those who do not? What about Black Americans who do not look like Henry Louis Gates Jr., who do not have his pedigree, his eloquence, his stature, his paycheck, who do not fit the White mainstream's conception of "bright," "clean," or "nice-looking"? What about those who look like Michael Brown or Freddie Gray, Renisha McBride or CeCe McDonald, Sandra Bland or Jordan Davis? What about the single mothers, the welfare recipients like those who a generation ago lived at Pruitt-Igoe? Do they deserve fairness too, or is fairness the privilege of the well-turned-out, the conformist, the employed, the happy, the "accepted"?

It is worth contemplating how "Gates and Crowley" and "Brown and Wilson" form the same basic narrative: a Black person doing something ordinary is subjected to heightened scrutiny for a suspected criminal act. Police confront the Black suspect, who responds with verbal hostility, whereupon that hostility becomes, for the arresting officer, the very confirmation of criminal behavior. This confirmation of criminality then becomes the justification for the use of force. Gates was doing something ordinary as he fiddled with his key; Brown and his friend, the dreadlocked Dorian Johnson, were doing something ordinary as they jaywalked in their own neighborhood. Brown, like Gates, reacted to the police officer's questioning with "lip." In Gates's case, the result was an embarrassing arrest that turned into a national incident. The Brown episode, as with many other incidents involving America's vulnerable, ended with his death.

That Brown's story also contained a petty crime—the stealing of the cigarillos—and a physical tussle may cloud the picture for some. This was likely the reason that the Ferguson Police Department released video footage of Brown's store theft during the same press conference in which they were forced to release Darren Wilson's name to the public. Their hope was that the public, including the Black community, would not invest its support in Brown if he was marked as a criminal. But, in fact, Brown's story highlights how respectability politics around who deserves public support and protection within the Black community, as well as the expansion of the market-driven punishment state, creates an environment where constitutional affordances like due process and protection from cruel and unusual punishment are reflexively denied to those considered part of the "criminal class."[86] Brown's story is a testament to how race and class, as well as other factors like gender, sexuality, citizenship, and ability status, conspire to create a dual set of realities in twenty-first-century America. For the powerful, justice is a right; for the powerless, justice is an illusion.

This is why the discourse of race is at once indispensable and insufficient when telling the story of Ferguson and other sites of State-sanctioned violence against Black bodies. Michael Brown, Tamir Rice, Jordan Davis, and Trayvon Martin were not killed simply because they were Black, although it is entirely reasonable to presume that they would still be alive if they were White. They were killed because they belong to a disposable class for which one of the strongest correlates is being Black. While it is hard to imagine that Brown would be dead if he were White, his death was only made more certain because he was young, male, urban, poor, and subject to the kinds of legal and social definitions that devalue life and compromise justice. His physical presence on Canfield Drive was due not only to his own personal experiences and choices but also a deeply rooted set of policy decisions, institutional arrangements, and power dynamics that made Ferguson, and Canfield, spaces of civic vulnerability. There is no formal poll tax to march against anymore, no segregation of the lunch counter.[87] But the kind of injustice that the story of Ferguson illuminates is just as insidious as the targets of earlier battles of the freedom struggle.

This is why the death of Michael Brown is not merely a throw-
back to a wounded racial past but also a thoroughly modern event.
It is not only the repeat of an age-old racial divide but also a statement of a relatively new public chasm that has been growing for
years. This divide is characterized by the demonization and privatization of public services, including schools, the military, prisons,
and even policing; by the growing use of prison as our primary
resolution for social contradictions; by the degradation and even
debasement of the public sphere and all those who would seek to
democratically occupy it; by an almost complete abandonment of
the welfare state; by a nearly religious reverence for marketized
solutions to public problems; by the growth of a consumer culture that repeatedly emphasizes the satisfaction of the self over
the needs of the community; by the corruption of democracy by
money and by monied interests, what Henry Giroux refers to as
"totalitarianism with elections";[88] by the mockery of a judicial process already tipped in favor of the powerful; by the militarization
of the police; by the acceptance of massive global inequality; by
the erasure of those unconnected to the Internet-driven modern
economy; by the loss of faith in the very notion of community; and
by the shrinking presence of the radical voices, values, and vision
necessary to resist this dark neoliberal moment.[89]

The stories of Ferguson, Baltimore, Flint, and countless other
sites of gross injustice remind us of what it means to be largely
erased from the social contract. They expose life on the underside
of American democracy, where countless citizens are rendered disposable through economic arrangements, public policy, and social
practice. They spotlight the nagging presence of the exploited, the
erased, the vulnerable, the dehumanized—those who are imagined,
treated, and made to feel like Nobody.

II.

Broken

Those who knew Eric Garner describe him as a "gentle giant." Like Michael Brown, the forty-three-year-old Garner was tall—six feet three inches—and very heavy. Over the years, he had added a few inches to his girth and now weighed 350 pounds.[1] Around the basketball courts at the Coney Island housing project where he grew up, Garner's nickname was "Big E."[2] Most of Garner's childhood friends went the way of so many youths raised in post-industrial American housing projects during the 1980s: pushed out of formal labor markets, they sold or used crack cocaine until they either were incarcerated or died in some random encounter. Garner, however, managed to survive those trying times. He even found work, holding a seasonal job as a horticulturist, planting trees with the New York City Parks Department. More recently, however, Garner's asthma, diabetes, and sleep apnea made it impossible for him to work a traditional job. Garner's health got so bad that he couldn't walk to the corner without being left completely breathless.

For money, the father of six occasionally sold loose cigarettes on the streets of Staten Island, where he lived. Cigarette taxes differ wildly from state to state, so much so that a pack that costs roughly six dollars in Virginia costs thirteen dollars in New York. As a result, smugglers buy cases of cigarettes from low-tax states and sell them on the black market in high tax-states like New York. Many New York City bodega owners engage in this practice, hiding the smuggled, untaxed packs in drawers behind their cash registers. The same is done by street vendors, who sell not only whole packs but also loose cigarettes, or "loosies"—one for seventy-five cents, two for a dollar. The loosie market is so popular in New York that more than half of the cigarettes purchased in the city have been smuggled from out of state.[3]

Staten Island's Bay Street was one place where these vendors regularly peddled their merchandise. There, at the corner of Bay and Victory Boulevard—near a park, a welfare office, and the docking station for the Staten Island Ferry—Garner and a handful of other men, almost all of them Black or Latino, worked the streets. The nearby shop owners occasionally complained about them, but the vendors had long ago become something of a fixture at this corner. Garner had been a welcomed presence there for years, a regular who played checkers with others on the curb and served as an unofficial peacekeeper, breaking up fights that would spill onto the streets from area bars.

In the spring of 2014, things changed when the loosie business on Bay Street was called to the attention of Chief of Department Philip Banks III, New York City's top uniformed police officer.[4] In addition to the illegal sale of cigarettes, reports were now coming in that drug sales and other crimes were on the rise in the neighborhood. Banks, following the logic of the day, decided to address these and other "quality of life" issues that he believed tended to make areas of bad crime worse when overlooked. Soon, police from the 120th Precinct were regularly on Bay Street, making arrests. Garner himself had already been cited several times when, on July 17 of that year, officers Justin Damico and Daniel Pantaleo approached him, ready to make another arrest. The policemen, both White, engaged Garner in conversation for two full minutes.[5] As the confrontation began to escalate, Ramsey Orta, one of Garner's friends,[6] pulled out his cell phone to record the scene.

On Orta's video, a clearly exasperated Garner is seen shouting at Damico and Pantaleo, professing his innocence and telling them to go away.[7] "I'm minding my business, Officer," Garner says to Damico, "please leave me alone." Damico persists. "Every time you see me you want to arrest me," a frustrated Garner continues. "I'm tired of it. It stops today." Damico is facing Garner when Pantaleo, dressed in plainclothes, moves in from behind and puts Garner in a choke hold. Garner is thrown to the ground by Damico, Pantaleo, and three other police officers who join the encounter. With his head pinned to the concrete sidewalk, Garner says to them, "I can't breathe."

"I can't breathe. I can't breathe. I can't breathe. I can't breathe. I can't breathe. I can't breathe. I can't breathe. I can't breathe. I can't breathe. I can't breathe. I can't breathe."

Eleven times.

Eric Garner would utter these desperate words eleven times before falling unconscious.[8] Minutes later, at Richmond University Medical Center, he was pronounced dead.

Unlike the details of the Michael Brown killing, which remain hotly debated, the story of Eric Garner carries with it a sense of unambiguous certainty. On the subject of the Garner killing, even those who reflexively defend the police and doubt claims of excessive use of force are compelled to wrestle with the realities of State violence. This is almost entirely due to the presence of Orta's camera phone, which placed the actions of the New York City

Police Department (NYPD) in full public view. The video from Orta's phone appeared for days on TV news outlets and went viral throughout the social media world.

Many found it hard to imagine what possessed two police officers—presumably trained to understand the difference between a felony and a misdemeanor, between a dangerous crime and a purely annoying one—to take down a fragile, unhealthy, unarmed man. Yes, Garner was *verbally* resisting arrest, but he clearly appeared to pose no physical threat to the five officers on the scene. And yet there it all was, not only the violent encounter but also the terrible, almost poetic plea that summed up so much of the relationship between America and its most vulnerable citizens: "*I can't breathe.*" And then, like a dog being put down, Garner expires before our very eyes. "Hands Up, Don't Shoot" might have been fiction in the most narrow and literal of terms, but "I Can't Breathe" was real on every level. In unedited video, the world saw a Black body perishing from injuries inflicted on him by police.

Days later, the official autopsy confirmed what the video appeared to show: Eric Garner died from "compression of neck (choke hold), compression of chest and prone positioning during physical restraint by police."[9] This report also served as a rejoinder to critics like Congressman Peter King, who attempted to blame Garner's death on his preexisting health problems.[10] To be sure, Garner's bronchial asthma, obesity, and heart disease were contributing factors. But as medical evidence and common sense both confirm, Garner died from the clear, direct, and violent actions of the New York City Police Department. The violent action, in this case, was a choke hold, a maneuver with an awkward and painful history within the NYPD, particularly since the dawn of the crack era.[11] Despite its relatively recent surge in use, the choke hold is as old as policing itself, and it has long been used with impunity on Black bodies.

In 1983, a case before the Supreme Court famously highlighted the challenge of redressing State violence against Black citizens in general and choke holds in particular.[12] The case involved Adolph Lyons, a Black man who was stopped by the Los Angeles Police Department (LAPD) for a broken taillight. After pulling his car over, Lyons was met by officers holding revolvers aimed directly at him. He was ordered to lean on his car, spread his legs, and put his hands on his head. When he complained that the key ring he was holding in his hand was giving him pain, the policemen put him in a choke hold, "Either the 'bar arm control' hold," wrote Justice Byron White in the court's opinion, "or the 'carotid-artery control' hold or both, rendering [Lyons] unconscious and causing damage to his larynx." Lyons recovered consciousness while face down on the ground, spitting up blood. He had urinated and defecated in his pants. After the violent encounter, the officer gave Lyons a simple citation and released him.

Lyons sued the LAPD for damages and injunctive relief, the latter meaning that he not only wanted to be compensated for his suffering but also wanted action taken against the LAPD to end its policy of using choke holds. The practice of applying choke holds on citizens, as Lyons pointed out, was not only excessive but discriminatory. From 1975 to 1983, the maneuver had resulted in the deaths of sixteen people in Los Angeles; twelve of those sixteen were African-American.[13] In the end, the court found it fit for Lyons to pursue damages but, on a 5–4 vote, refused to consider his claim for injunctive relief. The court reasoned that Lyons had standing to sue only for the injuries he had already suffered, not prospective injuries to himself or others due to a particular policy of the LAPD.

Supreme Court justices under the Burger Court, 1969–1986—
in contrast to the preceding Warren Court, which expanded civil
liberties, judicial power, and federal authority—had returned to a
belief that courts should not interfere with issues best handled by
local governmental institutions.[14] This shift only intensified the crisis
of injustice in addressing local police violence. If Blacks could only
use the courts to redress what was specifically done to them and not
to change the policies that enabled the damage to happen, then the
power of the federal judicial system, as Justice Thurgood Marshall
observed in his *Lyons* dissent, becomes "limited to levying a toll for
such a systematic constitutional violation."[15] Marshall reminded the
court of the words of then–Chief Justice Warren Burger, who had
argued in an earlier case for the importance of federal oversight to
ensure proportionality in police procedure. Burger suggested that
a "shoot to kill" order "might conceivably be tolerable to prevent
the escape of a convicted killer but surely not a car thief, a pick-
pocket, or a shoplifter"[16] and that if a jurisdiction did not recognize
such distinctions, we would all justifiably feel "wrath and outrage."
In light of the court's decision in *Lyons*, Marshall then added, "we
now learn that wrath and outrage cannot be translated into an order
to cease the unconstitutional practice, but only an award of damages . . . if the police adopt a policy of 'shoot to kill' . . . the federal
courts will be powerless to enjoin its continuation."[17]

If nothing else, Lyons's suit brought the use of choke holds to
the attention of the general public and, under pressure, many police
departments began limiting their usage. In 1985, the NYPD established a policy of discouraging choke holds unless officers felt their
lives were threatened and it was the "least dangerous alternative
method of restraint." In 1993, the department banned choke holds
even in such limited circumstances. As a practical matter, however,

these policy changes did not stop officers from using them. A year after the prohibition was put into place, twenty-nine-year-old Anthony Ramon Baez was tossing a football with his brothers in the Mount Hope section of the Bronx when the ball twice escaped them and landed on a police officer's car.[18] There was a confrontation, and a scuffle broke out among Baez and several officers. It was later charged that one of the officers, Francis X. Livoti, put Baez in a choke hold, asphyxiating him to death.

The incident became an instant controversy. Baez's family cried foul, and Livoti, who had a history of violent confrontations,[19] was charged with criminally negligent homicide. At the subsequent trial, there were accusations that the police officers who had been at the scene were adjusting their stories to close ranks around one of their own. Evidence from the Livoti trial also offered a clear picture of how fellow officers exploited a rule allowing them to avoid talking to investigators for forty-eight hours after an incident, a tactic that would allow them to coordinate their versions of events. This claim was bolstered by New York State Supreme Court judge Gerald Sheindlin, who said he had witnessed "a nest of perjury"[20] in his court during the trial. Still, Sheindlin acquitted the officer, insisting that while Livoti had indeed put Baez in a choke hold, the State had not proven that injuries from it had directly led to Baez's death. And, as in the story of Eric Garner, there were suggestions that Baez's poor health—he, too, had asthma and was said to have suffered an attack at the moment he died—was the deciding factor. Without the luxury of cell-phone video to show the truth, the sequence of events remained in dispute. After the verdict was announced, Baez's mother, stunned by the judge's decision to let her son's killer go free, remained alone in the front row of the courtroom, her Bible held tightly in hand. She then walked outside and fainted.[21] Four years later, a federal court convicted Livoti of the lesser charge of violating Baez's civil rights. Livoti was subsequently sentenced to prison.

In Garner's case, a grand jury composed of six Whites and six non-Whites listened to testimony from the police officers involved in the incident as well as twenty-two civilian witnesses.[22] They heard from forensic pathologists and officials involved in the training of police officers, and—despite repeatedly watching the cell-phone video from Orta, as well as two others bystanders—determined that there were no grounds on which to indict Pantaleo. Just one week before, a Ferguson grand jury had decided not to indict Darren Wilson. A year after the incident that took Eric Garner's life, his body lay in an unmarked grave at Rosedale Cemetery in Linden, New Jersey, twelve miles from Staten Island. There, Garner's body rests in a field of greens and browns interrupted only by one tiny American flag marking the resting place of a Vietnam veteran in the plot next to Garner's.[23]

In an odd twist, the City of New York announced an agreement to pay Garner's family $5.9 million, forestalling civil litigation. "Mr. Garner's death is a touchstone in our city's history and in the history of the entire nation," said Comptroller Scott M. Stringer as he revealed the deal—an odd, yet telling, choice of words, considering that a "touchstone" is a standard against which to judge other similar experiences. In essence, the city was willing to admit *responsibility* for Eric Garner's death without admitting *liability*. "Financial compensation is certainly not everything, and it can't bring Mr. Garner back," Stringer continued. "But it is our way of creating balance and giving a family a certain closure."[24]

In fact, real "closure" still eluded those who cared about Garner and victims of other such cases. In the same month that Garner was killed, the office of the comptroller established a database called

ClaimStat.[25] Through the database, visitors can examine the city's history of lawsuits filed for damages. ClaimStat shows that New York City payouts for claims of personal injury are budgeted at roughly seven hundred million dollars a year, which amounts to roughly eighty dollars per city resident. This number, according to the report's executive summary, is more than the *combined* budgets for the Department for the Aging, the city council, and New York's three public library systems.[26]

IN 1982, JAMES Q. Wilson, a political scientist, and George L. Kelling, a criminologist, coauthored an article for the *Atlantic*. The piece, simply titled "Broken Windows," offered a critique of American law-enforcement strategy.[27] At the time, police working in high-crime areas tended to focus on bigger crimes and ignore minor ones like graffiti, panhandling, and small-scale drug deals. Wilson and Kelling argued that this approach was wrongheaded, as tolerance for small-scale crimes leads to an atmosphere that encourages, within the same space, larger crimes to be committed. The analogy they used was a building where a broken window is left unrepaired. In both poor and wealthy communities, they found, the site of one broken window will lead to more broken windows, because a window left unrepaired coveys a message that the people in the neighborhood do not care. It is, to use their phrase, "untended property" and once it is perceived that property is "untended," disrespect and disorder follows.

Wilson's and Kelling's theory was laid out in some detail in the *Atlantic* article, surrounded by an informal history of American law enforcement. They pointed out that when city neighborhoods were more stable—that is, when the population was less likely to move

on from generation to generation—crime waves had a self-correcting
solution: the core population that could not or would not move anywhere else simply "reclaimed their authority over the streets." The
police officer helped here, as Wilson and Kelling observed, by serving
as a kind of "night watchman" patrolling the area. This is the neighborhood cop, as portrayed in many American movies, who knows the
town drunk, the kids who like to smoke behind the school, and old
man Duffy who keeps an illegal pistol tucked under his bed. The cop
maintains order, but only at the fringes. Yes, he could arrest old man
Duffy, but he doesn't. He could run the kids in for vagrancy, but he
does so only when he sees them spraying graffiti on the schoolhouse
wall, and even then he doesn't actually arrest them. Instead, the parents get a call from the station house and the teens are taken home
for a spanking. Here, the implicit understanding between the police
officer and the community that hires him is that there are official rules
and rules established by the neighborhood. Regardless of what the law
says, the neighborhood rules are the only ones worth enforcing.

Maybe that means that "drunks and addicts could sit on the stoops,
but not lie down," wrote Wilson and Kelling. "People could drink on
the side streets, but not at the main intersection. Bottles had to appear
in paper bags. Talking to, bothering, or begging from people waiting
at the bus stop was strictly forbidden." And so on. The important thing
is not what the rules are, but that there *are* rules and that those rules are
enforced, because the moment that the rules go unenforced, neighborhood decline would be inevitable. The "unchecked panhandler,"
wrote Wilson and Kelling, "is, in effect, the first broken window."[28]

Essentially, Wilson and Kelling were arguing that perception is reality: communities that appear ordered usually are ordered, and communities that allow disrespect for their rules tend to become communities where all rules, no matter how major, are soon disrespected.

But in saying that *the people* set the rules, they were also advocating for community control over policing. At the time, it was more common for police officers to patrol in cars; indeed, there had been data suggesting that it was more efficient to police that way. But in so doing, Wilson and Kelling argued, the police had abandoned the critical function of the beat cop. For it is the beat cop who projects the feeling that law enforcement is community work, not some distant, faceless power forcing conformity onto ordinary life. Proper policing, they argued, should be shaped "by the standards of the neighborhood rather than by the rules of the state."

"Broken windows" (or "order maintenance policing," as it is sometimes called) took hold like few theories in the history of law enforcement. In fact, one would be hard pressed to name another academic concept that has so completely transformed any area of public policy in the last fifty years. Along with the dramatic increase in incarceration to which it is directly related, broken-windows policing is the most significant development in law enforcement of the last thirty years. Although the term is often associated with Mayor Rudolph Giuliani of New York City, broken windows was actually being implemented in the city's approach to law enforcement long before Giuliani's tenure began in 1994. Giuliani's predecessor, the much-maligned David Dinkins, hired Boston native William J. Bratton to take charge of the New York City Transit Police. (At that time, the transit police were separate from the NYPD. Today, the two have been combined). Bratton had made a name for himself as head of the Massachusetts Bay Transportation Authority police in the early 1980s. Inspired by Wilson and Kelling's article, he targeted the small "nuisance crimes" that had created an atmosphere of disorder on the "T," Boston's subway system.[29] In New York, he brought the same approach, issuing an almost immediate directive to eject panhandlers from the subways.[30] On this mission, he had an ally in David Gunn, head of the New York City Transit Authority. Gunn had arrived a few years before Bratton became head of the transit cops, beginning his tenure by attacking the graffiti "menace" that he believed made the subways look like the picture of anarchy.

One of Bratton's biggest challenges was the practice of farebeating. It was estimated that more than 170,000 fares were lost each day due to people who jumped the turnstiles or otherwise slipped onto the system without paying.[31] The practices of farebeating ranged from the mundane to the ingenious. Back then, the New York subway system used tokens as fare: a metal coin that you slipped into a slot, allowing one revolution of the turnstile. Fare beaters would jam the slot with paper just enough so that the token dropped from view but did not turn the turnstile. Then, after an unsuspecting person had put a token into the slot and "lost" it, the fare beaters would return, lean over, and use their mouths to suck the token out of the slot. Entire stations were crippled by this kind of operation. Once the turnstiles did not work, the only way that a passenger could enter the station was through a gate being manned by part of the fare-beating crew, who would then demand a token in return for holding the gate open.

Fare beating was a classic example of Wilson and Kelling's theory in that the more fare beaters one saw operating with impunity, the more it seemed as though no one cared. People who would never have thought of jumping a turnstile thought, "Why should I pay if so many others do not?" and from there it was just a matter of time before a handful of fare beaters became an onslaught. There were many bigger issues facing New York City at the time, and fare beating was, by comparison, such a low-level crime that police essentially left the fare beaters alone. But, convinced that this was one of those visible crimes that contributed to an overall sense of lawlessness, Bratton changed the department's approach. He had the cops arrest token thieves and turnstile jumpers in droves—so many that he had to have buses outfitted with fax machines, phones, and processing personnel brought to the subway stations to facilitate the number of arrests. Once there, they ran warrant checks and found that a healthy number of the fare beaters had outstanding warrants for other crimes.[32]

Bratton was so successful at arresting people at subway stations that he was named the head of the entire NYPD when Giuliani became mayor. As police commissioner, Bratton applied broken-windows policing as citywide law-enforcement strategy. He found New York to be a place "that had stopped caring about itself," as he later wrote. "There was a sense of a permissive society allowing certain things that would not have been permitted many years ago . . . the epitome of what Senator Daniel Moynihan had described as a process of 'defining social deviancy down'—explaining away bad behavior instead of correcting it."[33]

The most famous image of the disorder of the 1980s was the so-called "squeegee men," bands of panhandlers who would approach cars at stoplights while holding a window cleaning device soaked with dirty water. The men would then begin "cleaning" the windshield of the cars, expecting a handout for their "work." If the drivers didn't give them money, they would stop their work halfway through, leaving windows smeared with grime. Bratton had them arrested too.

As Bratton explained in a book he wrote years later, the NYPD that he inherited was operated, like most American law-enforcement institutions, in a reactive fashion. It existed to apprehend criminals, not to prevent crime from happening in the first place. The implicit understanding within the department was that "[c]rime . . . was caused by societal problems that were impervious to police intervention."[34] By contrast, Bratton believed that a constructive police presence made crime less likely, and, indeed, crime did go down on his watch and that of his successors, leading a long decline that has lasted well into the new century. There were roughly 1500 homicides in New York in 1982; there were 340 in 2015.[35, 36, 37] Perhaps the clearest sign that broken windows had become the new State orthodoxy came in December 2013, when New York City's freshly elected mayor, the progressive Bill de Blasio, announced that under his administration, the NYPD would be led by none other than William J. Bratton.[38]

The case for broken-windows policing is compelling because it is lightly dipped in truth. Yet while there is a correlation between disorder (social and physical) and crime, research shows that this relationship is not causal. Simply put, there is no evidence that disorder directly promotes crime.[39, 40] What the evidence does suggest, however, is that the two are linked to the same larger problem: poverty.[41] High levels of unemployment, lack of social resources, and concentrated areas of low income are all root causes of both high crime and disorder. As such, crime would be more effectively redressed by investing economically in neighborhoods rather than targeting them for heightened arrests.

It is also worth noting that, despite the claims of politicians, law-enforcement officials, and academics, the idea of "disorder" is not an objective or universal one. Studies have shown that how individuals perceive disorder, and how they feel about disorder as it relates to crime, is highly subjective. More importantly, these perceptions are highly correlated to race and class.[42] Specifically, Black, Brown, and poor neighborhoods are seen as "disordered" more often than others and disproportionately targeted for intensified policing. In a sense, rather than policing neighborhoods based on their level of crime and disorder, we end up policing them based on their level of Blackness and poverty.

It is worth stressing that, despite the popular label of broken-windows policing, the strategies undertaken by the NYPD and other departments do not wholly reflect broken-windows theory. As noted above, Wilson and Kelling argued for an approach to policing that includes both intensified policing and heightened *community control* over the neighborhood. Some scholars of broken-windows theory have referred to this as "collective efficacy," or the amount of social cohesion and willingness to act for the common social good that exists within a community.[43] These scholars have shown that high levels of collective efficacy, even in neighborhoods with high amounts of disorder, are effective in reducing both crime and disorder.

Despite the evidence, the NYPD and other departments have eliminated community engagement from the policing equation, focusing almost exclusively on the aggressive policing of minor crimes. Intensified policing, when divorced from an engagement with the public, does little to improve collective efficacy. Instead, it increases fear of crime, corrodes community-police relations, and delegitimizes police in the eyes of residents. Rather than residents feeling invested in crime prevention, they become fearful of both the criminals and the police.

The often-heralded argument that broken-windows policing "works" is also worthy of considerable scrutiny. While it is indisputable that crime declined in New York during the broken-windows era, crime also went down in other major cities that did *not* adopt so-called broken-windows approaches.[44] Even within New York, Bratton's introduction of CompStat—a much-admired and much-copied[45] method of computer analysis that helps police departments target resources to high-crime areas—coincided with his enforcement of broken windows and may have been just as influential in reducing crime. Analysts who are inclined to say that broken-windows policing is the primary factor inducing lower crime rates will acknowledge that there is no way to prove this claim, since all we can do is speculate as to what would have happened if the policing of minor offenses had not occurred. And even if we *could* firmly establish that broken windows is the prime factor for lower crime rates, this still does not necessarily justify its use.

Without question, crime would be reduced if all laws were strictly enforced to the letter. For example, reckless driving would be minimal if state troopers were to strictly enforce the speed limit on the nation's highways, and loitering would cease if every gathering of teenagers on a corner resulted in a citation. Society, however, would never tolerate such rigorous enforcement in all neighborhoods. Instead, there would likely be cries that America had turned into a police state. But in many places, mostly poor and mostly Black, this has been precisely the consequence of broken-windows approaches. As with many well-intentioned policies, the execution has been imperfect, too often emphasizing the arrest of those committing nuisance crimes over the need for communities to control law-enforcement practices within their own neighborhoods. This flawed execution has also revealed a set of problems that, through incompetence or indifference, went unaddressed by the architects of the system.

A few years ago, civil-rights attorney Harvey Silverglate wrote a provocative text called *Three Felonies a Day*.[46] Silverglate's thesis was that the enormity of the federal criminal code had presented the government with an opportunity to charge anyone with a crime whenever it wants. After all, as the title suggests, all of us commit crimes regularly without even knowing it. And the "not knowing it"—that is, the absence of criminal intent—has increasingly become less of a defense due to the United States Congress. Over the years, the House and Senate have crafted numerous laws that have stripped away the long held mens rea ("criminal mind") requirement from the American justice system.

The conservative Heritage Foundation—which is as concerned with this development as the liberal American Civil Liberties Union (ACLU)[47]—estimates that there are more than 4,500 offenses in the federal criminal code and 300,000 more regulations that carry criminal consequences.[48] The foundation published some of the more absurd stories involving federal and state prosecutions, including a twelve-year-old child who was arrested for eating French fries on the DC Metro (no food is allowed on the train); a stay-at-home mom who was prosecuted for operating an unlicensed day-care center because she had let mothers drop their children at her house as they waited for the school bus; and a Florida businessman who was convicted of using plastic bags to import lobsters from Honduras in violation of an obscure Honduran wildlife regulation that the FDA had pledged to support.[49] The businessman, whose story has become something of a cause célèbre in conservative circles, was convicted and sentenced to ninety-seven months in prison followed by three years of supervised release.[50]

Of course, the intellectual and political concern of groups like Heritage and individuals like Silverglate is not the criminalization of the vulnerable per se but the growth of the administrative state and the considerable reach of federal law and overweening prosecutors. Still, the principles they espouse can be applied to state and local criminal law as practiced in the nation's poorest communities. It is here, after all, that broken windows and its political progeny have led to an equally intrusive and arbitrary police presence. In 1940, US attorney general and future Supreme Court justice Robert H. Jackson warned of the dangerous power a prosecutor can wield. In choosing *what* to prosecute, Jackson offered, he also chooses *who* to prosecute, free to "[pick] some person whom he dislikes or desires to embarrass, or . . . some group of unpopular persons and then [look] for an offense." In so doing, "law enforcement becomes personal, and the real crime becomes that of being unpopular with the predominant or governing group."[51] Today, particularly in our most vulnerable areas, the same can be said of the police officer.

WHEN IT COMES TO racial justice, South Carolina has always occupied a place of particular shame. It was, famously, the state that launched the Civil War, the first state to secede from the Union, and the home of Fort Sumter, site of the war's first battle. In 1871, alarmed by the level of racial violence initiated by the Ku Klux Klan, President Ulysses S. Grant suspended the writ of habeas corpus in several South Carolina counties in order to effect faster arrests and prevent sympathizers from letting suspects escape, thereby forcing some two thousand Klan members to leave the state.[52] (Abraham Lincoln is the only other US president ever to have suspended the writ.) In 1948, South Carolina's segregationist governor, Strom Thurmond, split from the Democratic Party over civil rights and challenged President Harry Truman in that fall's election, denouncing Truman's integration of the armed forces as "un-American" and asserting that no number of federal troops was enough to "force the southern people to admit the Negro race into our theaters, into our swimming pools, into our churches."[53]

The Dixiecrats, the short-lived segregationist faction of the Democratic Party, won four states in 1948, including South Carolina, and had a lasting impact on Southern politics. In fact, many people credit Thurmond and his party for the return of the Confederate battle flag to a place of honor in the Southern imagination and material culture. A few years after they displayed it at their nominating convention, the distinctive Saint Andrew's Cross was embedded into the Georgia state flag, and South Carolina was one of several Southern states that began flying the battle flag over its statehouse in the early 1960s.[54] Strom Thurmond went on to represent his state in the US Senate until he retired in 2003 at age one hundred, a span of nearly fifty years. Still, even with that cloudy history, it was hard to comprehend the level of violence and the resulting soul-searching that descended on South Carolina in 2015.

It began on Saturday morning, April 4, 2015, as Walter Scott, a fifty-year-old African-American warehouse worker was driving his 1990s-vintage Mercedes W124 sedan in North Charleston, South Carolina, and was stopped by White police officer Michael Slager for having a broken "third taillight." Their exchange, in the parking lot of an auto-parts store where they had pulled over, began innocently enough. As captured on a dash-cam video,[55] Slager approaches the driver's-side window of Scott's car and asks for his license. There is some discussion as to whether Scott, a father of four,[56] owns the car, and he tells Slager that he is in the process of buying it. Slager then returns to his patrol vehicle with Scott's license. Scott waits in his car briefly until, at just over two minutes into the video, he opens the door, gets out, and motions to Slager as if he wants to ask him something. Slager uses his loudspeaker to tell Scott to get back in the car. He does. Then, at 2:33, Scott opens the door and begins to run from the scene.

The rest of the story is picked up by the cell-phone video of Feidin Santana,[57] a twenty-three-year-old barber from the Dominican Republic who was walking to work when he heard the sound of a Taser gun and saw the two men struggling. Santana took out his phone and began recording the scene. His video picks up the picture just as Scott, who is unarmed, breaks free from Slager and begins to run once again. At the twenty-second mark, Slager pulls out his gun and starts shooting Scott from behind. Eight times, Slager shoots Scott in the back. Scott staggers and falls headfirst into the mud. [Santana can be heard saying, "Oh, shit," as he records the scene.] Slager walks calmly toward the body as if he were going to tie up a dead deer. Scott is immobile, yet Slager yells at him to put his arms behind his back. When Scott doesn't respond, the officer goes to Scott's body and places the arms there himself [0:58]. He handcuffs Scott. ["Oh, shit," says Santana again.] Slager jogs back to the place where they had presumably wrestled over the Taser. He picks something up [1:09]. Another officer arrives on the scene and appears to check Scott's body for a pulse [1:11]. Slager returns to Scott, stopping shortly before he gets to him, and appears to be speaking into his radio. A transcript of his dispatch, released later, quotes him as saying "Shots fired, subject is down. He grabbed my Taser." Slager then appears to drop something next to Scott's body. ["Fucking abuse," says Santana.]

Since he was killed by the police, we can only speculate as to why Walter Scott ran. There are certainly plenty of reasons for African-Americans to fear traffic stops in North Charleston. The city is 47 percent Black, with a police force that is overwhelmingly White. Seventy-six percent of traffic stops in North Charleston not ending in citations or arrests involve African-American drivers.[58] (In other words, these are stops where *there was no crime committed*.) According to the Scott family's lawyer, he was eighteen thousand dollars behind in child-support payments and had previously been arrested for his delinquency.[59] Scott was likely worried that this information would surface when Slager searched the police database, unleashing a chain of events that would put him back in jail. So he ran.

Without question, Walter Scott made some bad choices that day. But no bad choice—not the act of resisting arrest, not the alleged fight over the Taser, and certainly not the sprint from the scene—legitimizes the deadly force that was unleashed upon him. With yet another cell-phone video of police brutality posted on YouTube and repeatedly played on cable news shows, another phrase was added to the national protest lexicon: "Back Turned, Don't Shoot." But how about simply "Don't Shoot," whether back turned, hands up, smiling, frowning, cooperating, resisting, dancing, standing, or doing somersaults? Whatever one's posture or demeanor, so long as it is short of an imminent attack, there is simply no moral or legal justification for the kind of force used in the confrontation involved in the case of Walter Scott.

Excessive force of this nature is, in fact, often justified by law enforcement, media, and everyday citizens. Absent clear video footage, numerous Americans continue to give the "benefit of the doubt" to police officers, despite the growing evidence against them. Even when video evidence is available, such as in the now-classic case of Rodney King, excessive force is justified by playing into longstanding irrational fears of Black bodies as superhuman predators. Had the four police officers not beaten King so severely, defense attorneys argued, he would have harmed them and pillaged the rest of the community. In the absence of fear-based arguments, some point to the moral failings of the victim. In the case of Walter Scott, critics like CNN analyst Harry Houck have argued that Scott "would be

alive today if he stayed in the car like the officer had told him."[60]
While this is likely true, the more urgent and morally significant
hypothetical is that Walter Scott would be alive if Officer Michael
Slager had not unnecessarily shot him. Unfortunately, such logic is
rarely invoked when the victims are Black, poor, trans, queer, or
otherwise marked as disposable within the public imagination.

A few days after the death of Walter Scott, Clementa Carlos
Pinckney rose from his seat in the South Carolina state senate chamber, in the capital city of Columbia. An unusual politician, Pinckney held master's degrees in both public administration and divin-
ity. In addition to representing the 45th senatorial district of South
Carolina, which is comprised of parts of seven Lowcountry counties,[61] Pinckney was an ordained minister of the African Methodist
Episcopal Church. Having delivered many eulogies, he was adept
at helping audiences wring meaning from death, and the eulogy he
gave after the passing of Walter Scott was similarly affecting.

After drawing attention to the fact that he spoke to them in the
Christian season of Easter, Pinckney reminded his fellow senators of
the story of the risen Jesus gathering his disciples at Galilee and how
every disciple was there but one, Thomas. He talked about how,
when the others told him that they had seen Jesus, Thomas refused
to believe them. Only when he himself was able to see Jesus and
touch his wounds did Thomas acknowledge the risen Christ.

When we first heard on the television that a police officer
had gunned down an unarmed African-American in North
Charleston by the name of Walter Scott, there were some
who said, "Wow. The national story has come home to
South Carolina." But there were many who said, "There is
no way that a police officer would ever shoot somebody in

the back six, seven, eight, times." But like Thomas, when we were able to see the video, and we were able to see the gun shots, and when we saw him fall to the ground, and when we saw the police officer come and handcuff him on the ground, without even trying to resuscitate him, without even seeing if he was really alive, without calling an ambulance, without calling for help, and to see him die face down in the ground as if he were gunned down like game, I believe we all were like Thomas, and said, "I believe."

Pinckney's use of the story suggests that the video of Scott's death highlighted what so many Black Americans already knew—the regularly violent and dismissive treatment of a whole population—but few others were willing to acknowledge. "What if Mr. [Santana] was not there to record what happened?" Pinckney asked. "I am sure that many of us would still say, like Thomas, 'We don't believe.'"[62]

Pinckney appealed to his audience to allow "sunshine" into the process, and in so doing, to pass legislation mandating body cameras for all police officers so that people "are seen and heard and their rights . . . protected." He asked that all hearts go out to the Scott family and, graciously, to the family of Michael Slager as well, "because the Lord teaches us to love all." Finally, he asked that justice be done, a plaintive cry that would no doubt later resound in the ears of all who had heard it.

A little more than two months later, Pinckney was sitting with twelve others in a prayer group at his downtown Charleston church—a gathering of thirteen, like the Last Supper. An hour into the meeting, a newcomer named Dylann Storm Roof stood up. The world would later learn that Roof had a history of espousing White supremacy, once complaining to a friend that "Blacks are taking over the world." Using a .45-caliber handgun he had hidden under his jacket, Roof shot and killed nine of those with whom he had just prayed.[63] Clementa Pinckney, who was forty-one years old at the time, was among those murdered.

IN 2014, *New York Times* writer Sam Roberts approached George Kelling to get his views on the current status of broken-windows policing.[64] This interview took place one month after Eric Garner had died from a police officer's choke hold, and many had begun to see the incident as a by-product of a police effort that appeared to overcriminalize harmless rule-breaking behavior. Kelling defended his theory but agreed that, in practice, it had been distorted to focus too much on accumulating arrests and too little on the maintenance of order. "I've never been long on arrests as an outcome," he told Roberts. Rephrasing a corollary of his original concept—that communities need to adopt and enforce their own rules—he said that he thought that the policing of the selling of loosies was something that needed to be understood neighborhood by neighborhood and not in City Hall. "Is selling loosies disruptive to a community?" he asked. "Is it serious enough to pass a law against?" He also repeated another theme from his original essay, one that has been little mentioned: since so much disorderly street behavior is the product of untreated mental illness and drug dependency, he suggested that "social workers" should patrol the streets along with the police. "We shouldn't be using our jails as mental hospitals or drug rehabilitation sites."

Yet almost forty years since the publication of his original thesis, Kelling is like the scientist who has unleashed a power he can no longer control and is left now to wistfully recall what might have been. The concept of broken windows long ago lost its moorings and has become little more than an opportunity to arrest the vulnerable. This revisionist practice may have started with Mayor Giuliani himself, who is said to have preferred the term "zero tolerance"[65]—something which has caught on nationwide but which Kelling has rejected as smacking of "zealotry." When Baltimore publicly adopted "zero tolerance" policing in the early 2000s, for instance, it resulted in the arrest of one in six people and a federal lawsuit filed by the ACLU.[66]

By contrast, Kelling prefers to see his theory as the antithesis of zero tolerance, for it emphasizes police discretion. The result, though, has been the worst of both worlds: zero tolerance—that is, *no discretion* as to what can potentially lead to an arrest—exhibited for those whom the police *in their discretion* deem to be the worst troublemakers. And who do the police believe to be their best targets? In their *Atlantic* piece, Kelling and Wilson expressed concern that instead of focusing their attention purely on destructive behaviors, broken-windows police forces might resort to using "skin color or national origin" or "harmless mannerisms" as the "basis for distinguishing the undesirable from the desirable," and that in so doing they might "become the agents of neighborhood bigotry." In many places, we have witnessed just what the architects of broken-windows policing feared: that it would be used as a pretext for racist policing.[67]

In the months after Eric Garner's death, the *New York Daily News* assembled statistics on the number of summonses for nuisance crimes issued by NYPD officers. They found that from 2001 to 2013, 7.3 million citations were issued for everything from public urination and littering to possession of small amounts of marijuana and consuming alcohol on the streets, and that "roughly 81 percent" of these so-called offenders were either Black or Latino.[68] With regard to relatively more serious offenses, like unlawful operation of a motor vehicle or a minor in possession of alcohol, there was much less of a correlation to race, but arrests for loitering, having an open container, failure to have a dog license, and even spitting were more routinely visited on Blacks and Hispanics. In 2011, there were fifty thousand arrests for marijuana possession in New York City alone.[69] (Compare that number to the 1,500 recorded in 1980). In 2013, the 25th Precinct, which includes parts of East Harlem, issued summonses to nearly one in five residents. No wonder one local told the *News* that he felt like his neighborhood was "under martial law."[70]

It doesn't take much analysis to see what was happening here. In 2008 and 2009, Adrian Schoolcraft, a police officer in the 81st Precinct in Brooklyn, began secretly recording workplace conversations that revealed a strategy of underreporting serious crime statistics (in order to maintain the image that such crime was down) and the enforcement of a quota system that required officers to complete a predetermined number of nuisance arrests.[71] While his assertions were initially rebuffed by the city—Schoolcraft says he was forcibly confined to a mental ward as a way of intimidating him and burying his message[72]—an independent study involving two thousand retired NYPD officers later revealed such practices to be widespread not only in the 81st, but in precincts throughout New York.[73] (Schoolcraft sued the NYPD, and the case was settled in late 2015 for $600,000).[74] A separate suit brought by twelve Black and Latino officers claimed that they suffered a disproportionate burden to meet quotas with nuisance arrests (and punishment if they did not); one officer cited pressure to fulfill his quota by ticketing subway riders who occupied more than one space.[75]

Quotas are one of the dirty secrets of American policing, particularly in those places, like Ferguson, where ticket-writing is valued as a method of revenue generation for the department. But the larger point of discussion is how the demand to meet a quota would obviate the kind of healthy discretion that Wilson and Kelling had hoped the "night watchman" police officer would practice. Faced with a quota, police looking to meet departmental expectations are more likely to look for the easy targets that will round out their arrest numbers. In so doing, they are apt to follow the kind of conscious or unconscious social cues that lead officers, many studies conclude, to disproportionately arrest Blacks and Latinos.[76] As in virtually every arena of contemporary American social life, market values and an obsession with profits and so-called efficiency overdetermine how policing looks, feels, and functions in the lives of everyday people.

In the late 1990s, the broken-windows approach to law enforcement began to incorporate "stop and frisk" tactics—or, to use the more formal departmental phrase, "stop, question, and frisk," though the amount of "questioning" done has always been a matter of dispute. The technique of stop-and-frisk was not, of course, a new one. In fact, it was long ago vetted by the Supreme Court in its landmark 1968 decision in *Terry v. Ohio*, addressing police procedure and the Fourth Amendment's prohibition of "unreasonable" search and seizure. In *Terry*, the Warren Court acknowledged the intrusive nature of a stop-and-frisk. "It is simply fantastic," wrote Chief Justice Earl Warren himself, "to urge that [a frisk] performed in public by a policeman while the citizen stands helpless, perhaps facing a wall with his hands raised, is a 'petty indignity.'"[77] Yet, despite that, the court issued a nearly unanimous (8–1) and surprisingly pro-police ruling, setting out a method by which officers who had a "reasonable suspicion" of criminal activity could do a "carefully limited search of the outer clothing" of a suspect—that is, a "frisk"—in search of a weapon that could be used to do harm to the officer or others nearby.[78] This "reasonable suspicion" standard was something short of the "probable cause" standard that police had had to meet before *Terry*. Over the next two decades, the court expanded its understanding of such procedures even further, allowing "*Terry* stops" for suspicion of non-violent and minor crimes as well,[79] though the "frisk" was limited to those situations where the officer "reasonably" suspected that "the person stopped is armed and dangerous."[80]

Even with this relaxed standard, the rise in the number of such stops over the last fifteen or so years has been astonishing. Philadelphia,[81] Detroit,[82] Baltimore, and Gary, Indiana,[83] police departments have utilized the practice with new enthusiasm, but throughout the administration of Mayor Michael Bloomberg, which lasted from 2002 to 2013, it was New York, the crown jewel of broken-windows policing advocacy, that was center stage for stop-and-frisk. Consider these numbers: In 2002, there were roughly 100,000 *Terry* stops in the city; in 2011, there were 685,724. A little more than half of the 4.4 million stops conducted between 2004 and 2012 included a frisk for weapons, but, of those frisks, weapons were discovered in only 1.5 percent. Only 6 percent of the stops in this same period resulted in an arrest and 6 percent more in a summons. And of those stopped, more than half were Black; another 30 percent were Latino. In other words, for all this effort and all the indignity being foisted upon Black and Brown citizens, the takeaway was fairly minor.

In August of 2013, federal judge Shira Scheindlin, ruling in a class-action suit brought by several minority residents of the city, found the NYPD's stop-and-frisk policy to be in violation of the Fourth Amendment's *Terry* formulation and the Fourteenth Amendment's guarantee of equal protection of the laws. She criticized the practices of officers whose determination of "suspicion" was based on "furtive movements" like looking over one's shoulder, while also noting that "an officer's impression of whether a movement was 'furtive' may be affected by unconscious racial biases." (Compare this to Wilson's and Kelling's warning about the temptation to police "harmless mannerisms.") She wrote of the weight of the "human toll" of such stops, adding that "[w]hile it is true that any one stop is a limited intrusion in duration and deprivation of liberty, each stop is also a demeaning and humiliating experience." And she referenced both Earl Warren's original decision in *Terry*, when he declared that officers, in making a stop, "must be able to articulate something more than an inchoate and un-particularized suspicion or hunch" and the conservative legal lion Judge Richard Posner in a 2005 case that also turned on Fourth Amendment rights. "Whether you stand still or move, drive above, below, or at the speed limit," Posner wrote, "you will be described by the police as acting suspiciously should they wish to stop or arrest you. Such subjective, promiscuous appeals to an ineffable intuition should not be credited."[84]

Scheindlin insisted that she was not ordering an end to stop-and-frisk, only an adjustment to its practice so as to bring the NYPD within the bounds of the Constitution. But her opinion was delivered a couple of months before the 2013 mayoral election, and while the city immediately appealed the decision, the judge's strongly worded critique made police practice a central issue of the campaign. Today, some contend that it is the prime reason that Bill De Blasio, then a little-known Democratic candidate, won the mayoralty; among those seeking to occupy Gracie Mansion, De Blasio alone had criticized the Bloomberg administration for its use of stop-and-frisk. Soon after becoming mayor, De Blasio decided to drop the city's appeal of Scheindlin's decision, and the use of stop-and-frisk dropped substantially. But his decision to install

William Bratton as chief of police leaves little room for comfort.
Bratton has admitted that when he was chief of police in Los Angeles, from 2002–2009,[85] his officers resorted to "stop and frisk"
even more frequently than their counterparts in New York.[86]

IT IS ROUGHLY 1,700 miles from the heart of Manhattan to Hempstead, Texas, the seat of Waller County, a place so sparsely inhabited
that its population would not even qualify as a single NYPD precinct. But the ticky-tacky pursuit of the vulnerable is just as common
here as in New York. Broken-windows policing, though, is less of a
factor here than good old-fashioned racial animus. Cemeteries remain
segregated—White people buried in one place; Blacks in another.
As recently as 2004, a local resident sued the city, and won, for not
maintaining Black burial grounds with the same attention it maintained White ones. In 2007, when DeWayne Charleston, a justice of
the peace, tried to break the cemetery "color barrier"—arranging for
the Black cemetery burial of an unidentified White woman who had
been brutally murdered and left by the side of the road—he was rebuffed by a local judge. The judge argued that the Black cemetery
charged too much money for a pauper's grave ($426 more than the
White cemetery), but there were plenty of locals who nodded their
heads in a silent understanding that it was still race, not money, that
guided this decision.[87] Charleston later told the *Guardian* that Waller is
the "most racist county"[88] in Texas, though, sadly, in a state that ranks
third in the nation in the number of lynchings (after Mississippi and
Georgia),[89] there are plenty of others that could vie for that title.

Waller is home to Prairie View A&M University, established
in the Reconstruction era as the segregated Alta Vista Agricultural
and Mechanical College of Texas for Colored Youth. Prairie View's

student body of roughly eight thousand is 84 percent African-American.[90] These numbers stand in sharp contrast to the racial demographics of Texas A&M University's campuses, where only 3 percent of the 41,000-member undergraduate student body is Black.

Sandra Annette Bland was a 2009 graduate of Prairie View A&M. She majored in agriculture, played in the school band, and was a member of the Sigma Gamma Rho sorority. After graduating, she returned to her native Chicago, where she worked for Cook's Direct, a food-service equipment-supply company. It was also during this time that she became politically active. After the events in Ferguson, Bland had become an ardent supporter of the Black Lives Matter movement.

In the summer of 2015, Bland accepted a job at her alma mater. Friends report that she was excited to return to Texas, where she was to begin work as a program associate with the university's extension division.[91] It was there, on July 10, her first day back in Waller County, that she was pulled over by a Texas state trooper named Brian Encinia. Once again, video cameras[92]—one on the officer's dashboard, another held by a bystander—provided a front row seat to the action.[93] Encinia approached Bland's car and informed her that she had been stopped for not signaling a lane change. Bland had not been speeding or otherwise driving recklessly. She was not under the influence of alcohol. After gathering her documents and writing up her citation, the officer returned to Bland's car and stood by her driver's-side window. Perhaps noticing that the woman looked unhappy, he asked her if everything was "okay." Bland responded.

"I'm waiting on *you*," she said, clearly annoyed. "This is *your* job. I'm waiting on *you*. When are you going to let me go?"

"I don't know," said Encinia. "You seem very, really, irritated."

"I *am*. I really *am*. I feel like it's crap what I'm getting a ticket for.

I was getting out of your way. You were speeding up, tailing me, so I move over and you stop me. So, yeah, I am a little irritated, but that doesn't stop you from giving me a ticket, so write your ticket."

"Are you done?" said the officer.

"You asked me what was wrong," said Bland. "Now I told you."

As tense as that exchange may have seemed, it was remarkable how suddenly it escalated and how quickly the foul scent of confrontation filled the air. Encinia asked Bland to put out her cigarette. She refused. He asked her to step out of the car. She refused. He told her to step out or he would "remove her." Bland, her voice dripping with indignation, asked "I am getting removed *for a failure to signal?*" In a business in which officers count on compliant targets, Bland was no easy statistic. The impertinent style of this courageous young Black woman was clearly getting under Encinia's skin. He called for backup. He opened the door and reached in to forcibly remove Bland. He told her that she was under arrest. Bland asked, "For what?" He again demanded that she get out of the car. "I will light you up," he said, holding his Taser, the ghosts of the Big House inflating his lungs. "Get out. Now!"

At that, Bland did get out, continuing to mock the officer, her voice running on incessantly, boldly, delivering staccato language bullets. "You are doing all of this for a failure to signal," she reminded him. "Let's take this to court." Under the officer's order, Bland moved to the side of the road, onto the property of a local church. She was now out of view of the police car's dashboard camera, but the microphone continued to pick up their exchange, and a bystander's cellphone camera would later show what had actually happened.[94]

"You feeling good about yourself?" Bland continued with Encinia. "Turn around," he told her. Their voices were raised, verb crossing verb. "Are you fucking *kidding* me?" said Bland as Encinia handcuffed her. "You are full of shit. . . . South Carolina got y'all bitch asses scared." And then, again, "I can't wait till we go to court. Oh, I can't wait." Encinia told Bland to get on the ground. "Don't it make you feel real good, don't it?" Bland blasted him, "a female for a traffic ticket. Don't it make you feel good, Officer Encinia? You're a *real* man now."

There would be no appearance in court for Sandra Bland. She was put in Cell Block 95 of the Waller County jail, where three days later she was found hanging from a transparent plastic garbage bag that had been fashioned into a noose and then tied around a metal barrier in her cell. The official autopsy report, issued a day later, declared Bland's death a suicide.[95]

In the aftermath, debate ensued about whether or not Bland actually committed suicide. Jail officials claimed not only that Bland killed herself but that she had had notified them of a previous suicide attempt the year before.[96] Bland's family, however, insisted that Bland had shown "no evidence" of ever having attempted suicide.[97] While Encinia was ultimately fired for failing to follow proper protocol, subsequent investigations supported the State's suicide claim.[98] Still, even if Bland died exactly the way jail officials claim, this does not absolve the State of gross levels of wrongdoing.

After stopping Bland for failing to signal before a lane change—a clear but relatively minor and often overlooked infraction—Officer Encinia escalated the situation. Rather than merely handing Bland a ticket, he decided to question her about being "irritated." He then demanded that Bland put out her cigarette, a request that had no basis in the law. It was only when Bland refused to comply with his request that Encinia ordered her out of the car. Although he later insisted that he took her out of the car for safety reasons—a claim that was ultimately rejected even by his own department—it was clear that Encinia was punishing Bland for her attitude. As Black feminist scholar Brittney Cooper points out, "[Encinia] firmly expected to be able to harass a citizen going about her business and have her be okay with it. He expected that she wouldn't question him. He wanted her submission. Her deference. Her fear."[99]

This is not an uncommon expectation of Black women and girls, who are disproportionately arrested (compared to their White and Black male counterparts) for minor crimes because their behavior is deemed by law enforcement to have "violated conventional norms and stereotypes of feminine behavior"[100, 101] These patriarchal norms demand that women remain quiet, passive, and deferential in the face of State (read: male) authority. For Black women and girls, these oppressive norms are compounded by longstanding social narratives that also depict them as immoral, angry, violent, and emasculating.[102] This increases the likelihood that interactions between Black women and law enforcement will end in unnecessary violence, criminalization, and even death. It is precisely these dynamics that heighten the suspicions of many observers regarding Bland's alleged suicide.

Many have also found it implausible that Bland would kill herself just hours before her sister was coming to bail her out, and just days before she was set to begin a new job about which she was excited.[103] To them, Bland's death was yet another in a long line of suspicious deaths of Black people while in State custody. On one hand, these suspicions reflect a healthy skepticism of the police based on the long history of anti-Black violence and systemic dishonesty within every dimension of the criminal justice system. On the other hand, they reinforce a troubling sense of silence and shame around mental health, particularly within the Black community.[104] In a sense, many people needed to see Bland's mental health "exonerated" before she could be a worthy and respectable victim. All of this, however, ignores the fact that Bland's death, suicide or not, is directly linked to the actions of the State.

After her violent arrest, Bland was taken to jail, where she spent three full days because she was unable to come up with the refundable five-thousand-dollar bond, or even the non-refundable five hundred dollars necessary to pay a bondsperson. Given her mental health history, and the fact that she posed no demonstrable threat to the community, it would have been in everyone's best interests to release Bland as quickly as possible. Instead, like much of America's incarcerated population, Bland was forced to remain in jail simply because she did not have enough money to get out. While the bail system was designed to ensure that defendants return to trial, it has become yet another form of punishment wielded only against the economically vulnerable. As a result, 83 percent of people currently in American jails remain there for no other reason than that they cannot afford to pay their bail.[105] It is entirely reasonable to suggest that if Bland had raised the money to pay bail—or, more importantly, if she had not been forced to exchange money for her freedom in the first place—she would still be alive today.

On her jail intake form, Bland indicated that she had previously attempted suicide. She also told police and jail officials that she suffered from epilepsy (to which Officer Encinia responded, "Good") and was currently taking Keppra, an anti-epileptic drug known to cause suicidal thoughts. Despite these bright red flags, and despite the fact that most female jail suicides take place within the first four days, jail officials failed to place Bland on suicide watch.[106] If they had done so, jail officials would have been required to conduct face-to-face observations every fifteen minutes rather than the standard sixty minutes. Further, the Texas Commission on Jail Standards determined that the jail failed to meet the hourly observation standard in Bland's case.[107]

In July 2015, the same month of Bland's death, five other Black women also died in police custody: Kindra Chapman, an eighteen-year-old Alabama woman, committed suicide after only two hours in jail for cell-phone theft; fifty-year-old Joyce Curnell died in South Carolina's Sheriff Al Cannon Detention Center after experiencing medical problems while being held on a shoplifting charge; Ralkina Jones, thirty-seven, was in jail in Cleveland Heights, Ohio, for less than forty-eight hours due to a domestic dispute when she was found unresponsive in her cell; Alexis McGovern, twenty-eight, was found dead in her bed by St. Louis County jail officials; and forty-two-year-old Raynette Turner died two days after being arrested for shoplifting and sent to a jail in Mt. Vernon, New York. [108]

Many argue, perhaps correctly, that jail officials and police had no desire to kill these and other Black women. Such arguments presume that it is negligence and indifference, rather than malicious intent, that lead to their tragic deaths. While this may be true, it does not negate the fact that these women ultimately died because of a series of unnecessary actions by the State. Debates about whether those in power wanted to kill them or were simply indifferent to their well-being only serve to determine whether the violence done to them was direct *State violence* or a form of *State-sponsored violence* through willful ignorance. In either case, Sandra Bland was ultimately a casualty of a broken criminal justice system that criminalizes vulnerability and, more specifically, Black womanhood.

III.

Bargained

arilyn Mosby was just thirty-five years old when she strode to the steps of the Baltimore War Memorial on May 1, 2015. The eyes of the nation were upon her. She was the youngest chief prosecutor in any major American city[1] and one of the least experienced. Less than a year before,[2] Mosby, then a litigator for Liberty Mutual Insurance, had surprised Baltimore politicos by challenging incumbent prosecutor Gregg Bernstein in the election, an undertaking many thought had little chance for success. Yet after she ran a strong campaign focused on "getting tough" with repeat violent offenders, rooting out corruption within the Baltimore Police Department, and addressing Baltimore's history of police brutality,[3] Mosby won the race in an upset. It would be just four months into Mosby's term when the city was rocked by two weeks of protest and rebellion over the death of Freddie Gray.

Gray was a twenty-five-year-old Black man who was arrested, ostensibly, for carrying a switchblade. While in police custody, Gray died from injuries suffered to his spinal cord brought on by the physical treatment of the officers involved. He was yet another casualty in the nation's sudden burst of very public episodes in which unarmed

Blacks had fatal encounters with police.[4] In a speech she delivered at her alma mater, Tuskegee University, the previous October, Mosby expressed frustration with prosecutors in St. Louis and New York who had failed to bring indictments for the killings of Michael Brown and Eric Garner.[5] Now it was Mosby's chance to show that she was different—that in Mosby's Baltimore, police would not get away with such evident brutality.

Mosby did not disappoint. To the shock of many in attendance that Friday, most of whom were expecting a routine announcement of a continuing investigation, the young Black prosecutor—a native of Boston who admits to having felt harassed by police at various moments throughout her own life—announced that she would bring charges on the six Baltimore police officers involved in the arrest and detention of Freddie Gray. Mosby looked triumphant as the crowd, and the broader social media world, responded with cheers. As in the case of Michael Brown, the circumstances surrounding the death of Freddie Gray were at once sickening and symbolic. For many, there was something satisfying about watching a person in power finally striking back against injustice.

But why was Gray arrested in the first place?

The incident happened at the corner of North Avenue and Mount Street outside the Gilmor Homes housing project where Gray was raised. While Gilmor is a low-rise housing development built in 1942,[6] it had followed the trajectory of St. Louis's Pruitt-Igoe, gradually becoming a hotbed of drugs and crime. A telling example of how bad conditions in Gilmor had become was a lawsuit filed in late 2015, which claimed that repairmen sent there by the Housing Authority of Baltimore City would demand sex from women in exchange for their services. Those who refused were forced to live with leaky faucets, peeling paint, and continued rodent infestations.[7]

Still, in the West Baltimore neighborhood of Sandtown-Winchester where the Gilmor Homes are located, there is plenty of misery to go around. Nearly a third of its population is living at or below the poverty level, unemployment is around 20 percent (double the rate for the city), and the streetscape is a pockmarked scene of abandoned and boarded-up row houses interrupted by liquor stores and tobacco outlets, twice as many per capita as can be found in other parts of the city.[8] Incidents of lead-paint poisoning here are triple the average for the rest of Baltimore. In fact, Freddie Gray and his siblings suffered lead poisoning when they were children. So, ironically, did Officer William G. Porter, one of the policemen pursuing him that day, who grew up eleven blocks away from where Gray lived, their birthdates just two months apart.[9]

According to the Baltimore police, the confrontation with Gray began when he made "eye contact" with an officer. While eye contact is generally received as a sign of respect within Western cultures, when it comes to police and Black citizens, it is often interpreted as disrespect or even outright aggression. This is not a new phenomenon, but rather a practice that dates back to ancient times. As David Brion Davis points out in his monumental history of slavery, *Inhuman Bondage*, slaves in Mesopotamia were known as *iginu'du*, which translates as "not raising their eyes,"[10] an illustration of their degraded state and "social death." For Blacks during the Jim Crow era in America, to make eye contact with Whites was likewise considered to be an act of rebellion.[11] And in Baltimore in 2014, more than 150 years after the Emancipation Proclamation, a young Black man making eye contact with a police officer is still regarded as a sign of guilt, an act of disrespect, and an affront to State power.[12]

When Gray locked eyes with a passing bicycle cop, he ran. Several officers pursued him.[13] When they finally apprehended him, they discovered the knife in Gray's pocket, which was neither illegal nor used to threaten anyone. But the officers aggressively arrested him anyway, folding him up, said one bystander, "like a piece of origami."[14] This led to one of Mosby's twenty-eight charges: "fail[ing] to establish probable cause for Mr. Gray's arrest, as no crime had been committed."[15] A cell-phone video shot by a bystander suggests that Gray was already complaining of being injured as the police dragged him to their vehicle. But his complaints did not stop the police from giving him a "rough ride" back to the station house, "rough ride" being a term police used internally to describe a manner of driving meant to inflict harm on the passengers held in the rear of the van.[16] The ride ended in tragedy. "Mr. Gray," said Mosby, "suffered a severe and critical neck injury as a result of being handcuffed, shackled by his feet and unrestrained inside the B.P.D. wagon."

The key term here was "unrestrained." Gray, who had been irate with the officers, was never strapped into place with a seatbelt. Instead, while his arms and feet were held immobile, he was left to be thrown around the vehicle in gruesome fashion. When he cried out for medical attention, he was ignored. For this, the prosecutor decided to seek second-degree "depraved heart" murder charges—that is, murder committed not with premeditation but with an "extreme disregard for human life"—against Caesar Goodson Jr., the officer who was at the wheel of the van.[17]

FOR ALL THE PRAISE that Mosby received for daring to charge "Johnny Law" with homicide, as one Black blogger put it,[18] for all the applause and her almost instant national celebrity, there is reason to pause and reflect on the speed of her decision. Prosecutors in Ferguson and New York and other municipalities—like Cleveland, where twelve-year-old Tamir Rice was hastily killed by police bullets—might have been slow, even reluctant, to charge police with misconduct. By contrast, Mosby, who decided to bring the charges against the officers herself and not wait for a grand jury, was working at a pace and via a method common to today's criminal justice system. When it satisfies us—and answers a very public and necessary call for justice, as in the case of the Freddie Gray incident—we cheer it. Yet the discretionary power reserved for a prosecutor like Mosby, power that allows her to bring whatever charges she wishes upon whomever she wishes whenever she wishes, is in fact one of the great flaws of the American legal system. And while this power arrangement may have worked to the pleasure of many Black people in the case of Freddie Gray, it largely serves to further oppress people of color. As the late Harvard law professor William J. Stuntz wrote, "[d]iscretion and discrimination travel together."[19]

This is not the system of fairness that the architects of American criminal justice envisioned, even if they were only imagining it for White male landowners. It is not even the system romanticized in popular culture, with its emphasis on the rights of the accused, arguments being played out before a jury of one's peers, and judges guiding the process according to eternal principles of fairness. And it is certainly not the system dictated by the Fourteenth Amendment, with its demand for "equal protection of the laws."[20] Despite these lofty ideals, despite the paeans to justice etched on the entryways of our courts, our current system is actually carried out in two places that ultimately compromise justice: first, in the mind of the prosecutor, and second, behind closed doors, where that same prosecutor and a defense lawyer (who is all too often an overworked and underpaid public defender) work out the details of a plea deal. Here they dispose of lives—especially the lives of the vulnerable—with astonishing alacrity. Amazing though it may seem, it is estimated that 97 percent of federal cases and 94 percent of state cases end in some kind of deal.[21, 22] As Supreme Court justice Anthony Kennedy acknowledged in his *Lafler v. Cooper* majority opinion in 2012, "Ours is a system of pleas, not a system of trials."[23]

Plea bargains—guilty pleas induced by "promises of favor"—were considered to be inadmissible by eighteenth-century English courts. These jurists believed that "a confession forced from the mind by the flattery of hope, or by the torture of fear, comes in so questionable a shape . . . that no credit ought to be given to it."[24] As late as the Civil War, the US Supreme Court found them unconstitutional. But quiet bargaining between prosecutors and defendants nonetheless became commonplace, so much so that the court finally endorsed the constitutionality of plea bargains in 1971, deeming them "an essential component of the administration of justice."[25] In *Lafler*, they took that approval one step further, extending the constitutional right for effective assistance of counsel to include guidance provided not only to those who go to trial but to those determining whether to take a plea deal or not.[26] That was a decision that took the plea bargaining process out of the realm of "necessary evil" and into the place of, to borrow a phrase from Justice Antonin Scalia's dissenting opinion in *Lafler*, a "constitutional entitlement."

But before we become too comfortable with substituting a deal-making process for a fact-finding process that aims to discover the truth, we must consider what is lost in the process. We pay a considerable price for a system that puts so much power in the hands of the state officer bringing the charges, that obscures the determination of outcome from public view, that finds no facts and hears no witnesses, that involves no judge nor jury and only a minimal role for defense counsel. There is a reason why the founding generation of American settler-colonialists, in preserving the right to a jury trial, described it as "sacred," "inviolable," "ancient," and "inestimable."[27] One wonders what James Madison would say if he could see the end run most prosecutors make around that right today, and how they have turned the pursuit of justice into a "bargain."

As William J. Stuntz argues in *The Collapse of American Criminal Justice*, Black and Brown citizens, immigrants, the poor, and those without formal education are the most likely to suffer from this systemic shift in criminal procedure.[28] In the last chapter, I discussed at length how the discretionary power of police leads to the arrest of Blacks at a disproportionately higher rate than Whites. When those arrested reach the next stop within the criminal justice system, they find more of the same. Despite the fact that Blacks and Whites use recreational drugs at roughly the same rates, Blacks are nine times more likely to be imprisoned for drug crimes than Whites, and three times more than Latinos.[29] As Stuntz argues, the system also works cruelly in reverse: "The more poor people and Black people in the local population, the less likely that victims of criminal violence will see their victimizers punished."[30] In other words, Blacks receive more of the kind of policing that puts them behind bars and less of the kind of policing that protects them from danger.

One reason for this structural inequality is the close tie between criminal justice and politics. At the state and local level, where the criminal process most commonly plays out, district attorneys and judges are *elected*. (Only the District of Columbia, Connecticut, Rhode Island, New Jersey, and Delaware use a system of appointed prosecutors.[31]) The logic of this arrangement was that the electoral process would allow "the People" to keep a check on an overreaching prosecutor or a judge who disregards the law. Such an arrangement only functions, however, when the majority is invested in the process. This leads to an uncomfortable juxtaposition. On one hand, the Constitution protects minority rights. Yet on the other hand, those rights are protected by institutions that are subject to the whims of the political process, leaving them vulnerable to the abuse (or indifference) of the majority.

This contradiction is further complicated by the fact that district attorneys are typically elected countywide. This is problematic because counties—particularly those that include large urban populations—can incorporate widely disparate population groups. This is why the people of largely White Clayton, Missouri, vote in elections for the same prosecutor as people in largely Black Ferguson, and why the fate of Darren Wilson was therefore left in the hands of Robert McCulloch, the St. Louis County prosecutor. In that case, McCulloch—perhaps anticipating the kind of criticism he might receive for being detached from the realities of Black life in Ferguson—opted to send the case to a grand jury. Yet even here we see the distorting effect of politics. Grand juries are intended by design to reflect the racial makeup of the community in which the crime occurred. But the recognized "community" for the Michael Brown killing was St. Louis County, with its predominantly White demographic, not Ferguson. That, in essence, is like saying that Scarsdale and the North Shore of Long Island occupy the same social, cultural, or political space as the Bronx.

As more and more middle class families moved from the cities to the suburbs, lured by a range of policy arrangements that also relocated necessary resources, they helped to create more dangerous neighborhoods in the cities they abandoned. Yet the political community of the "county" included both the city and, predominantly, the suburbs. This meant that power over criminal justice was given to voters with less of a personal or material investment in a fair and functioning criminal justice system. For those suburban voters, the election of prosecuting attorneys became little more than a rubber stamp, an extension of an anonymous bureaucracy. McCulloch, for instance, has been the St. Louis County prosecutor since 1991,[32] often running unopposed in county elections. By contrast, Blacks, whether through election or appointment, are deeply underrepresented in the prosecutorial ranks. A recent survey in California, for instance, found that the state Department of Justice had just 11 Black attorneys out of a staff of 368, a number that amounted to roughly 3 percent. [33]

While politics play a role in how prosecutors are elected and whose interests they protect, they are also largely responsible for how the power of the prosecutor has grown substantially in the past forty years. Prior to the introduction of mandatory minimum sentencing and sentencing "guidelines,"[34] sentencing in America was a power reserved to judges, who had discretion to consider a multitude of factors in deciding a sentence. These factors included the defendant's character and personal context, as understood through the judge's conversation with a probation officer. But things quickly changed as crime rates rose substantially in the 1960s and 1970s, creating the political will for an intensified "War on Drugs." In prosecuting this war, Congress, and then individual states, became more involved with assigning stiff sentences to individual crimes. These sentences were not limited to drug crimes but extended to laws punishing child pornographers, identity thieves, and those committing repeat offenses as represented by California's notorious "three strikes and you're out" law.[35] A case in point is the federal Anti–Drug Abuse Act of 1986, which set mandatory minimum sentences for drug possession and sale.[36] In theory, the act was intended to prevent sentencing disparities as well as to "get tough" on big-time drug dealers without having to depend upon judicial discretion. It achieved neither.

The act included a 100–1 differential between sentences for possession of crack cocaine and powder cocaine. This proved problematic because the cheaper-priced crack was largely popular among poor Black drug users, while powder cocaine was more prevalent in affluent White communities. The consequence: a facially neutral public policy that nonetheless targeted Black drug users disproportionately.[37] Since the law considered anyone even remotely involved with a drug sale as a "dealer," the law also punished small-scale drug users, petty drug dealers, and even police lookouts as if they were drug kingpins. As a result, the person standing on the corner selling a five-dollar vial of crack was placed in the same category as the person transporting multiple kilograms of the drug. An equally important but less considered outcome of the mandatory-minimum approach was that it did not end sentencing disparities for these or other crimes. Instead, it merely shifted sentencing discretion from the judge to the prosecutor, who, in negotiating with the defendant, ultimately decides what the State will charge. In essence, this shift didn't get rid of arbitrary judges, it simply turned prosecutors into de facto judges.

These "guidelines" have not only altered the division of labor within the criminal justice system, they have radically changed the nature of American justice itself. Gone is the veneer of temperance and evenhandedness often associated with the judicial process. In its place is a cutthroat deal-making process in which the prosecutor holds the sentencing guidelines out as a threat, saying, essentially, "Either take my offer or take your chances in court, but if you lose in court, you will face nothing less than this statutorily defined sentence, with no chance that the judge will grant you anything else."

In 2004, Massachusetts federal judge William G. Young, an appointee of Ronald Reagan, wrote a scathing opinion on the system.[38] Judge Young cited the "sophistry" of prosecutors who, following the guidelines, offer a "discount" on sentencing if the defendant "accepts responsibility" for the crime. This admission of guilt, wrote Young, has nothing to do with the kind of moral achievement that would be represented by a perpetrator actually stipulating to the failure of their actions and expressing regret for them.[39] In fact, the prosecutor, and the broader system, has no material interest in that result. Instead, the prosecutor's conduct is motivated by little more than promoting the government's interest in minimizing "the trouble, expense, and uncertainty" of a jury trial. Individual prosecutors have little room to resist this arrangement, as the entire system is structured (and budgeted) to effect this outcome. Again, issues of fairness, mercy, and justice become subordinate to neoliberal notions of efficiency.

Another casualty within the current framework is the truth itself. Instead of determining what actually happened in a particular case, the prosecutor and defendant engage in "fact bargaining," a process by which they agree to a version of events that corresponds to the sentencing guidelines and garners a mutually agreed upon punishment.[40] As a result, we often never find out what actually happened in a particular case. Before presenting their offers to frightened, confused, and intimidated defendants, prosecutors are likely to work from nothing more than a few notes dashed off by the arresting officer, with almost no consideration given to the defendant's version of events.[41]

Judges are complicit in this charade. In what has become something of a surreal exercise, judges continue to order probation officers to prepare pre-sentencing reports on the defendant's personal history even though the reports will have no impact on the term of punishment. They then address the defendant as if they have mulled over the details of the case and the sentence. In truth, these details have already been worked out by the prosecutor and, in this situation, the judge is nothing more than a prop in a judicial process devoid of actual judicial decision making. While these practices are nothing new, they have now become the primary method of adjudication on the federal, state, and local levels. Even misdemeanors are pleaded out, meaning that prosecutors and defense attorneys carry caseloads that make a mockery of the term "process." Legal journalist Amy Bach, for instance, tells the story of a public defender in Georgia who handled 1,493 cases in only four years. Of those 1,493 cases, only 14 (less than 1 percent) went to trial.[42] Over and over again, defendants, most of them Black and nearly all of them poor, rose from "rickety dark wooden benches" and "one after another" pleaded guilty, a rhythm that the attorney, without an ounce of irony, described as "*a uniquely productive way to do business.*"[43]

Of course, there is a need for some level of plea bargaining. No one would expect every case of reckless driving, public intoxication, and petty theft to require the time, procedural rigor, and expense necessary for a full trial. But when so much happens in concealed quarters, we deprive ourselves and the accused of a key dimension of the process. The Sixth Amendment right to a public trial is just that—a right that can be waived by the defendant at her will. Still, it is important to reflect on the word "public" and its meaning in this context. As legal scholar Akhil Reed Amar has written, nowhere does the Constitution provide the right to a *secret* trial.[44] Why? Because the Constitution is a document that lays out not only the rights of the individual but also those granted to "the People"—*the public.* The purpose of this arrangement is to ensure republican government by letting citizens witness their *public* officials in action and judge them accordingly in the next election.[45]

Unfortunately, since modern American society, as with all things in the current neoliberal moment, prioritizes privatization and individualism, the very notion of *the public* has become disposable. As the current criminal-justice process shows, no longer is there a collective interest in affirming the value of the public good, even rhetorically, through processes of transparency, honesty, or fairness. No longer is there a commitment to monitoring and evaluating public officials, in this case prosecutors, to certify that justice prevails. Instead, we have entered a moment in which all things public have been demonized within our social imagination: public schools, public assistance, public transportation, public housing, public options, and public defenders. In the place of a rich democratic conception of "the public" is a market-driven logic that privileges economic efficiency and individual success over collective justice.

But this is not merely an abstract intellectual argument about the pitfalls of free-market fundamentalism and its logics. We must ponder the practical consequences of a legal system so obsessed with efficiency that it does not even pretend to be interested in locating truth. We must consider the danger and corruption that inevitably accompanies a system that engages in backroom dealing 97 percent of the time. And we must reassess a system that usurps arbitrary power from judges only to give it to prosecutors. While prosecutors like Marilyn Mosby may use that power in the interest of justice, they are merely "hitting a straight lick with a crooked stick." The system is broken.

LIKE MICHAEL BROWN BEFORE him, Freddie Gray was an unlikely centerpiece for a social movement. He never held a formal job and earned most of his income by selling drugs on the street. His father was absent. His mother struggled with heroin addiction. His stepfather had had his own run-ins with the law.[46] Criminal charges had been filed on Gray in more than twenty cases, five of which were still open when he died. Most of these incidents involved narcotics offenses, though he had also been cited for assault and for destruction of property. Still, no less than Elijah Cummings, US Representative for Maryland, gave a eulogy at Gray's funeral in Baltimore's New Shiloh Baptist Church. As he did, three representatives from the Obama White House sat among the congregation.[47] The purpose of their attendance was clear: to stop the violence that was likely coming to these streets. Though his life was short and complicated, Gray, again like Michael Brown, had become a symbol to rally around.

The uprisings that followed Gray's death—the worst Baltimore had seen since the assassination of Martin Luther King in 1968—were devastating to the city. Demonstrators destroyed storefronts and threw rocks, bottles, and jagged slabs of concrete at police officers working to quell the uproar. They looted Mondawmin Mall, a seven-hundred-square-foot shopping center named for the Algonquian spirit of the corn. In one particularly tragic scene, the protesters set ablaze a sixteen-million-dollar Baptist church–sponsored community center and apartment complex that, half built, had been a sign of hope to the neighborhood's elderly.[48]

Still, to suggest that the violence was unnecessary or entirely unjustified would be to misunderstand the complexity of the story. Even calling the actions "riots" rather than "rebellions" or "uprisings" obscures the principled outrage that animated many acts of resistance that occurred in the aftermath of Gray's death. For many in Baltimore, as in Ferguson, the rebellions were an attempt to scar public tissue, to draw attention to a deeply troublesome and long-standing state of civic affairs. By destroying government property, they were attempting to momentarily disrupt the affairs of a State that was systematically killing them. By tearing down commercial businesses, they were aiming to strike a blow against the crippling machinery of late capitalism, which had created the conditions for social deprivation and economic vulnerability. Their actions are an extension of a long tradition of political militancy that does not dismiss nonviolence as a tactic but refuses to fetishize it as an overarching philosophy against an inherently violent State.

Violence is not foreign to Baltimore. Ever since drugs began to ravage its once-sturdy neighborhoods, the city has been regularly ranked among the top ten most violent places in America. The reality of this dubious distinction was made all too clear in 2002, when a fire destroyed the home of Angela Dawson, a crusader against the neighborhood drug trade. Dawson had filed complaints with police about the dealers who worked near her family's row house. The police's response to the Dawsons: they should move. But the family stayed—that is, until the night when one of the dealers arrived, kicked in the front door, dowsed the stairs with gasoline, and started the blaze that would kill Dawson, her husband, and their five children, aged nine to fourteen.[49] After standing for years as a charred ruin, a symbol of the lawlessness of Baltimore's streets, the house was replaced by a community center.[50]

The city is shown with considerable accuracy in the popular HBO series *The Wire*, a gritty and pessimistic portrayal of what series producer and creator David Simon once called "The Killing Streets."[51] Former Baltimore police commissioner Edward T. Norris, who pleaded guilty to using police funds to buy personal gifts and served time in prison, plays himself in the series.[52] Norris, who is now a morning FM radio cohost in Baltimore, was credited with reducing major crimes in the city by 27 percent; crime continued to decline through 2011 before rising again more recently.[53, 54] There are now roughly as many homicides in Baltimore each year as there are in New York, which has thirteen times the city's population.[55] In July 2015, three months after the violence that followed Freddie

Gray's funeral, Baltimore realized a dark milestone: the city suffered its deadliest month since 1972. There were forty-five homicides, including a fifteen-year-old stabbed to death by a thirteen-year-old in a dispute over a cell phone[56] and an expectant father who was gunned down a month before his child was born. His girlfriend told the *Baltimore Sun* that she still texts his phone and sends it pictures of their baby girl.[57]

In the midst of this misery, Baltimore police go about their work with a decided recklessness. Simon recalled that when he began working the police beat in Baltimore decades ago, officers treated "probable cause" as "whatever you thought you could safely lie about when you go into district court." Then, like now, a prolonged stare got you in handcuffs. "You know what probable cause is on Edmondson Avenue?" Simon recalls officers saying. "You roll by in your radio car and the guy looks at you for two seconds too long."[58] Yet since the department was sued in 2006 by the ACLU and the National Association for the Advancement of Colored People (NAACP), which charged that the employment of zero-tolerance policing exceeded the bounds of acceptable law enforcement, the city had pulled back from the "mind boggling" number of arrests it was making in the early 2000s.[59]

Baltimore citizens have also had to tolerate a police department known for corruption. In addition to the scandal that brought down Norris, fourteen police officers pleaded guilty in 2012 to accepting kickbacks from a body shop where they would have cars towed after accidents in exchange for cash.[60] Far worse, several officers were convicted of entering the drug trade themselves, spreading heroin around the very streets that they had been sworn to police.[61] Ironically, the work of two of these officers was exposed through the controversial drug dealer–produced 2004 DVD *Stop Snitchin'*, which—two years after the death of Angela Dawson and her family—put would-be informers on notice that cooperating with the police would result in their deaths.[62] Even as they threatened those that might snitch on them, the drug dealers exposed cops who would shake them down for their product and later sell it for profit.

In 2014, a *Baltimore Sun* report found that in the preceding four years, more than one hundred people had won judgments or earned settlements for police brutality, among them a fifteen-year-old boy, a pregnant woman, and an eighty-seven-year-old grandmother who had suffered abuse while coming to the aid of her wounded grandson. The city paid out roughly six million dollars[63] to these and other people on charges of broken "jaws, noses, arms, legs, ankles" as well as "head trauma, organ failure, and even death" suffered during "questionable arrests,"[64] and such payouts continue. As recently as October 2015, the city paid $95,000 to a woman who claimed that she, like Freddie Gray, was subjected to a "rough ride" by police.[65] All of these claims likely represent only a small percentage of the people who were actually assaulted. Imagine how many others never reported such crimes or had their reports discarded or ignored.

Despite the fact that police brutality has become a popular grievance of a large segment of our society—particularly Black, Brown, and poor folk—many Americans remain unaware of this reality. This is due to the nature of settlements, which end lawsuits before the issues can be adjudicated, leaving the public in the dark as to what actually occurred. The conditions of the settlements prohibit the recipient from disclosing information to the news media or making any other public pronouncement on the police conduct that prompted the payout. Like the arrangements struck by prosecutors with criminal defendants on plea bargains, police brutality is a business negotiation resolved through deal making—contracts, essentially—drafted in the impenetrable shadows.

In September 2015, Baltimore mayor Stephanie Rawlings-Blake announced that the city had agreed to a wrongful-death settlement with Freddie Gray's family. In agreeing to pay $6.4 million,[66] more than the combined payout in the one hundred previous settlements mentioned above, the city did not admit liability. The city's actions here almost certainly compromised the criminal process that was yet to unfold. To many, like Harvard law professor Alan Dershowitz, Marilyn Mosby's quick indictment of the officers had been more about "crowd control" than justice.[67] And the wrongful-death settlement, rightly understood, was less about restitution for the Gray family than about hard economic realities; the deal, which preempted any civil suit by the Gray family, would save Baltimore the cost of protracted litigation. As one White Baltimorean told a reporter for the *New York Times*, the settlement was nothing but "riot insurance."[68] Rather than justice, it was political convenience, self-interest, and ever-present market logic that prevailed in the city.

MORE THAN FIFTY YEARS ago, a petty criminal by the name of Clarence Earl Gideon made an impassioned plea to the highest court of the land. He made the plea using a pencil and sheets of lined paper provided to him by the Florida prison where he was an inmate, having been convicted for breaking into a pool hall and robbing its bar of some wine, cigarettes, and a small amount of money. Not accustomed to the intricacies of the language of the law, Gideon nonetheless knew to title his page with the Latin phrase in forma pauperis or "in the form of a pauper," which allowed the petition to proceed without the usual filing fees and with some tolerance for error. Still, Gideon could not have known that his petition would also make him famous.

The crux of Gideon's complaint was that when the State of Florida refused to provide him with the assistance of a lawyer, they had denied him his constitutional right to due process as guaranteed by the Fourteenth Amendment. Though Gideon was White and lived before the onslaught of the drug war, his life had many of the hallmarks of social vulnerability today. His father died when he was three, and Gideon left home when he was fourteen. From there, he lived the life of a drifter who went in and out of prison for years at a time. He married four times and fathered three children who were taken away from him by child-welfare authorities. He suffered serious health problems. Unable to afford counsel to defend him against his latest charge, Gideon conducted his own defense, even calling a character witness on his own behalf. Still, Gideon recognized that his knowledge of the law, and lawyering, was insufficient to give him a legitimate chance at success in court. Unsurprisingly, he lost. While serving out a five-year sentence, he wrote his petition to the Supreme Court.

In *Powell v. Alabama*, the 1932 decision that grew out of the tragic story of the Scottsboro Boys, the Supreme Court had already found that in capital cases there was such a right to counsel, albeit limited to situations where the defendant was "incapable adequately of making his own defense because of ignorance, feeblemindedness, illiteracy, or the like."[69] In that case, nine Black, illiterate defendants ranging in age from thirteen to twenty had been falsely accused of raping two White women while on a train in Alabama. In an atmosphere where "crowd control" also figured largely—the town, it was said, had formed a lynch mob, and one defendant described the courtroom as "one big smiling White face"[70]—all nine were convicted and sentenced to death. Counsel for the defense had been assigned by the State, but under circumstances that made it impossible for them to be anything but ineffectual, which was, of course, the State's intention.[71] That led the high court to intervene and reverse the defendants' convictions on the basis that they had been denied "effective appointment of counsel." But its ruling was narrowly drafted, and in a subsequent decision, *Betts v. Brady* (1942), the court affirmed that this right did not extend beyond capital cases. Now Gideon was asking the justices to overturn *Betts* and grant a constitutional right to counsel for all indigent defendants as a rule.

The court, as it turned out, was ready for such a challenge. When it took up the case, it resulted in a victory for Gideon, one of the landmark decisions of the Warren era. The Warren Court, led by its chief justice, the Republican former California governor Earl Warren, is perhaps best known for its decisions that deemed segregation and anti-miscegenation laws unconstitutional. Just as important, however, the Warren Court extended the rights of the criminally accused in ways that fundamentally changed the nature of law enforcement in America. In light of the discussion above about prosecutorial pressure on the innocent to plead guilty, it is worth revisiting Warren's own opinion in *Miranda v. Arizona,* which established the requirement that police must inform criminal suspects of their rights before interrogating them. Warren pointed to "the compulsion inherent in custodial surroundings" where "no statement obtained from the defendant can truly be the product of his free choice."[72] The discovery of a right to counsel for even the poorest among us was a decision of monumental importance, one that would radically alter the criminal justice system. Unlike *Miranda* and other significant Warren Court decisions on criminal procedure that were decided on narrow votes and prompted harsh dissents from minority justices, *Gideon* was a unanimous decision, almost uniformly praised by lawyers, the press, and the general public alike.

One might have expected that Warren, who had been not only a politician but a prosecutor as well, would have anticipated the problems encountered in real-world applications of principles established from the bench. Consider, for example, the practical failures of *Brown v. Board of Education*, such as the loss of teacher jobs and the ultimate resegregation of schools and neighborhoods.[73] Still, it is unlikely that he would have conceived of just how many problems the application of *Gideon* would encounter. Just as the promise of *Miranda* has been undermined by the shift of power to plea-hungry prosecutors, so has *Gideon*, in practice, long ago lost its original luster. Anyone still crowing over how the Warren Court elevated American criminal justice to a more righteous plane should spend a day in the office of a public defender.

This situation is not new to our times. In 2004, the American Bar Association (ABA) issued a report, *Gideon's Broken Promise*,[74] that summarized hearings it had held for the fortieth anniversary of *Gideon*. The ABA's report concluded that "thousands of persons are processed through America's courts every year either with no lawyer at all or with a lawyer who does not have the time, resources, or in some cases the inclination to provide effective representation." As a result, "defendants plead guilty, *even if they are innocent*, without really understanding their legal rights or what is occurring."[75] To veterans of the bar, the report's charges must have had a familiar sound to them. In 1982, on the twentieth anniversary of *Gideon*, the ABA held similar hearings with similar conclusions. Since then the system had only grown worse.

The most egregious examples of the system's failures boggle the mind. In a capital case in Texas, the lawyer assigned to represent the defendant repeatedly fell asleep during the trial. The defendant, a gay man, also claimed that the lawyer made anti-gay slurs against him. When the defendant appealed the trial court's verdict, claiming ineffective assistance of counsel, a panel for the Fifth Circuit acknowledged that the attorney did indeed fall asleep. They argued, however, that the defendant had not proved the attorney was sleeping for the important parts of the trial.[76] Another Texas attorney in a capital case (Texas has executed more than five hundred citizens—the most of any state—since the Supreme Court lifted the ban on capital punishment in 1976) failed to meet the deadline for filing a federal petition for a habeas review of his client's case as the client faced execution.[77] The man was put to death in February 2015, and the attorney suffered no consequence for his irresponsible actions, continuing to be assigned new cases. But more disturbing than these egregious examples of incompetence and indifference to justice—and there are dozens more of them—is the broader public-defender system. Ultimately, the system fails because those assigned to represent and defend our most vulnerable citizens are chronically overworked and underpaid. Also, with the all-powerful prosecutor running the show, their jobs are largely reduced to managing paperwork.

Journalist Amy Bach spent years following the activity in courtrooms and prosecutors' chambers and unearthed consistent patterns of injustice. Despite the premium Americans long ago placed on an adversarial system, in which two sides argue to a reach a battle-tested outcome, Bach found prosecutors, judges, and defense attorneys working together as if they were members of a close-knit club, a "tag team" operating with speed to "charge the accused, assign a lawyer, prosecute, plead, sentence"—and all "with slight regard for the distinctions and complexities of each case."[78] While this arrangement creates greater efficiency and easier workflow for officials, it only further compromises the work of justice. Employees can go home on time and, freed from the adversarial relationship prescribed for them, prosecutors and defense lawyers can be the best of friends. Why? Because they have engaged with none of the social awkwardness and tension that accompanies the struggle to locate truth and justice. The public defender, from this posture, serves as little more than a clerk assisting in the administration of guilty pleas.

Bach also found persistent constitutional violations just about everywhere she went. She saw defendants plead guilty without a lawyer present and defendants who had no idea what they were pleading guilty to. She even witnessed a prosecutor announce to a room full of defendants that they could either choose to work with a public defender—Bach describes him as "a tired-looking defense lawyer sitting at a table with his back to the crowd"[79]—or move things along more quickly by speaking with someone from the prosecutor's office first. The prosecutor, showing that she fundamentally misunderstood the law, later explained to Bach that this was not a constitutional violation since people were making an affirmative decision not to utilize the public defender. "People often know that they are guilty," the prosecutor said, "and want to hear what the offer is." Guilty or not, more than half of those in the room opted to go to her first.[80]

When the Supreme Court ruled in *Gideon*, it made it necessary for states and counties to offer legal counsel to the poor. The problem, however, is that the court left it up to individual states to determine how best to provide indigent defense. As a result, there are more than fifty public-defender systems, each observing widely different standards, adding up to a fractured and dysfunctional application of the Supreme Court's mandate.[81] Pennsylvania's is among the worst. While most states passed the responsibility for providing for indigent defense over to their counties, Pennsylvania is one of four states[82] (along with Utah, South Dakota, and Arizona) that does so without state funding or state oversight.[83] As a result, the abuse of the *Gideon* principle there has become rampant.

One particularly appalling situation was uncovered a few years ago in Luzerne County, home to the city of Wilkes-Barre, when it was found that 1,866 juveniles had appeared before the county's juvenile court without counsel. With no one there to object on their behalf, the youths were sentenced to harsh terms to be served out in private, for-profit detention centers. It later turned out that the owners of these centers were providing two of the judges kickback money—to the tune of $2.6 million—in exchange for the draconian sentences.[84] This example likely does not represent the norm—though the current trend of privatizing public institutions makes such deals more common than many would like to acknowledge—but it nonetheless spotlights a larger problem. The systematic elimination or marginalization of defense attorneys from the process allows for irregularities both egregious and ordinary, well-intentioned and venal, to routinely occur. Without proper checks and balances, corruption, abuse, and injustice become the norm.

Another major issue with criminal defense is the "flat-fee system," the most common method for providing public defenders. Within this system, which is used by 64 percent of the nation's counties,[85] a judge provides a contract to private attorneys to represent every defendant that comes before them. Proponents of the flat-fee system argue that it provides support to overworked public defenders' offices and offers necessary cost savings for cash-strapped cities. Like all market-based solutions, however, the flat-fee system prioritizes economic efficiency over the fundamental interests of the public.

Because of their relatively low pay rates, flat-fee systems tend to attract less experienced lawyers. This heightens the chances of defendants receiving poor representation and shifts workloads to appellate courts due to the increased frequency of procedural errors.[86] Within a flat-fee system, attorneys are paid the same amount regardless of the complexity or severity of the case. This creates a conflict of interest between defendants and their attorneys, as the financial costs of zealous representation—such as hiring investigators, expert witnesses, and requesting records—all subtract from the attorney's profits. Essentially, it is in the best interest of the flat-fee defense attorney to do as little work as possible. These attorneys are also financially incentivized to please judges, who are responsible for giving them their contracts. This further encourages flat-fee attorneys to push cases through the system as quickly as possible. In fact, some counties provide financial incentives—essentially bonuses—to the public defender for doing so. Once again, the entanglements of the market compromise proper adjudication of the law for the vulnerable.

In theory, the Warren Court's discovery of procedural rights for the criminally accused should have made our system of justice considerably more rigorous in its pursuit of the truth and less susceptible to the mob rule that has targeted the poor, the Black, and the Brown for most of our history. And it has, for those rare few who actually get into the courtroom. But since these same procedural rights have dramatically increased the cost of a criminal trial, trials have become something that the State, short on resources, tries desperately to avoid. That it has addressed this problem by moving the role traditionally occupied by the judge to the office of the prosecutor is wholly unacceptable, for it short-circuits the principle of defense, particularly indigent defense, potentially putting the same level of abuse back into the system that the Warren Court's constitutional findings were meant to erase.

One year after the death of Freddie Gray, very little has changed in Baltimore on the most fundamental levels. As citizen uprisings have subsided, complaints of police harassment and racial profiling have persisted. Although Mayor Stephanie Rawlings-Blake decided not to pursue reelection, as of this writing the city's Democratic machine has all but ensured the ascendance of yet another political insider, State Senator Catherine Pugh, to the mayoralty. While policy conversations have turned toward more progressive solutions—such as drug treatment over mass incarceration, investment in economically vulnerable neighborhoods, and massive education reform— very few of these conversations have been translated into concrete change on the ground. And despite the State's aggressive commitment to prosecuting the officers involved in Freddie Gray's death, nothing has been done to repair a system that prosecutes, judges, and sentences millions of vulnerable citizens with the stroke of a single pen—and without any semblance of justice.

IV.

Armed

It was November 23, 2012, "Black Friday" of Thanksgiving weekend. Brevard County, Florida,[1] software developer Michael Dunn was driving back from his son's wedding in suburban Jacksonville.[2] Dunn's fiancée, Rhonda Rouer, was with him. The two, who had been drinking rum and Cokes at the wedding,[3] planned to return to their room at the Sheraton hotel to check on their dog, Charlie, who was staying there with them. But first, they decided to stop and pick up a bottle of wine; they hadn't drunk any at the wedding reception because red was all that had been served and Rouer wanted to drink white.

At roughly 7:30 p.m., they pulled into a Gate gas station and convenience store.[4] Dunn parked his black Volkswagen Jetta to the immediate right of a red Dodge Durango with several Black teenagers inside. They were parked so close, it was later observed, that the space between them would have made it hard to open the door of either car. The teens had just spent the afternoon at the St. John's Town Center mall in Jacksonville, hanging out and looking for girls.[5] Their car thumped to the sound of rap artist Lil Reese's "Beef": "Fuck nigga, you don't want no beef / In the field we play for keeps."[6] Dunn, who is White, turned to Rouer and muttered something about how much he loathed "that thug music." Rouer said "Yes, I know," then went into the store to buy the wine and some potato chips. Tommie Stornes, the driver of the Durango, was also inside the store looking for cigarettes and gum. The others— Dunn and the three remaining teens, including seventeen-year-old Jordan Davis—stayed back in their respective cars.

As he waited, Dunn leaned out the window and asked the young men if they would turn down the music. "I can't hear myself think," he added. They did as he asked. But then, Davis, who was seated in the right rear passenger seat, ordered Tevin Thompson, who was seated in the front passenger seat, to defy Dunn. "Fuck that," he said. "Turn the music back up." Thompson did as he was told. With his window down, Davis pointed his finger at the older man and said, "Fuck you." There is discrepancy between the witnesses as to what else Davis may have said,[7] and Dunn would later argue that Davis appeared to have a weapon, despite the fact that there were no weapons anywhere in the car. But all seem to agree that their face-off reached a head shortly after Stornes returned from the store, dancing to the music, oblivious to what had been going on, before getting back into the driver's seat.

As Stornes started to back out of the parking spot, Dunn continued his heated exchange with Davis. He looked squarely at the teen and said, "Are you talking to me?" Davis replied, "Yes, I'm talking to you."[8, 9] At this point, Dunn reached over to his glove compartment, pulled out a gun, opened his door,[10] and started firing toward the rear of the Durango at precisely the place where Davis was sitting. He then got out of the car and went down on one knee, into a shooter's stance, continuing to fire at the teens even as the car was moving away.[11]

From inside the convenience store, Rouer heard a "pop, pop, pop" sound.[12] "What was that?" she asked the clerk, unaware that it was gunfire. After a second "pop, pop, pop," the clerk began to look for cover. "Oh my God, someone is shooting," she said. "Someone is shooting out of their car, I swear to God!"[13] Seeing through the window that the gunman was Michael Dunn, Rouer, while unnerved, still assumed that he was not the aggressor. She even attempted to reassure the clerk that she "did not need to worry about it" because Michael was a "good guy with a gun" and he was going to "protect you."[14] Still, when Rouer hurried outside, leaving the chips and wine on the counter,[15] she froze briefly at the scene: the man she saw as her future husband had just shot up a vehicle carrying four innocent teenagers and was now replacing his revolver in the glove compartment and demanding that she get in their car at once.[16]

Without alerting the police to what had just happened, the two made a quick exit to their hotel. There, safely in their room, Rouer changed her clothes while Dunn took Charlie outside to "go potty." They ordered a pizza, and Dunn mixed a rum and Coke for each of them[17]—stronger, Rouer admitted, than they had been drinking earlier. They then watched a movie and went to bed. It was not until the following morning, after turning on the local news, that they heard that Jordan Davis, the boy in the back seat who had gotten into a verbal confrontation with Dunn, had died. Even then, the couple simply got in their car and drove home to Satellite Beach, Florida. Of the ten bullets fired by the "good guy with a gun," two had lodged in Davis's legs. A third had gone through his liver and both lungs before "shredding" Davis's aorta.[18] The whole episode, as the title of a documentary later emphasized, had taken three and a half minutes.[19]

. . . .

FOR ALL THE PROBLEMS within the American judicial system, it is
even more stunning how much faith has been placed in extrajudicial
outcomes. You can hear it in the arguments against gun control,
with progun advocates arguing that criminals and terrorists will not
risk violence against civilians if there is a high probability that the
civilians are armed, ready, and willing to fire on them. You can find
it in the increasing thirst that police departments have for big guns—
military hardware—that are by their very nature not the tools of
self-defense or law enforcement but the equipment of armies at war,
arsenals of destruction. And you can discover it in the language of
our public discourse, including the legislative zeal for "Stand Your
Ground" laws that are turning our citizenry into a vigilante force
and our streets into a violent free-for-all reminiscent of the Wild
West. If neoliberal America is engaging in a war on the vulnerable,
vindicated by a murderous perversion of the frontier code, it is recruiting the rest of us to join in.

The history of the law of homicide is an interesting thing to
behold. It is the Englishman William Blackstone who provides us
with its foundational principle. In his *Commentaries*, the eighteenth-
century legal thinker parses the crime into three categories: justifiable, excusable, and, of course, felonious.[20] The justifiable homicide
is the one committed by order of the State. It exonerates the executioner fulfilling the capital sentence pronounced on a convicted
criminal—homicide "where the law requires it." Excusable homicide
is when the killing happens by some "misadventure"—an accident,
perhaps brought on by one's negligence, but nonetheless an act committed without intent. Killing done in self-defense also falls into this
category. However, to qualify as "excusable" (a term, by the way,

which is not equal to "justifiable" and does not render the person committing the act faultless), "it must appear that the slayer had no other possible means of escaping from his assailant."[21] The law does not recognize a "right of attacking," Blackstone says—one cannot start a fight and then claim self-defense in pursuing it. Even more than that, the one who eventually kills "should have retreated[22] as far as he conveniently or safely" could to "avoid the violence of the assault" and should do so "from a real tenderness" at the thought of "shedding his brother's blood."[23] Blackstone's point is that the right to defend oneself should not be mistaken for the right to kill.

There has long been a significant exception to this doctrine of retreat: the "castle doctrine." Blackstone wrote that "the law of England has so particular and tender a regard to the immunity of a man's house, that it stiles it his castle, and will never suffer it to be violated with impunity."[24] Under these circumstances, when faced with an attacker threatening one's place of living, a homeowner need not run. Indeed, with certain restrictions, she would be "excused" for killing her intruder. The precedent actually goes back even before Blackstone, to the 1604 decision of the great English barrister Edward Coke. In what is known as Semayne's Case, Coke declared a home to be not only a place of "repose," but a "fortress, as well for his defence against injury and violence."[25]

Some manner of "castle doctrine" has been part of American common law since before the nation's founding; one could even argue that the Fourth Amendment to the Constitution is built, in part, on it. But there has also been a parallel line in America, as much cultural as legal, that objects to the idea of "duty to retreat" in absolute terms. Whether it be in one's "castle" or anywhere else where one has a right to be, retreating is often interpreted as cowardly and fundamentally un-American.[26] This sense has occasionally been referenced in American legal decision making, as when the early twentieth century Justice Oliver Wendell Holmes Jr., writing for the Supreme Court in *Brown v. United States*, found that it was too much for the law to expect that a person under attack would have the opportunity to soberly consider his or her option to retreat. "Detached reflection cannot be demanded in the presence of an uplifted knife," Holmes famously wrote.[27]

This argument addressed the issue of "imminent threat" that colors all self-defense law, but it was not the only principle informing Holmes's opinion. Writing about the case to his friend Harold Laski, Holmes declared that "a man is not born to run away," and indeed it is this sense of honor, more specifically masculine honor, that America has added to the English common-law doctrine of self-defense.[28] An earlier Supreme Court had described this as the "true man" doctrine, as in a "true man, who is without fault" is "not obliged to fly from an assailant who by violence or surprise maliciously seeks to take his life or to do him enormous bodily harm."[29] The thinking of Holmes and others was informed by a dangerous conception of patriarchal masculinity that imagines "true manhood" as an identity that must be constantly protected through various forms of violence.[30]

Until recently, there had been little effort to codify the "castle" or, for that matter, the "true man" doctrine. But over the past few years, state legislatures have been rushing to write laws that extend the reach of the castle to include not only a person's physical residence but his body as well. In essence, these new laws declare that a person's body is as much a castle as a brick-and-mortar abode. Of course, few of the conservative politicians—libertarians aside— who have pushed the extension of the castle doctrine would see the clear resonance with the argument for women's reproductive rights that would naturally flow from such an idea. After all, at its ideological core, this doctrine is about male identity, male property, and male bodies.

The move to extend the castle doctrine began in Florida in 2005, with the passage of the first "Stand Your Ground" law. Despite the fact that crime was already down nationwide, the state's politics were largely shaped by the energy and money being deployed by special-interest groups. A campaign by one of the boldest lobbyists for the National Rifle Association (NRA)—the group's former president, Marion P. Hammer, whose efforts on behalf of gun rights had already earned her a place in the Florida Women's Hall of Fame—is widely credited with having forced the issue on a pliant legislature.

The bill, which passed 39–0 in the Florida senate and 94–20 in the state House,[31] differed from common-law doctrine in that it carried a presumption that the person using deadly force against an attacker has, by definition, the required level of fear to be considered as acting in self-defense. Based on this presumption, the bill said that there need not be any attempt to retreat from such a fight, and that those who kill under such circumstances do not even necessarily have to go to trial. Instead, they can achieve immunity from both civil and criminal prosecution by convincing a judge at a pretrial hearing that the shooting was justified. Florida governor Jeb Bush, who signed the bill into law, derided four hundred years of legal reasoning when he declared that the "Stand Your Ground" law revised a duty-to-retreat doctrine that defied "common sense."[32]

Florida was only the beginning. Though the late Sarah Brady, then head of the Brady Campaign to Prevent Gun Violence, expressed her disgust with the state[33] and vowed to fight similar measures as they emerged across the country, she was no match for the NRA and its allies.[34] Urged on by the gun lobby, the American

Legislative Exchange Council (ALEC), an organization that brings together business representatives and state legislators to write model legislation supporting conservative causes, brandished the Florida law as a prototype for the rest of the country.[35] The council, which is funded by donors that include the Koch brothers[36] and dozens of the nation's top corporations (many of which later withdrew when ALEC's claimed nonprofit status came under fire), successfully pushed the Florida law nationwide. Today there are forty states that have castle doctrine laws—that is, they have created statutes, rather than relying on the common law—and twenty-four that have extended the reach of the doctrine to situations outside of the home.

A 2007 study by the National District Attorneys Association[37] found that the appeal of "Stand Your Ground" laws came from beliefs that are strongly contradicted by facts: that terrorists are around every corner, that the criminal justice system works to protect criminals, and that the due-process rights of lawbreakers are valued over the rights of victims. "People want to know we stand on the side of victims of crime instead of the side of criminals," said Republican lawmaker Dennis Baxley, who sponsored Florida's law the year after the NRA had given him its 2004 Defender of Freedom Award.[38, 39] While no one can dispute that sentiment, many people, especially those in law enforcement, have seen Florida's law as encouraging, not discouraging, lawbreakers. Seven years after the law was enacted, Miami's police chief penned an op-ed in the *New York Times* decrying not only the law itself but the message it sent: that every argument can be taken to its natural extreme, that road rage and drunken outbursts need not be reined in, and that even deadly force can, in this new environment, be treated with immunity.[40]

There was one other reason the National District Attorneys Association study found for the rise of "Stand Your Ground." The easing of gun regulations across the nation meant that more guns were now available, resulting in pressure to find more opportunities to use them. By this logic, the new "Stand Your Ground" laws were only keeping up with a trend, one that had grown both organically and with the support of the NRA. That trend was the growing perception that we live in a gun-loving culture. This message became entangled with citizens' frustrations about what they perceived to be an unresponsive government, and a growing sense that they were less in control of their own lives. To these Americans, it all seemed to add up to a society that looks a lot like the one their frontier forefathers knew, one in which individuals, and not the government, were the guardians of their own safety. It was as if America was waking up from the twentieth century to discover that it had retreated to the nineteenth.

We can blame the Supreme Court, in part, for this. For over two hundred years from the nation's founding, the Second Amendment was viewed as protecting the rights of citizen militias. The very words "well regulated militia" are in the amendment itself, as in, "[a] well regulated Militia, being necessary to the security of a free State, the right of the people to keep and bear Arms, shall not be infringed."[41] But in 2008, the court reversed itself on its view of the Second Amendment—first invalidating a District of Columbia law that restricted handgun ownership in what is a federally controlled jurisdiction, and then in 2010 doing the same to a Chicago ordinance, thereby imposing the interpretation of an individual's right to a firearm on all state and local governments as well.

The late justice Antonin Scalia, who wrote the opinion for the court's narrow (5–4) majority in the DC case, based his reading, in part, on a particular understanding of the Constitution's use of the word "people."[42] For most of American history, the word has been read as a collective noun—the people as a community comprised of all of us. It appears in the preamble to the Constitution as part of one of the most famous lines in American history: "We the people . . ." But in his reading, Scalia made a distinction between those places where "people" describes a power—here, in the preamble, a collective understanding of the term was the correct one—and those places, like the Second Amendment, where it describes a right. The latter, he asserted, should be compared to the use of the term "people" in the First Amendment, where the framers describe the "right of the people peaceably to assemble, and to petition the government for a redress of grievances."[43]

While an assembly by definition requires more than one person, it is the individual's right to assemble with others that is being protected by the First Amendment. Surely, the framers did not intend to deny a single person the right to petition, and only to provide that right to, say, a group of lobbyists. Still, it is a remarkable thing for a court to overturn such a longstanding doctrine as that which has defined Second Amendment jurisprudence. It is even more startling to see this shift motivated by the logic of Scalia, an ostensibly "originalist" justice who spent thirty years on the Supreme Court deriding landmark liberal rulings as representative of an "activist" agenda. Indeed, if there is an activist agenda today, seeking to subvert the people's will as expressed by the nation's legislatures, it is one pushed by the political right. In 1991, Supreme Court chief justice Warren Burger—a conservative, appointed by Richard Nixon—challenged Scalia's interpretation, telling *PBS NewsHour* that the idea that the Second Amendment protected an individual right to a firearm "is one of the greatest pieces of fraud, I repeat the word 'fraud,' on the American public by special interest groups that I have ever seen in my lifetime."[44]

. . . .

For strategic reasons, Michael Dunn's attorneys opted not to seek immunity under "Stand Your Ground."[45] Since it was unlikely that a judge would grant the motion for such a high-profile case, Dunn's attorneys decided not to even try, as it would give the prosecutors an early peek at his defense strategy. A first trial on the charge of first-degree murder then ended in a deadlock when jurors split over whether Dunn, responding to Davis, was acting to protect himself as allowed by the law. Noting that Dunn continued to fire at the car well after it had begun to pull away, the jurors did, however, find him guilty of second-degree attempted murder. When the state then moved to try Dunn again on the first-degree murder charge with respect to Davis, it won a conviction, and Dunn was sentenced to life in prison without the chance of parole.[46]

Still, even without his attorneys seeking immunity, "Stand Your Ground" loomed large in Dunn's two trials. In each case, when the judge gave instructions to the jury, he reminded them that if Michael Dunn was in a place where he had a right to be, he had no duty to retreat, that he had the right to "stand his ground" and meet "force with force, including deadly force if he reasonably believed that it was necessary to do so to prevent death or great bodily harm to himself."[47] In fact, a juror from the first Dunn trial described the dilemma she experienced during deliberations. She felt that there were things that Dunn could have done besides shooting, including "roll the window up, ignore the taunting, put [his] car in reverse . . . move a parking spot over."[48] These options would have figured prominently in any decision had the case been tried before 2005—in all likelihood leading to a swift first-degree murder conviction—but all of them, in effect, amounted to some manner of "retreat." And in

2014, "retreat" was not something demanded of someone who, like Dunn, felt threatened. For anyone who sensed that level of danger, "Stand Your Ground" was a license to kill.

So why did Dunn sense he was in danger?

Why did he claim to see a gun when no gun was ever found?

Of course, we could simply assume that Dunn was lying about seeing a gun in an attempt to avoid punishment. While this may or may not be true, it is also helpful to consider the social cues to which he was responding. Specifically, there was the recognition of loud music—"thug music," as Dunn called it, by which he meant Black music. The term "thug," in this case, was not used merely as an expression of musical taste. Rather, Dunn was making judgments not only about the music but also about the types of people who create and listen to such music. For Dunn, "thug music," along with the assumed race, class, and gender of the young men in the car, may have served as markers of violence.[49] To Dunn, the teens themselves were thugs—and thugs have guns.

Now, from at least one perspective, Dunn might have been justified in thinking that Davis had a gun. After all, a lot of people in Florida have guns. In fact, this kind of confrontation is precisely what the "Stand Your Ground" proponents imagine our proper future should be: "You have a gun and I have a gun and, because we both know that, we do not dare escalate an argument." Its historical antecedent is the Dodge City standoff of pulp fiction and its most recent geopolitical appearance is the mutual assured destruction doctrine of the Cold War. But if that dynamic is supposed to prevent rather than incite violence, why did it not work out that way here? One possible reason is that in order to work, this "standoff" conception required only that Dunn brandish his weapon to remind Davis that he was armed, not that he actually shoot it. But more likely it is because when Marion Hammer, the NRA, and ALEC promoted their prototype of the "Stand Your Ground" law, it wasn't the safety of people like Jordan Davis and his friends that they had in mind. It was the White masculine pride of people like Michael Dunn.

This is where the problematic notion of the "true man" from history returns. One of the ideas behind "no duty to retreat" is that he who is "right" should not have to run from those who challenge him. Michael Dunn had a right to be where he was. To have to endure the insults being flung his way, move his car to another parking space, or drive off to another convenience store, all to avoid confrontation with one who was "wrong"—well, that, according to the logic of "Stand Your Ground," would be not only unfair but unmanly. The prosecutor highlighted this theme when he offered that Dunn's rage at Davis emerged not because he feared that Davis had a weapon but because he knew that Davis had a "big mouth" and that he felt disrespected by it. "That defendant didn't shoot into a carful of kids to save his life," he told the jury. "He shot into it to save his pride."[50]

The idea that "Stand Your Ground" empowers the "good guy with a gun" is central to its appeal, which is central to a worldview promoted by the NRA. In November 2014, the organization issued an open letter to all members, signed by its executive vice president, Wayne LaPierre.[51] The missive, which was titled "Is Chaos at Our Door?" was timed to the midterm election and opened with a photograph of a knife-wielding, black-masked figure reminiscent of the Islamic State in Iraq and Syria (ISIS) executioner Jihadi John, superimposed on a typical American suburban neighborhood scene. The text of the letter begins with a familiar attack on the press. "You won't hear this from the mainstream media," writes LaPierre, before quoting from an article from the mainstream *Wall Street Journal* on the threat that terrorists will use an electromagnetic pulse to wipe out the nation's power grid, leaving us all to fend for ourselves in the darkness. "Imagine your world blanketed by pitch black," the NRA chief continues. "You have no lights, no electricity. Phones don't work. Even the battery-powered radio you keep for emergencies picks up nothing but static—if it powers up at all."

What would it be like to endure such a horrific attack? Well, according to LaPierre, it would be as if "our nation was plunged back into the 1800s": no electricity, no gas, no Internet, no food, our hospitals rendered useless to fight the onslaught of Third World diseases arising from the absence of clean water or sanitation. LaPierre then expands upon his image with references to two recent times when things did "go black": in 2005, with Hurricane Katrina, and in 2010, with the earthquake in Haiti, both of which events rendered hundreds of thousands of poor Black people homeless, desperate, and roaming the streets. From his evocation of images from pre-Emancipation America to his conjuring of images of Black civic disorder, LaPierre is anything but subtle in his appeal to White nationalist terror and solidarity.

LaPierre tells his membership that if terrorists do not do us in, then Mexican drug lords or Chicago gangs (like the ones, he tells us, that live near President Obama's home) will. According to LaPierre, there are twenty thousand gangs with a total of more than a million members in America. And what about the immigrants, "the waves of drug smugglers, kidnappers, sex-slave traffickers and criminals of all kinds who invade our country from the south every day"? Add those to the criminals being released by our federal justice department—13,500 a month from California prisons alone—and you have a society where enemies lurk in every corner. "For all you know, you pass them in your car on your way to work."

Terrifying though this vision of modern America may seem, LaPierre is just beginning. "Even if you take the terrorists and criminals out of the picture," he offers, "chaos is an ever-present danger to America today—especially when you factor in the undercurrent of social unrest that seethes beneath the surface of much of our society." Remember, LaPierre is writing less than four months after the killing of Eric Garner, less than three months after the killing of Michael Brown, and after the street rebellions that these killings inspired. In his writing, LaPierre conjures images of everything from peaceful protests to sporting events degenerating into riots, shootings, and other forms of civic disarray. The picture, particularly for economically vulnerable White males feeling threatened by America's changing demographics, is horrifying. But the key here is not so much LaPierre's vision of America, distorted and manipulative as it may be, but rather his solution to it: strap up and prepare yourself. Faced with a world that has decayed into an arena of primal aggression, there is no room to embrace a sense of community or shared public values. There is only one thing left to do: reach for your gun. The police cannot be counted on to defend us. "The government can't—or *won't*—protect you, either," pronounces LaPierre. "Only *you* can protect you." Only you.

Along with such florid descriptions of a dystopian future, the NRA publishes a magazine, *American Rifleman*. The monthly has been around since 1923, and to scan the covers that have graced it since its founding is to witness a replay of America's history with guns. In the early years, there were painterly scenes of duck hunters and other sportsmen. Military heroes, winners of rifle competitions, and pictures of historic firearms and shooting ranges are favorite topics of the 1940s, '50s and '60s. By the late twentieth century, when the organization became more overtly political, there were appeals to resist the "anti-gun frenzy" sweeping the nation, for readers to stand up for liberty and vote for those who will respect the Second Amendment. More recently, however, the magazine has become a showcase for personal firearms, semi-assault rifles, and stories of glory in a column the editors call "The Armed Citizen." The message is clear: America is under attack, and it must be defended by any means necessary.

IF TRAYVON MARTIN HAD been a little older and lawfully carrying a gun on February 26, 2012, the situation might have turned out differently. Under such circumstances, Martin, and not his killer, might have been a poster child for the NRA's Second Amendment campaign. Martin, of course, was the gray-hoodie-wearing seventeen-year-old Black boy who was staying with his father and his father's fiancée at a gated town home community in Sanford, Florida, when he was confronted by George Zimmerman, a neighborhood watch volunteer who had already reported Martin to 911 as appearing "real suspicious" and "up to no good."[52, 53] Martin, who was unarmed, had just gone to a 7-Eleven convenience store to pick up some Skittles for his younger brother and a can of Arizona Iced Tea for himself.[54] The NBA All-Star Game, which they had been watching, was at halftime.[55]

As he returned, Martin felt Zimmerman's eyes on him. Speaking by phone to a friend, Rachel Jeantel, the teen told her that there was a "creepy-ass cracker"[56] following him. Meanwhile, Zimmerman, who was known to police as a "wannabe cop" who frequently—perhaps too frequently—called in tips, was keeping a running account of Martin's every movement. "It's raining and he is just walking around, looking about . . . looking at all the houses," he said to the dispatcher. "He's got his hand in his waistband and he's a Black male. . . . These assholes, they always get away."

Just as the dispatcher was telling him that an officer was en route to the scene, Zimmerman noticed that Martin was running. He went in pursuit. "Are you following him?" the dispatcher asked. "Yeah," said Zimmerman. "Okay," he replied. "We don't need you to do that."[57] But Zimmerman continued. On the phone with Rachel Jeantel, Martin mentioned that he thought he had escaped Zimmerman, then a moment later announced that he, in fact, had not. The last words from Martin that Jeantel would ever hear were the first he spoke to Zimmerman. "Why are you following me for?"

We do not know precisely what happened from there, largely because we only have Zimmerman's side of the story. But we do know from several 911 calls placed by other residents that the two ended up in a brief and violent scuffle. While Jeantel lost contact with Martin, their call was still connected, and she could hear the sounds of movement in the grass and someone saying "Get off" before the phone went dead.[58] She thought it was Martin speaking, but Zimmerman claims that it was actually he who was calling for help. He argues that Martin had pinned him down and was banging his head on the sidewalk and that, in response to this, he finally pulled his 9-mm Kel-Tec semiautomatic pistol,[59] a firearm similar to those used by many police officers, and shot Martin dead.

Since Martin—carrying Skittles and tea, returning home from a trip to the store—was in a place where he had the right to be, and since Martin was the one being pursued in the night by a man with a gun (Zimmerman was not a police officer and, however one might describe his "community watch officer" role, he was not in uniform), you would think sympathy would fall to the teenager to act in self-defense, to "stand his ground." And if he had had a weapon—his own Kel-Tec semiautomatic—the NRA itself should have been there in the rain, cheering him on to use it. Of course, the actual result couldn't have been further from a story of self-defense. Instead, the story of Trayvon Martin's death, in terms of the response from the Sanford police and later in a Florida courtroom, became the tale of a scary Black teenager who didn't have a gun, but invented one by turning the concrete sidewalk into a weapon just as deadly; a boy who was not the victim but rather the aggressor. And why? Because he did not flee, because he dared to confront Zimmerman, because he did not retreat, because he ventured to assert himself as a true man. "We know he had the opportunity to go home, and he didn't do that," said Zimmerman defense attorney Mark O'Mara, of Martin. "The person who decided this was going to become a violent event was the guy who didn't go home when he had the chance to."[60] O'Mara's statement, which the jury ultimately found persuasive, underscores an unspoken but repeatedly confirmed understanding: the right to self-defense and "true manhood," however corrupt an idea it is, does not include Black citizens.

It mattered little that Zimmerman had profiled Martin as "up to no good" only because he was walking slowly and using a hoodie to cover his head (it was raining in Sanford that evening), and then because he started to run (a normal reaction to being followed in the dark by an unknown person). What mattered was that Zimmerman had not seen him before and he was Black. In a posttrial press conference, after Zimmerman had been acquitted of all charges, O'Mara continued to display a pattern of logic worthy of Lewis Carroll. He declared that the sole reason Zimmerman had been charged with a crime was because of his race, that it was he, and not Martin, who had been profiled. Once it became clear that Zimmerman was White and Martin Black, he argued, that fact alone served

as a convenient way to see this story through a racial prism, to assert
a racial agenda, and to refuse to recognize the incident for what it
was: an act of self-defense. The idea that Zimmerman was acting on
a racial motive, said O'Mara, was simply not borne out by the facts.

Yes, it is hard to legally argue that Zimmerman killed Martin
because he was Black. Absent a clear pattern of deep-seated racist
behavior closely associated with the criminal event in question, it
is next to impossible to prove beyond a reasonable doubt that racial
hatred has spurred anyone to act on any impulse. This is why the
repeated attempts to charge a White person who kills a Black person
with a hate crime, in violation of that Black citizen's federal civil
rights, are little more than an exercise in political theater. Even if
we could faithfully assert that race was indeed a factor, certainly
there may be others; the human brain is a complex organ and every
act is pushed forward by a multitude of impulses. Zimmerman, for
example, likely also held Martin in suspicion because he was young
and male. But this is where an analysis can be tragically stalled: just
because race cannot be isolated or proven in a court of law as a motivating factor does not mean it can be eliminated.

The important thing to behold is that, based upon nothing more
than a demographic outline, Zimmerman held Martin in such suspicion that he denied him the basic human right of freedom of
movement. Even worse, he did so not as an officer of the law but,
to use the NRA's syntax, as an "Armed Citizen." Like the defense
team in the Michael Dunn case, O'Mara opted not to argue that
Florida's "Stand Your Ground" statute justified Zimmerman in his
killing of Martin. But can anyone doubt that the new enthusiasm
for State-sanctioned vigilantism informed the jury's decision in this
case? And even if we do not argue race was the primary motivator,
is there not something else to behold, something very disturbing, in

the image of an unarmed teenager lying dead and unnamed while the killer holding the gun that killed him is briefly questioned and then allowed to go home? (Martin had no identification on him— he was, after all, a teenage boy—but, as *New York Times* columnist Charles Blow has written,[61] the police that night did not even afford him the dignity of a search through the community to inquire if a teenager was missing.)

Even if we were to grant that there was indeed potential evidence for an argument of self-defense, why were the police so ready to believe Zimmerman that they simply questioned him and let him go? Why did it take six weeks of national outrage for the State to finally move to arrest the shooter? Is it possible that they were so inured to the denial of rights to a victim who fit Martin's description that those rights were not even given a cursory consideration? Sadly, the poster boy of this story turned out to be George Zimmerman, not Trayvon Martin. Two and a half years after he shot the bullet that ended a teenager's life, Zimmerman could be found at an Orlando gun show wearing a T-shirt promoting a local firearms shop. The neighborhood watch volunteer was now a celebrity of sorts—strangers approached him to say "God bless you," as if he were a war hero—and still carrying his 9-mm, semiautomatic handgun.[62]

IF EXTRAJUDICIAL DISPUTE RESOLUTION has been sanctioned on our streets, it has a counterpart on the other side of the spectrum in the gross militarization of our police. Even as we have handed some of the responsibility for policing over to the "Armed Citizen," we have been turning the police themselves into a small-scale army. *Washington Post* journalist Radley Balko describes the trend as developing in three stages.[63] The first was in response to the Black Power movement and the race riots of the 1960s, which prompted a "War on Crime." The second was in concert with the War on Drugs. The third came with 9/11 and the so-called "War on Terror." At each stage, the use of the "war" meme was a convenient way of both raising public awareness of a civic crisis and also justifying the use of extraordinary tools and tactics to resolve it. The police, after all, can fight crime, but you need an army to fight a war.

The nation's first Special Weapons and Tactics, or SWAT, team was established by the Los Angeles Police Department in response to the 1965 race riots in the neighborhood of Watts. The unrest, which resulted in the death of thirty-six Blacks and the arrest of four thousand more,[64] erased much of the national goodwill that had been established (at least superficially) by the civil rights movement. This led to a conservative backlash that operated under the premise of "law and order." Still, there were concerns within the LAPD that a military-style assault unit (in its original conception, the "A" in SWAT stood for "attack")[65] violated the mandate of a civil police force. There were also worries that if a police force began to be organized and trained like an army that it might soon look and act like an army. But fear of more riots and pressure from a public that felt crime was running out of control won over the departmental brass. The original notion was that the SWAT team was to be employed reactively—that is, in response to an event, not to initiate one—which was at least consistent with the role of a police force looking to restore order. But from the start, that limited mission was scrapped. The LAPD's new SWAT team was used for the first time on the local office of the Black Panthers in an early-morning raid on December 6, 1969.

The attack came at a time when the Black Panther Party was at the high point of its influence in the Black community and generating considerable alarm among the broader American public. In fact, anyone tracing America's history with guns should pause to consider the ironic contrast of that era with today. Back in the mid-1960s, Black Nationalist leaders like Malcolm X were publicly contemplating the choice between "bullets" and "ballots," and deadly confrontations between police and Black activists were common. In this climate, efforts to push through restrictions on gun ownership were embraced by conservative lawmakers motivated by the specter of the armed Black invader. At the same time, Black activists, convinced that gun-control advocates aimed to disarm the Black community, asserted their gun rights as fervently as NRA activists do today.[66] History shadowed the Black Power movement's concerns, as gun laws had been adopted throughout the South during Reconstruction in an effort at disarming Black militias resisting the violence of the Ku Klux Klan.[67] "I see no reason why on the street today a citizen should be carrying loaded weapons," said then California governor Ronald Reagan in response to the Mulford Act, a 1967 California gun-control bill that repealed the open carry of firearms.[68] On May 2, 1967, thirty "armed Negroes" invaded the chamber of the California statehouse carrying pistols, rifles, and shotguns as they protested the legislation.[69]

The 1969 Los Angeles SWAT raid was aimed, ostensibly, at a cache of illegal firearms. But few doubt that the Panthers themselves were the real targets. The attack came only days after police in Chicago had murdered the charismatic Fred Hampton, head of the Illinois chapter of the Panthers, in a raid ordered by State's Attorney Edward Hanrahan. Hanrahan had been waging a "war on gangs," which Hampton described as a "war on black youth."[70] The killing, which gained the approval of the editorial writers at the *Chicago Tribune* (their headline read "No Quarter for Wild Beasts"),[71] had fueled anticipation that more raids were in the works in other major cities.

The Los Angeles shootout lasted over three hours, and the two sides exchanged more than five thousand rounds. In an attempt to finish off the attack, LAPD acting chief Daryl Gates asked for a grenade launcher from the Marine base at Camp Pendleton. Yet because it involved a civil action—the use of military hardware on a domestic enemy holed up in a building in one of the nation's largest cities—his request was greeted with alarm. The Marines told him that he would have to get clearance from the Pentagon, which, after enlisting the help of Los Angeles Mayor Sam Yorty, he did. "The story is remarkable," writes Radley Balko, not because Gates's request was granted but because of the care and worry that went into the consideration of it. "About twenty years later, the Pentagon would begin giving away millions of pieces of military equipment to police departments across the country for everyday use—including plenty of grenade launchers."[72]

Today, SWAT teams are everywhere, and SWAT raids—still a relative rarity as recently as 1980—are now conducted roughly fifty thousand times a year, most of them to serve warrants or execute drug raids.[73] In fact, one would be hard pressed to find a decent-sized municipality that does not have its own paramilitary operation. Irvine, California, for instance, is perhaps the safest city in America,[74] yet its police department has a nine-ton Ballistic Engineered Armored Response vehicle (BEAR)[75] fitted with gun ports and a rotating turret at top. When it was acquired back in 2004 on a federal government grant, it was seen as ready to "carry officers into gunfights, breach buildings, help rescue hostages, and better prepare Irvine for biological warfare and terrorist attacks," reported the *Orange County Register*.[76] But it has only been used five times since then and only to deliver a felony search warrant or approach a barricaded suspect. It has never been fired upon. Many federal agencies, including the

Bureau of Land Management, the US Fish and Wildlife Service, the Department of Agriculture, and the US Railroad Retirement Board have their own SWAT teams as well.[77]

The first big ramp-up in police militarization came with the decision of the Reagan administration to allow the military to assist in the drug war. Then came a further expansion of the police power to seize assets. Finally, there was the move to end the exclusionary rule, whereby evidence gathered illegally cannot be used in court. With each step, military assets became more central to ordinary policing. Ironically, the "castle doctrine" figured here too—not because it allowed for protection of the home from the invasion of a criminal intruder but because historically it was primarily intended as a means of limiting the intrusion of the civil servant issuing a warrant.

The Fourth Amendment was written out of the experience that the American colonists had with capricious and arbitrary searches conducted at will by British authorities—in particular, the "writs of assistance" employed to enforce tax and import laws. (The term "assistance" referred to a court requesting that sheriffs and other officials carry out its orders). These writs were general warrants that allowed the authorities to enter private homes to confiscate smuggled goods. What was particularly onerous about them was that they were, for all intents and purposes, permanent: once a writ had been issued, it was good until six months after the demise of the king who held power when it had been written. This meant that a writ could last decades.

When King George II died in 1760, it fell to the new king, George III, to renew the writs that had been in force before his ascension. The colonists demanded hearings to challenge them, and the orations given at those hearings by the colonial lawyer James Otis Jr. were so powerful that John Adams later remarked that they were the "spark" that led to the American Revolution.

Otis's appeal before the court ultimately failed, but it only followed that the nation's founders would later enshrine the principles that he had espoused in their constitution. Thus, the Fourth Amendment requires that searches and seizures can only be conducted with "probable cause"—not some vague suspicion, as the British had often followed—and with a warrant issued by a judge "particularly describing the place to be searched, and the persons or things to be seized."[78] In practice, this has meant that government agents serving a warrant can only do so with certain restrictions, among them that they "knock and announce" their arrival and allow enough time for the resident to respond. Only then can the officer, if barred by the homeowner, proceed to a forced entry.

For most of American history, these rules were respected. But beginning in the 1960s, and more so throughout the 1970s and 1980s, exceptions began to be made as the nation aggressively pursued the War on Drugs. The first crack in the doctrine came with the willingness to let police force their way into homes without knocking if they believed that announcing their arrival might prompt the suspect to destroy evidence. Then came the "no knock" warrant specifically allowing police to storm a residence without having to make that judgment in the moment. There were discussions of "loose search" warrants too—reminiscent of the "writs of assistance"—under which police would be allowed to search several destinations with the same warrant, though these were never adopted. Aware that Blacks were disproportionately the targets of these adjustments to the rules, several civil rights groups were among those who protested them.[79] But they were not the only ones.

Perhaps the most disturbing shift in American search-and-seizure policy came with the attack on the exclusionary rule. The Supreme Court long ago decided that if police violate the Fourth Amendment's provisions on forced entry, then the evidence that they discover is tainted ("fruit of the poisonous tree")[80] and cannot be used in court.[81] The decision was handed down in the court's liberal Warren era, much to the chagrin of conservative dissenters who would argue that criminals would get off on "technicalities." But the rule was defended by others as a way of discouraging bad police practice. Still, increasingly, the rule has been eroded as Republican presidents have assumed power and put their imprimatur on the court.

First, the court permitted the government to use the poisonous-tree evidence so long as it was being presented to convict someone other than the person whose privacy rights had been breached. Then it allowed the evidence even if the warrant had been improperly drafted—that is, with, say, an innocent clerical error. In 2006, the justices allowed for evidence that was obtained despite violating the "knock and announce" provision of Fourth Amendment practice. And in 2011, Chief Justice John Roberts, writing for the majority, asserted that Fourth Amendment violations can only be used to deny evidence if the violations are systemic or egregious.[82] Good-faith errors do not, Roberts said, reach the threshold of interests that the Fourth Amendment was intended to protect.

By this standard, it has become all but impossible for such claims of unconstitutionality to hold up in court. Consider, for instance, the recent case of a group of Latino day laborers in Danbury, Connecticut, who were picked up by an undercover police officer posing as a contractor and dropped off at a parking lot where agents of US Immigration and Customs Enforcement awaited them. The men, who then faced deportation, argued that the officers lacked "probable cause" and had targeted them purely because they looked Latino.[83] But a three-judge panel of the Second Circuit Court of Appeals denied that their Fourth Amendment rights had been violated since they "self-selected" to go with the "contractor."[84] Whatever questionable tactics the police may have employed, they did not rise to the "egregious" level that the Supreme Court has established as the new standard. As a result of these changes, police officers have been given even greater latitude to wage war on neighborhoods and treat citizen homes like occupied territory.

THOUGH KATHRYN JOHNSTON HAD resided in the Atlanta neighborhood called the Bluff for seventeen years, her family worried about her. Ninety-two years old and living alone in an area known for its hundreds of empty, boarded-up houses, drug dealing, and prostitution,[85] Johnston was vulnerable. The Bluff had the highest crime rate of any neighborhood in the city, the most active heroin business in the entire Southeast, and a level of poverty that made it feel like an island of desperation.[86] (Like many sites of civic terror, the hellish conditions in which Johnston lived were present at the doorstep of Atlanta's economic epicenter, just a short walk from the Georgia Dome and the headquarters of the multinational corporation Coca-Cola.) A neighbor told the *New York Times* that Johnston was scared and almost always stayed inside her house. "She wouldn't even come to the door for me unless I called first."[87] Another elderly neighbor had recently been raped. Concerned for her safety, Johnston's niece had given her a gun to protect herself—a "rusty revolver" is how it was later described—and there were bars on the windows and on her front door to defend against burglary. Yet when a break-in finally did happen to her home at 933 Neal Street NW, it wasn't the nefarious effort of one of the area's many drug dealers. It was the Atlanta police.

Around 7:00 p.m. on November 21, 2006, eight narcotics officers stormed Kathryn Johnston's home on a mission to serve a warrant.

Since it was drugs they were after, they had convinced a judge to issue them a warrant to enter without knocking. On recordings of police radio traffic that were later released, one of the officers can be heard saying "Elderly female on the location . . . with a handgun," and referring to Johnston as the "perp."[88] Still, their intended target was a drug dealer. Earlier in the day, they had approached a small-time pusher from the neighborhood and, after arresting him, asked for a lead. The officers were short of their quota of arrests for the month and were in search of an easy mark. The dealer, in desperation, pointed out Johnston's home. The cops then lied to the judge who issued them their no-knock warrant, telling him that they had an informant who had done a "controlled buy" of crack at the house when in reality none had occurred. The police arrived that night with crowbars to peel back the bars on Johnston's door and a ram to push it in. When they finally made their entry, Johnston, no doubt believing that the men were the intruders she had long feared, met them with her gun. She fired one shot, missing her target. In response, the narcotics officers returned a barrage of bullets, thirty-nine in total, striking Johnston dead.

The officers, aware of their mistake, then moved to cover it up. They attempted to recruit an informant to lie and say that he had indeed bought cocaine there, though he refused to go along with them and later told investigators of the plot. The officers planted drugs in the house. Protests erupted in the Bluff. One, organized by the New Black Panther Party,[89] rallied outside Johnston's home. Another, in a nearby church, demanded that the officers be held accountable for Johnston's death. Two of the three officers eventually owned up to their lies and pleaded guilty to charges of manslaughter, the third pleaded guilty to lesser charges. But in a subsequent investigation of the Atlanta Police Department (APD), federal prosecutors found this was far from an isolated incident. Rather, police regularly lied to get warrants[90] and were so focused on meeting performance requirements that they often cut other corners.

More than ten years have now passed since Johnston died. A mural depicting her has been painted on the window of her now abandoned home,[91] making it a memorial of sorts. In response to the Johnston episode, an Atlanta Citizen Review Board[92] was established, providing a place where people can bring complaints about official misconduct. But five years out, it has been described as more symbolic than substantive, resented by the APD, a watchdog with no teeth.[93] The APD adjusted its procedures for requesting warrants to ensure a more rigorous standard would be applied. But in 2013, two ex-officers filed complaints in federal court arguing that, much like the officers in the Johnston case, they were being forced to meet strict quotas for arrests. The Georgia state legislature considered a bill to define and limit no-knock warrants, yet, years after it was introduced, the bill languishes in the state House.[94]

Meanwhile, the State-sanctioned war on citizens, guilty and innocent, continues.

V.

Caged

Had Michael Brown survived his assault by Officer Darren Wilson, or if the incident between Brown and Wilson had never even happened, inevitably, Brown would have had another encounter with the criminal justice system. By his early twenties and almost certainly by his late twenties, Michael Brown would have been accused of, confessed to, or been found guilty of a crime, *whether he committed the crime or not*. He would have gone where so many members of America's "disposable" populations ultimately go: prison. This reality is not particular to Brown; Trayvon Martin and Jordan Davis were equally vulnerable to the same fate. Men like Freddie Gray, who had already served time related to drug arrests and a few misdemeanors, are even more susceptible, part of a bounce-and-return cycle that is well known within America's most vulnerable neighborhoods.

The racial disparities here are quite stark. African-Americans make up roughly 13 percent of the American population but 36 percent of the 2.2 million Americans incarcerated today. Roughly one in nine Black men between the ages of twenty and thirty-four is now in prison. As impressive a statistic as this is, it does not account for those who have just been released from prison or those who, caught in a prosecutor's tangled web, are almost surely on their way there. Nor does it account for those who are on probation or parole, factors that more than *triple* the number of Black men affected to somewhere around six million. These numbers are so staggering that they lead to the tragic assumption that far more likely than not, Trayvon Martin, Michael Brown, and Freddie Gray would have ended up behind bars—not because they were inherently criminal but simply because they were born Black and male.[1]

In America, prison is as much a part of a young poor Black man's life as graduate school is a part of the lives of the young, White, and affluent in Chevy Chase, Maryland, or Scarsdale, New York, Santa Monica, California, or Evanston, Illinois. Among Black men in their thirties, it is more likely that they have been in prison than that they have completed a four-year college degree.[2] If today's trends continue, a full third of the African-American male population will spend some time in their lives behind the thick walls of a penitentiary. While a stint in the armed forces was the common experience that united American males of all races during the years of the military draft, it is prison that unifies large sectors of the Black American male experience today. Such a comparison goes beyond the superficial since incarceration, like war, is traumatic, has its greatest impact on the lives of the young, and visits horror not only on the one serving time but also on family, friends, and other loved ones. Thanks to the well-documented trend that has positioned America as the world's leading incarcerator-nation, one in every twenty-eight American children has a parent in prison.[3] Nearly half of these children—46 percent, to be precise—are Black. It is no surprise that in 2013, the popular PBS children's show *Sesame Street* deemed it appropriate to include a new Muppet character, Alex, whose chief identifying characteristic is that his father is serving time.[4]

Racial disparities in America's prisons have led some authors—most notably, Michelle Alexander in *The New Jim Crow*[5]—to conclude that mass incarceration of the kind that we have seen in the last quarter-century is nothing more than another phase of race-based social control, like slavery and Jim Crow. Alexander's analysis is far from hyperbolic. Blacks under Jim Crow could neither vote nor serve on juries; they were legally denied education, employment, and housing. The same can be said today of the convict, even when the crime committed is nonviolent—maybe even a "victimless crime" like drug possession; even when she has served her time in prison, paid her debt to society, and is now officially an "ex-con";[6] and even when she exercised no bad judgment other than admitting to a crime, perhaps under pressure from an overzealous and overempowered prosecutor. While there may be 2.2 million people in American prisons today, that number triples, again, when we consider those whose felony convictions have resulted in disenfranchisement,[7] creating a dent in our democratic process. In six southern states, the number of people disenfranchised by felony convictions represents no less than 7 percent of the voting-age population. Thirty-one states and the federal government prevent felons from serving on juries,[8] resulting in nearly a third of the population of Black men being so barred. And while Black unemployment is double that of the White population, unemployment among Black former inmates is substantially higher yet.[9] As Michelle Alexander argues, we have not ended the racial caste system in America, "we have just re-designed it."[10]

Alexander's trenchant analysis tells only part of the story. The trend toward incarcerating more African-Americans is matched by the trend toward incarcerating more Latinos, the trend toward incarcerating more women (more than two hundred thousand in jails and prisons at present, up 646 percent since 1980),[11] and the trend toward incarcerating more new immigrants. It is, after all, the establishment of an irreversible system worthy of the imagination of Sweeney Todd, profiting from the exploitation and further subjugation of the powerless. Indeed, nearly all of the vulnerable populations discussed throughout this book face an increasing risk of ending up in the grip of the American prison system. If there is a "new Jim Crow," it is joined by a new "Jane Crow," a new "Diego Crow," and a new "Jim Crow Jr." The number of women of all races behind bars has increased almost 20 percent in the last five years and, while the number of youth in custody has gone down from a peak of 105,000 in 1997 to 54,000 today,[12] the number of *youth being tried as adults* remains high.[13] No fewer than forty-six states utilize judicial-transfer laws—many of them passed during the crime panic of the last twenty or thirty years[14]—that leave the decision to shift a trial from juvenile court to adult court up to the suddenly all-powerful prosecutor.[15] It's a simple dynamic: gather up all the unwanted, "unnecessary" peoples—anyone who poses a threat to the commanding social order, to the hyperindividualism of our market-driven times, anyone whose very presence might force us to consider a shared public responsibility or expansion of the social safety net—and put them in a cage, where they will be invisible to the rest of us. We do not want to know that the vulnerable exist.

PRIMITIVE THOUGH THE PRISON may seem, it is a relatively modern institution. In many ways, it is a distinctively American institution. During medieval times, what George Washington called "the gloomy[16] age of Ignorance and Superstition," criminals were sentenced to the recesses of castles or the galleys of ships, or transported to distant colonies. The English, for instance, sent many criminals to their colonies in America and, later, Australia.[17, 18] In colonial America, criminals were put in stocks or cages, displayed in public squares, or lashed by whip to the cheers of onlookers. Some were simply put to death, usually by the rope of the public gallows. Jails were not used for punishment per se; they were where you parked the accused until a trial could be arranged or a punishment settled, with the jailer making a handsome profit off of the inmate in the meantime, charging sums for his bread and bed. As late as the eighteenth century, despite growing concern from religious groups—particularly the Pennsylvania Quakers—there was still little to no thought given to "reforming" the criminal. The idea was to cut the outlaw class from the body politic like a tumor and cast it out to where it would never be seen again.

This ethic of punishment changed with the dawn of the Enlightenment and, in the United States, with the American Revolution. There was, at first, a rush to rid the country of the harsh English criminal statutes that imposed capital punishment for ordinary crimes like burglary and robbery. In this, the new Americans were adopting the philosophy of Cesare Beccaria, the eighteenth-century Italian thinker whose works were read by John Adams and Thomas Jefferson. Beccaria argued for proportionality in criminal punishment, insisting that when a sentence of death is required by statute for even minor theft, "the severity of punishment of itself emboldens men to commit the very wrongs it is supposed to prevent."[19] Colonial juries, unwilling to assign a man to the gallows for a petty crime like thievery, had often acted to nullify the law. Refusing to find a thief guilty not because he did not commit the crime but because they did not wish to see him hanged for his error, they routinely opted to set him free instead. (Some have suggested that Black juries today adopt the same approach, declining to convict Black defendants when they have been charged with nonviolent crimes.)[20]

Early Americans also had the somewhat naïve belief that crime was only a product of the economic and political repression inflicted upon the colonists by the English crown. For this reason, they believed that crime would become a rarity in a truly republican society.[21] It was, in a way, a continuation of a prerevolutionary attitude—an attitude common to medieval Europe—that understood crime as an aspect of social exclusion. In Old England, as in colonial America, it was the "outsider" who received the greatest punishment. The wanderer, the vagrant with no stake in the community, was disconnected not only from society's benefits but from the responsibilities that come with social cohesion. And mere shame, like that elicited by a term in the stocks, was not enough to deter him from future lawlessness.

It comes as little surprise to note, then, that vagrancy laws were folded into the Black Codes of the post–Civil War era, which helped reinforce the notion of exclusion by criminalizing homelessness, unemployment, and arbitrarily conceived offenses like "using insulting language in the presence of a female."[22] These codes, combined with the loopholes of the Thirteenth Amendment that abolished slavery *except* as punishment for a crime, conspired to create easy end runs around the Emancipation Proclamation.[23] Simply put, slavery was allowed if Blacks committed crimes, so nearly everything they did was criminalized.

Even today, despite the Supreme Court having ruled that most vagrancy laws are too indefinite to pass constitutional scrutiny, many communities use vagrancy as the legal justification for forcing the homeless into shelters or, better yet, out of town.[24] Various incarnations of the crime of "vagrancy" are fundamental to the execution of the broken-windows philosophy of crime reduction discussed in chapter 2. The notion of a malevolent otherness—a message to the vulnerable that says "you don't belong among us; you could *never* belong among us"—has also become pervasive in our social discourse.

Of course, crime did not stop with the establishment of republican government, so Enlightenment sensibilities turned to the prison as a more humane approach to punishment. By the time Andrew Jackson took office as president, a new concern had developed, one that saw liberty itself as an encouragement to deviancy. In a society that demonstrated such a preoccupation with freedom, that so distrusted rules and institutions, went the thinking, order had to depend upon the self-policing character of its people. Instead of receiving brutal forms of punishment, criminals needed to learn methods for arresting their moral drift.

The result was the growth of prisons as reformatories. Hard work, isolation, and the reading of the Bible would correct the path of the criminal, it was thought, allowing the prisoner's return to society as a law-abiding citizen. Two prisons best exemplified this trend: the Eastern State Penitentiary in Philadelphia—where prisoners were held in solitary confinement for the entirety of their incarceration— and the Auburn Prison in Auburn, New York, where inmates would sleep in isolated cells but come together to eat and work. In each case, the notion of *penitence*—the root of the word "penitentiary"— was key. The belief was that the criminal needed monastic isolation to reflect on the crimes he had committed and, by so reflecting, he would be cured of his defect. In this sense, the American prison became the epitome of the social theory of crime—change the criminal's environment and you will change the criminal. And yet, at the same time, prisons were a clear demonstration of the principle of equality; people were people, whatever their origins, and if they ran astray, they merely needed a "correction" to be restored to a place of equivalence with their neighbor.

This new kind of prison was so different, so radical, it attracted curious visitors from all over the world. The French aristocrat Alexis de Tocqueville came to America in 1831 to study the Auburn and Philadelphia systems (his treatise on American prisons with Gustave de Beaumont[25] preceded his much better known *Democracy in America*); in 1842, Charles Dickens visited the Eastern State Penitentiary in Philadelphia. Tocqueville was impressed.[26] Dickens was repulsed.

Like many people today, the great English novelist and author of *David Copperfield* and *Oliver Twist* had idealized the American democratic experiment, believing that it would offer proof that the poor of Europe suffered from exploitation at the hands of the ruling class while here, in a republic of virtue, in a truly egalitarian society, the "common man" thrived. His visit, which he chronicled in the splenetic and tendentious *American Notes for General Circulation*, disappointed him. Dickens was offended by Americans' coarse manners (especially by the practice of chewing and spitting tobacco), nauseated by the moral transgressions of slavery, turned off by Americans' gross materialism, and deeply unsettled by the nation's hypocrisy.[27] America was "not the republic I came to see," he wrote a friend, ". . . not the republic of my imagination."[28] He had found, in America, "old vices in new forms."[29]

While Tocqueville viewed the American prison as a moral victory over previous forms of State-sponsored brutality, Dickens expressed a special repugnance for the American criminal justice system. To him, the practice of incarceration reflected a "slow and daily tampering with the mysteries of the brain" that was "immeasurably worse than any torture of the body."[30] He was equally troubled by solitary confinement, which he found inhumane and perhaps worse than execution itself, in that an inmate "never hears of wife or children; home or friends; the life or death of any single creature. He sees the prison-officers, but with that exception he never looks upon a human countenance, or hears a human voice. He is a man buried alive; to be dug out in the slow round of years; and in the meantime dead to everything but torturing anxieties and horrible despair."[31, 32]

While the intention of these institutions was reform, the outcome was quite the opposite. By the middle years of the nineteenth century, the penitentiary had become a monstrous place of overcrowding, filth, and disease. Despite its original philosophy, it relied on corporal punishment, including lashing and other more inventively cruel practices, to enforce discipline.[33] There was still a pretense toward rehabilitation—the Auburn System becoming the favorite model, joined now by the Elmira System (another New York prison, where vocational education and preparation for reentry into society were emphasized)—but idealistic theory almost uniformly fell victim to the harsh realities of practice. The new prisons had "substituted the pains of intention," Michael Ignatieff explains in one of the seminal studies of prison history, "for the pains of neglect."[34]

Ignatieff is one of a handful of scholars—the philosopher Michel Foucault, the sociologist Erving Goffman, and the historian David J. Rothman are three others—whose reconsiderations of American prison history and ideology animated the academic conversation of the mid- to late twentieth century.[35] Together, they agreed that the way to understand the penal institution—American or otherwise—was to see it less as an institution of reform than as an institution of control, total control, as might be found in a laboratory performing experiments on mice. The object of experimentation here was not only the criminal, but also the poor and the insane, lumped together in a vast project under the title of "asylum." The term "asylum," despite its overtones of protection and shelter, was abused to mean the coercion of human personality and consciousness, the eradication of difference, and the practice of social control. Foucault, unique among scholars, posited that the true goal here, hidden behind a sympathetic mask, was a political and "disciplinary" one: relegate the criminals of the lower class to prison, among other equally controlling social institutions like schools, factories, mental institutions, and army service, and they will produce "docile bodies" that cannot challenge the ruling elite, cannot lead the inevitably bloody revolt.

But even if we do not attach ourselves to the French philosopher's fertile imagination, the facts alone are something to behold. Prison is a fate that has been repeatedly reserved for the vulnerable, the weak, the outcast, and the disadvantaged; long after the idealism that accompanied its beginnings faded into a Hobbesian nightmare, we have continued to send such people there. It is hard to imagine any other institution in American society that has so failed to meet its professed goals—rehabilitation, correction, deterrence—and yet continues unimpeded. It is as if we are so invested in the theory of our experiment that we cannot admit to the prison's fatal flaws, lacking both the nerve to scrap it and the radical imagination to replace it.

FOR ANYONE OBJECTING TO the contemporary trend toward mass incarceration, there is an awkward fact to confront: nationwide, *crime has gone down*. Murder is down to rates not seen since the 1960s. Robbery is down. Reported rape is down. The numbers reached their nadir around 2011 and have risen slightly since,[36] but the trend is undeniable. The dip has led many to argue that, however unattractive the American prison regime may be, perhaps it does work.

Crime is going down, and perhaps it is going down *because we have locked up all the criminals* and made those who contemplate crime pause before the terror of the cell.

That was, after all, the unfortunate idea behind the recent rise in mandatory minimum sentences: the abandonment of any rehabilitative principle in favor of a return to the very thing the architects of the prison had derided, a mere cage for the "irredeemable." America's era of mass incarceration can roughly be dated to 1973 and the passage of what are known as the Rockefeller Drug Laws, which mandated harsh minimum sentences for drug users and placed drug dealing as a crime on par with murder. They are named for Nelson Rockefeller, the governor of New York—who, ironically, was a liberal Republican, back when such types were more common.

The drug laws served to shore up the New York governor's credentials with the right wing of the Republican Party at a time when he still harbored presidential ambitions. At that time, his archnemesis in the party, President Richard Nixon, was waging a popular "War on Crime." (Though Rockefeller never became president, he was appointed vice-president under Gerald Ford when the latter ascended to the presidency upon Nixon's 1974 resignation.) But to say that Rockefeller supported harsh terms for drug users and drug dealers *only* because of politics would be too simple. Like many other Americans, from journalists and politicians to everyday White citizens, Rockefeller too had grown frustrated by the surge in crime that followed the urban "riots" of the 1960s and was largely attributed to the increase in the drug trade. And while he had long looked upon drugs as a social issue, not a criminal issue, and certainly not a racial issue, Rockefeller took a dramatic turn on the subject in 1972, moved, he said, by an epidemic so crippling it demanded priority over all other social ills.[37] The drug menace, he said, had created a "reign of fear."

The timing was critical, both for Rockefeller and the nation. In the years leading up to the governor's decision to pursue strict drug laws, the drumbeat of protest coming from within the walls of New York state prisons was reverberating louder and louder. In August 1970, inmates at the Tombs, the decrepit and overcrowded facility on the Lower East Side of Manhattan where Black Nationalist Marcus Garvey wrote his autobiography as a prisoner in the 1920s,[38] rebelled. Rioting soon spread to many of the city's other jails. Then, a month later, prisoners at Auburn—the very same prison that had initiated the Auburn System back in the 1830s—seized control of the facility, holding fifty people hostage and using the public address system to declare "Black Solidarity Day," rallying inmates into a boycott of their work duties. The siege, which lasted just eight hours, was later dismissed by the superintendent as the work of "400 or so militants," adding that most of them were "colored people." While he made it sound like a small group of troublemakers, that number amounted to roughly a quarter of the facility's incarcerated population. A state investigation, conducted later, was more forthright. It found the rebellion at Auburn to be a sign of things to come, "the breakthrough . . . of a volcano which is seething under virtually every prison in this state and nation."[39]

To cool the tension, some of the leaders of the riots at the Tombs were summarily shipped off to Attica, an upstate prison near Buffalo, New York. Ironically, it was there, in September of 1971—just over a year after the uprising at the Tombs—that a significantly larger rebellion occurred, this one involving 1,200 prisoners and resulting in "the bloodiest encounter between Americans since the Civil War."[40] Inmates who were subjected to overcrowding and harsh conditions that, among other injustices, allowed them only one bar of soap and one roll

of toilet paper per month, erupted over the disciplining of two prisoners caught engaging in a fight. The rebelling prisoners took charge
of the facility and held guards and other administrative personnel hostage. Tensions quickly escalated. What started as a confrontation over
discipline evolved into a conflict over racial injustice and a dispute
over the very legitimacy of imprisonment. A guard was killed. Three
inmates were also killed, reportedly in scuffles with one another.

The protesters issued a manifesto calling out the "unmitigated
oppression wrought by the racist administration of the prison." This
was not, they made clear, a rage that could be eased by superficial
improvements like improving the quality of the lunch meat in the
cafeteria. "We are MEN!" they pronounced. "We are not beasts
and do not intend to be beaten or driven as such. The entire prison
populace has set forth to change forever the ruthless brutalization
and disregard for the lives of the prisoners here and throughout the
United States. What has happened here is but the sound before the
fury, of those who are oppressed." The group set forth demands,
among them amnesty for the rioters, safe transportation to a "non-
imperialistic" country, and federal government intervention.

Four days in, frustrated with the lack of progress toward a solution and unwilling to accede to demands that he come to Attica
to personally negotiate with the prisoners, Governor Rockefeller
ordered a police attack on the complex. The tear gas and bullets
arrived at precisely the moment when the rioters were poised with
knives at the throats of their hostages. One who survived had a gash
wound that required fifty-two stitches,[41] yet autopsy reports later
confirmed that all of those who died—all ten hostages and twenty-
nine inmates—were felled by police gunfire, the violence of the
State, not by the actions of the prisoners.[42]

Once the stalemate had ended and the police had retaken the facility, rumors—*unfounded*—that the prisoners had castrated guards
and stuffed their genitals in their mouths fueled a shocking level
of new institutional brutality. Recently revealed doctor testimony
shows that, in addition to being wounded in the rectum by broken
bottles and clubs,[43] prisoners were deliberately tilted off the stretch-
ers on which they were carried. There were also the claims of
a National Guardsman who saw prison guards beating inmates
with nightsticks, referred to in the prison as "nigger beaters," and
poking them in the rectum and the groin.[44] Others remembered
seeing cigarette burns on the inmates. All of this testimony was
consistent with the claims of prisoners and their families in the decades since the event. Criminal investigators knew of these claims
at the time, yet they declined to pursue legal action. In the end,
sixty-two inmates were indicted for their actions in the rebellion
and only one prison guard.

The Attica prison rebellion is acknowledged in all the standard
histories of the 1970s, yet the extent of its significance becomes clear
only when viewed from the distance of the present moment. The
place itself is important to the story. Attica was opened in 1931 in
response to yet another episode of rioting at Auburn (this one in
the 1920s)[45] and at the New York state prison in Elmira. While it
followed the standard "Big House" design of other prisons (thirty-
foot walls, fourteen gun towers),[46] Attica was to be a "convict's par-
adise," as the *New York Times* described it then, featuring "beds with
springs," windows allowing for streaming sunlight, and a radio in
every cell for entertainment. At the prison's opening, citizens of the
town of Attica were so eager to embrace their new "residents" that
they brought food and contributions for the prison library, and even
sponsored motion-picture shows in the mess hall.

As if caught in the same rhythm that undercut reform in the prisons of the nineteenth century, Attica soon devolved into its own hell. Not only did conditions deteriorate, racial tensions increased as the population of the prison became increasingly African-American. There were 2,243 inmates at Attica at the time of the riot, and all but one of the 398 guards were White.[47] Emboldened by the achievements of the civil rights movement of the 1960s, African-American prisoners—many of them members of the Black Panthers, the Nation of Islam, Nation of Gods and Earths, and other Black Nationalist groups—were asserting a new political confidence, not only at Attica but nationwide.

In the midst of the Attica standoff, the prisoners requested that a group of outside representatives be established to negotiate on their behalf, and among those to whom they entrusted their fate were Nation of Islam national spokesman Louis Farrakhan, Black Panther leader Huey Newton, Clarence Jones, publisher of the Black newspaper *Amsterdam News*, and the radical civil-libertarian lawyer William Kunstler. Side by side among the group with those who had been inspired by the civil rights movement of the 1960s were those who had only been disillusioned by it, radical Black Nationalists who felt that integration was a sham and that the only legitimate response to White supremacy was resistance commensurate with centuries of State-sponsored and State-issued violence.

In the days after the riot at Attica had been put down, Nixon asked the governor if the rebellion had been "basically a black thing." Rockefeller told him that it had indeed been. Yet it was not *only* Black. An influx of new White middle-class prisoners, many of them brought to the prison on drug charges, had helped to fuel the resistance with claims that they too were being held as "political prisoners." Earlier in the year, inmates calling themselves the Attica

Liberation Faction had mailed a set of demands, calling Attica and other prisons "the fascist concentration camps of modern America." Contrary to the public narrative, this was not a mere riot. It was a wholesale, and principled, rebellion.

The head of corrections for New York state was Russell Oswald, a reformer known for his successes in Massachusetts and Wisconsin.[48] He had been in the top job just a few months but had already declared his intention to improve the system, offering law libraries, work-release programs, and home furloughs. But Oswald's continued zeal for reform put him in a different place from others in the administration, including Rockefeller. The New York governor had lost his enthusiasm for rehabilitation; Vincent Mancusi, the "institutional superintendent" (warden) running Attica, never had any. Home for Mancusi was a Georgian mansion on the Attica prison grounds adorned with his own private putting green, and it was said that he used prison labor to iron his shirts and do his laundry.[49] Caught at the center of the drama of Attica, Oswald acceded to many of the rebels' demands, so many that some in the Rockefeller administration felt that he had not been tough in a moment that required toughness. But he had stood firm on a demand that he fire Mancusi and on another that the prisoners be given amnesty for their actions.

Oswald's career never fully recovered from Attica; he left his job a little more than a year after the revolt.[50] Later, in a book on the subject, he described the riot as indicative of a time when "the disinherited and the villainous, the alienated and the pawns, the flotsam and jetsam of society, and a new generation of revolutionary leaders focused on the prisons as their point of leverage."[51] The question, he argued, was whether the revolt would be seen for what it was—a cry for justice from the depths of society—or as confirmation that the "disinherited" deserved nothing more than the back of the hand.

We now know the answer. While the federal courts would eventually force the state to pay eight million dollars to the Attica inmates and their families as compensation for their suffering (as part of the settlement, the government did not admit to any wrongdoing),[52] the conclusion about Attica in the public mind was not that the convicts had legitimate grievances and that the state had acted rashly, and criminally, in resorting to violence. Rather, the takeaway narrative was the opposite: that the inmates had been treated too sympathetically, that corrections institutions dedicated to rehabilitating criminals were ill-conceived relics of failed liberal social policies, and that the evidence showed that rehabilitation simply does not work. It only followed, then, that in the ensuing years it was Rockefeller—the very politician who was at the center of the Attica revolt—who would be among those who shifted crime policy, specifically drug laws, away from rehabilitation and toward the most brutal forms of punishment.

There were a few during this time who saw the Rockefeller Drug Laws for what they would become. New York City mayor John Lindsay called them "impractical, unworkable, and vindictive." Some conservatives worried that they would put police at greater risk since the confronted criminal, knowing the fate that his arrest would bring, might be more willing to kill than give himself up, thus increasing the likelihood of violent crime. To answer those who worried that the state courts could not handle the burden of laws that would lead to a dramatic increase in arrests, Rockefeller proposed a fifty-million dollar expansion of the court system and the appointment of dozens of new judges.[53] He was a man on a mission, and his mission was to "restore the rule of law." When Rockefeller appeared before a legislative committee, New York assemblyman Arthur Eve confronted him by describing the

approach as "ghetto genocide." The governor (who already de-
spised Eve) countered by quoting a Harlem minister who said that
in fact "genocide" was already being waged in the ghetto, and it
was the drug dealers who were waging it.

The fact that some Black leaders joined the crusade for Rockefeller's harsh drug laws gave cover to conservative politicos who
wanted to "turn back the clock on racial progress" since it allowed
them to emphasize that the laws were "race-neutral." While these
laws were in fact racially neutral—a prerequisite for post–civil rights
era legislation—they nonetheless had race-targeted applications and
implications. The Rockefeller Drug Laws—copied in their toughness by dozens of states and the federal government—would be enforced predominantly on minority populations, leaving White drug
abusers comparatively untouched.

As the seventies rolled on, signs of the "rightness" of the new
tough approach to crime appeared, it seemed, everywhere. A study
on the "effectiveness of correction treatment" released in 1975
came to the disturbing conclusion that the criminal was incapable
of being reformed.[54] The biggest proponent of that study, the sociologist Robert Martinson, later renounced its findings, but the
die had been cast. "It requires not merely optimism but heroic assumptions about the nature of man," wrote Harvard academic and
neoconservative James Q. Wilson in the influential book *Thinking
About Crime* (published around the same time), "to suppose that a
person . . . should, by either the solemnity of prison or the skill-
fulness of a counselor, come to see the error of his ways and to
experience a transformation of his character."[55]

By the 1980s, a new, parallel approach to drugs had also settled in,
evoked with almost comic simplicity by First Lady Nancy Reagan,
whose "campaign" was summed up in three words: "Just say no."

Absent in this slogan was any acknowledgement of dependency, any nod to the demographics that tied drug use to social crises like unemployment, any discussion of social neglect and the abandonment of the poor and the mentally ill. This was the personal-responsibility policy counterpart to the War on Drugs—another three words, equally simple and equally disturbing, which actually dated back to the Nixon administration but had been taken to heart in incidents like the Attica uprising and other episodes of State-sanctioned violence. Using the language of war to attack a social problem worked to distort the image of those who suffered, just as propaganda in real wartime serves to distort the image of the enemy into a subhuman monstrosity. In both instances, there is the need to transform the object of our rage into something hateful, deserving not of our mercy but of our brutal assault.

In the early 1990s, during the administration of President George H. W. Bush, a project was launched by the Department of Health and Human Services (HHS) to determine if there was a violence "gene." The underlying premise of the study was that violence was not a learned behavior capable of being "un-learned" through rehabilitation or, better yet, explained by a deeper understanding of the underlying social conditions of degradation that nurture violence. It was, instead, an aspect of genetics (read: "race") that required a psychotropic solution. The biggest proponent of this theory at the time, and the director of the HHS project, was Maryland psychiatrist Frederick Goodwin, who publicly justified the study by comparing the inner city to a "jungle" where "hyperaggressive" and "hypersexual" "monkeys" operate without the kinds of civilizing social structures that would curb violent behavior. Goodwin was forced to resign shortly after these comments, and the "violence initiative" was eventually abandoned.[56] Yet he was only saying what others in power were thinking—and kept thinking, *and kept saying.* In 1995, political scientist John DiIulio Jr. warned of a coming epidemic of "superpredators," marauding youth who are at once "radically impulsive" and "brutally remorseless." The "thickening ranks" of this new species, he wrote, along with support from William Bennett and John P. Walters, could be expected to "murder, assault, rape, rob, burglarize, deal deadly drugs, join gun-toting gangs and create serious communal disorder"—and all that without fearing "the stigma of arrest, the pains of imprisonment, or the pangs of conscience."[57]

The superpredator, the three men warned—"fatherless, Godless, and jobless"—could at that moment be found in minority and urban communities, but he would soon be "flooding the nation's streets," arriving "in waves over the next twenty years,"[58, 59] an onslaught that could only be stemmed by more arrests and longer prison sentences. Notably, Bennett was the head of the White House Office of National Drug Control Policy under President George H. W. Bush, and Walters served in the same capacity under President George W. Bush. The term "superpredator" was also used under the Democratic Clinton administration—by both President Bill Clinton and then First Lady Hillary Clinton, who also publicly advocated for the policy—to justify the Crime Bill (formally, the Violent Crime Control and Law Enforcement Act) and three-strikes legislation, both of which led to the expanded incarceration of people of color.[60] As for DiIulio, he eventually came to regret his predictions, his use of the term "superpredator," and even the prison solution itself, as all were being used to justify State initiatives to try more juvenile offenders as adults. After advocating that more money be spent supporting church programs, he became head of the White House Office of Faith-Based and Community Initiatives under the younger Bush.

In the fight over whether the criminal was "one of us" gone bad and in need of help, or "one of them" who was fundamentally flawed and disposable from the body politic, the "one of them" theory had won. It was, in a way, as if the whole notion of a social policy solution to crime had been abandoned—as if the "safety net had become a dragnet"[61]—in what seemed like a disquieting reversion to the pre-Enlightenment notion that the bad are inherently bad and therefore need to be sent away from the rest of us, banished, like the thieves on a galley ship.

EVEN IF WE CONCLUDE that mass incarceration is a bad idea, either as an ethical project or as public policy, we still must contend with the fact that its expansion has coincided with a steep decrease in crime. Surely, it would be convenient to say that crime has gone down because we locked up all the criminals, justifying the "tough on crime" logic of the late twentieth and early twenty-first centuries. And of course, some of the downturn is attributable to increased incarceration. But there are so many other factors that have contributed to this turn of events that a clear conclusion on causality continues to befuddle social scientists. A recent study done by the Brennan Center for Justice[62] analyzed fourteen theories, among them the impact of legalized abortion, the overall aging of the population, the waning of the crack epidemic, an increase in the number of police patrolling the streets, and an increase in the effectiveness of statistical analyses in targeting police resources where they're needed. Others have pointed to the banning of leaded paints and gasoline, which were believed to interrupt cognitive development and result in more aggressive behavior; the use of new crime-resistant technologies that

made car theft and robbery less successful and therefore less attrac-
tive; the arrival of "right-to-carry" gun laws working as a deterrent;
the reinstatement of the death penalty; the use of new psychiatric
medicines that control aggressive behaviors; and the relative success
of the American economy in the 1990s and early 2000s (as compared
to the stagnant '70s and corrective '80s).[63] No single one of these
theories in and of itself can explain the downturn in crime, but neither does mass incarceration.

Even if increased incarceration was indeed a factor, perhaps even a
major factor, in the decline in crime, the rate and manner of increased
incarceration is not justified by the resulting reduction in crime. Consider, for instance, the accepted fact that—the "superpredator" image
notwithstanding—most crimes are committed by young adult males.
This finding goes back to the early nineteenth century, when one
of the first sociologists, Frenchman Lambert Adolphe Jacques Quetelet, used data to demonstrate that criminal activity rises to a peak
in the late teens and early twenties before beginning a dramatic decline throughout the rest of life. Quetelet's observation, which was
focused on his native country roughly two hundred years ago, has
carried across cultures and time. More recently, it has been supported
by studies that show that the frontal lobe of the brain, which helps
humans understand the consequences of their actions and develop a
sense of conscience, remains underdeveloped until the age of twenty-
five. This lack of development can lead to rash and risky behaviors,
a fact referenced by Justice Anthony Kennedy in his 2005 Supreme
Court opinion finding that the imposition of the death penalty on
juvenile offenders violated the Constitution's Eighth Amendment ban
on "cruel and unusual punishment."[64]

Certainly the arrest statistics today demonstrate the time-
honored disparity in criminal activity across age groups. In 2013,

for instance, more than half of all criminal arrests were of people under the age of thirty,[65] and three-quarters of those arrested were male. So how do we justify the fact that the prison population now includes 113,000 inmates over the age of fifty, more than five times more such prisoners than it did twenty-five years ago, many of them serving terms for crimes committed in the first blush of youth?[66] The system appears to function in what students of the law would describe as an "overbroad" fashion; that is, it punishes far more people far more harshly and for far longer than is necessary to achieve the desired results.

The expansion of the number and length of prison sentences is, of course, a by-product of the shift of power from judges to prosecutors discussed earlier. But it is not only the prosecutors who are to blame here. There are also the legislatures—like the New York state legislature under Rockefeller, and dozens of others—that have imposed harsh minimum sentences on crimes, leaving judges little to no discretion in punishment.

My short tour of the history of the American prison skipped over the critical years of the so-called Progressive Era, in the early decades of the twentieth century. It was during this time that indeterminate sentences were introduced, allowing for time-honored criminal-justice phrases like "one to five years," which in practice meant that a convict demonstrating good behavior representative of rehabilitation could be released earlier than one who did not. The thought was that this would provide hope for a future, an impetus for private reform, and a role for prisons not only to punish and rehabilitate but also to prepare inmates for reentry into the world with skills they had lacked on their previous tours.

Beginning in the 1970s, that logic was discredited by a political consensus that judges and parole boards assigning these indeterminate sentences were too lenient, and that as a policy such practice made for untenable disparities. Parole boards could, for instance, determine that a sentence of eight years to life could be fulfilled in even less than eight years, at times allowing convicted murderers out of prison after three or five years, a practice that particularly infuriated tough-on-crime conservatives. But the indeterminate sentence also came under attack from liberals who found that Whites fared better than Blacks[67] when judges and parole boards were allowed to exercise such subjectivity. They argued for a system that would apply the same punishment for the same criminal act, regardless of the race of the offender, the community in which he lived, the circumstances of the offense, and the sympathy (or lack of sympathy) of the judge or parole board. It was not Nelson Rockefeller nor Richard Nixon nor any other Republican but the Democratic Massachusetts senator and liberal icon Edward M. Kennedy who, in 1977, declared the indeterminate sentencing system to be nothing less than a "national scandal" with judges "free to roam at will, dispensing ad hoc justice in ways that defy both reason and fairness."[68]

All of this may have been true, but the lingering question is whether the solution to the problem was disproportionate to the problem itself. With both Republicans and Democrats agreed on the need to end indeterminate sentencing, the result was legislation ending parole for federal offenders and creating a US Sentencing Commission that would set guidelines, including mandatory minimum sentences for some crimes. (The Supreme Court later adjusted these guidelines to be strictly advisory.) The 1994 Crime Bill, sponsored by Democratic senator Joe Biden, went even further, calling for more juveniles to be tried as adults, the building of more prisons, an end to the Pell Grants that had allowed inmates to earn college degrees while in prison, a "three strikes" provision mandating a life sentence upon conviction for a third federal crime, and a provision making gang membership a crime in and of itself. When Bill Clinton signed the measure into law, he ensured that the pattern of mass incarceration started by his predecessors would continue well past the end of his presidency.[69, 70] "If lengthy mandatory minimum sentences for nonviolent drug addicts actually worked," wrote federal judge Mark W. Bennett almost twenty years after the bill's signing, "one might be able to rationalize them. But there is no evidence that they do. I have seen how they leave hundreds of thousands of young children parentless and thousands of aging, infirm and dying parents childless. They destroy families and mightily fuel the cycle of poverty and addiction. In fact, I have been at this so long, I am now sentencing the grown children of people I long ago sent to prison."[71]

An approach that cures one ailment but creates another even more debilitating one is not a cure at all. Sure, mass incarceration has an impact on crime. How could it not? Similarly, a mandatory highway speed limit of twenty miles per hour would have a dramatic impact on car accidents, and a ban on the sale of fatty foods would have a dramatic impact on heart disease. Still, we would never institute such measures; our respect for liberty is, at least in the abstract, too great. Why, then, have we been so willing to construct a prison system that denies freedom, destroys families, shrinks democratic participation, fails to rehabilitate, and decreases the life opportunities of our most vulnerable citizens?

THERE ARE TWENTY-NINE STATE prisons in Michael Brown's home state of Missouri. The most notorious facility, the Missouri State Penitentiary, in Jefferson City, was opened in 1835; James Earl Ray escaped from it in 1967, a year before assassinating Martin Luther

King Jr.[72] It closed in 2004 and is now a popular tourist site. In what is something of a mockery[73] of the suffering that went on there, visitors can go on overnight "ghost tours" or join the annual "prison break" fun run, for which they don striped T-shirts suggestive of prison attire and sprint through the penitentiary as if on an escape route.[74] The Jefferson City Correctional Center, which replaced the penitentiary, now houses roughly two thousand convicts. The Potosi Correctional Facility, about an hour and a half south of St. Louis, holds the forty-some Missouri prisoners now on death row. Built in 1989, it is home to eight hundred inmates in a space designed for five hundred; 54 percent of its inmate population is Black.

There are also ninety-seven county and city jails in Missouri, including the Taney County Jail, in Forsyth, which is near the Arkansas border. The county was named for Roger B. Taney, the author of the Supreme Court decision in the case of Dred Scott (*Scott v. Sandford*, 1856) that denied citizenship to all African-Americans, slave and free, and helped lead the country to the Civil War. (There is also a Taney Road in Baltimore, a short distance from where Freddie Gray was apprehended, and a Taney Street in Philadelphia; and until 2011, there was a largely African-American middle school in Maryland so named. The school has since been re-christened Thurgood Marshall Middle School.)

There are fifty-four state prisons in New York, including Auburn, the oldest continuously operated prison in America, and the fabled Attica, which today houses 2,240 inmates, most of them Black or Latino, watched over by 600 guards, still all but a few of them White.[75] In March of 2015, three Attica guards pleaded guilty to charges that they had beaten twenty-nine-year-old African-American prisoner George Williams, breaking his collarbone and both of his legs. The guards were dismissed from their duties but faced no jail time.

Florida, where Trayvon Martin and Jordan Davis died, has an interesting mixture of State-run and privately run prisons. There, private prison management has become so much a part of the state's correctional system that the GEO Foundation, a charitable arm of a worldwide private prison management company that operates several Florida detention facilities, recently arranged to pay six million dollars for the naming rights to the football stadium at Florida Atlantic University. The plan appeared successful until members of a student-led movement called Stop Owlcatraz (referencing the notorious island prison of Alcatraz and Florida Atlantic's sports teams, whose mascot is a burrowing owl) objected to having their arena bear the name of a company that makes profits off of incarceration.[76] In cancelling the plan, university officials said they did not want to be drawn into the debate over private versus public management of prison facilities. Yet the "debate" seems to have already been won, at least in Florida. The Bay Correctional Facility (population 964), in Panama City; the Gadsden Correctional Facility (pop. 384), in Quincy; the Graceville Correctional Facility (pop. 1,875); the Lake City Correctional Facility (pop. 888); the Moore Haven Correctional Facility (pop. 980); and the South Bay Correctional Facility (pop. 1,936)[77] are all privately run. This pattern in Florida reflects a broader and ever-growing crisis of prison privatization in America.

While American prisons have been alternately imagined as indispensable goods or necessary evils, both visions have been exploded in the era of prison privatization. When prisons are privatized, issues of crime and justice are taken out of the realm of ethics or morality and placed squarely within the culture and logic of the free market.

In doing so, the mission of rehabilitating or even punishing people is trumped by the market-driven goal of maximizing shareholder wealth. Further, market-based notions of "efficiency" prompt prisons to divest from everything but the crudest institutional resources. Healthful foods, mental health resources, and educational programs all become fiscal fat that must be trimmed by the prison in order to maximize the bottom line. In simple terms, we have created a world where there is profit in incarcerating as many individuals as possible for as little money as necessary.

But the issue of prison privatization is a symptom of a much larger illness. Whether prisons are publicly or privately administered, mass incarceration itself is largely indebted to an overarching "prison-industrial complex," which can be defined as the "the overlapping interests of government and industry that use surveillance, policing, and imprisonment as solutions to economic, social, and political problems."[78]

As a result of this marriage of government and industry, the economic fate of many American cities is inescapably linked to the existence of prisons. For example, in places like Susanville, California, the area's three prisons account for 60 percent of the city's jobs.[79] The prisons also have contracts with local businesses like the Morning Glory dairy, which gets 25 percent of its revenue from the prison economy.[80]

For some, the expansion of prisons is an opportunity to expand political power. Prison inmates are counted among a town's residents, creating large gains in the official town population. In Susanville, the town population has been nearly doubled by prison residency.[81] With this heightened population comes increased resources for roads, schools, and public services, as well as political representation for those living outside the prison. Under such circumstances, it is easy even for well-intentioned citizens and politicians to endorse "tough on crime" legislation, zero-tolerance policies, and prison construction. After all, their very lives depend on it.

But it goes deeper than that. The prison has become not only a fertile site of investment but also a catchall for the consequences of our failure to invest in other social needs. In the 1980s, President Reagan cut funding for mental health services, causing the closing of mental health facilities around the country and prompting a broader trend of state and local divestment from mental health resources.[82] Many mentally ill citizens were released to their families, adult homes, or, far too often, the streets. Three decades later, the mentally ill represent approximately 20 percent of the nation's state prison population. American state prisons currently hold ten times more mentally ill citizens than the country's mental institutions.[83] By divesting from mental health resources and allowing increased numbers of mentally ill citizens to relocate from mental health facilities to prisons, we have effectively warehoused some of the most vulnerable among us—the mentally ill.

Similar arguments can be made about the homeless. Over the past few decades, we have failed to invest in resources like affordable housing, mental health support, and adequate unemployment benefits, all of which reduce homelessness rates. At the same time, we have seen the rise of "quality of life" laws that prohibit activities like panhandling, camping, eating, sitting, and sleeping in public spaces. With the creation and selective enforcement of these laws among our most vulnerable citizens, being homeless has effectively become a crime.

These are just two among countless examples of how the prison system, with its market logic and growing indifference to rehabilitation, becomes a holding pen for all of our social, political, and economic contradictions. Whether a person is homeless, mentally ill, drug addicted, or simply poor, the prison has too often become our go-to solution. As sociologist Loïc Wacquant suggests, this approach reflects a deeper social crisis. Rather than invest in social or medical solutions to our collective problems, we have uncritically accepted the existence of the punishment State as the ultimate answer.[84]

TEXAS AND CALIFORNIA, THE largest states in the country, have the highest prison populations, topping two hundred thousand prisoners each. But the states with the highest incarceration rates remain those of the old Confederacy: Louisiana, Texas, Alabama, Georgia, and Mississippi are all among the top ten. All eleven Confederate states have people on death row, as do the twenty other states where capital punishment is legal. Since 1976, when the Supreme Court lifted its ban on capital punishment, there have been 1,413 executions, nearly half of them of non-White convicts; 528 of those executions occurred in Texas; 112 in Oklahoma.[85] There are now 3,002 inmates on death row nationwide; more than half of them are Black or Latino.[86] Before the Supreme Court's 2005 decision banning juvenile executions, 366 juveniles[87] had been put to death. Twenty-two of them were executed in the years since the restoration of the death penalty; of these, eleven were Black.[88]

Until the Supreme Court ban, Indiana was one of many states that allowed for teenage defendants to be sentenced to death. It was there, in 1985, at the height of the push for law and order, that the story of Paula Cooper gained international attention. Cooper was just fifteen when she was convicted of the horrific 1985 murder of Ruth Pelke, a seventy-eight-year-old Gary, Indiana, woman. On May 14 of that year, Cooper and three other teenage girls from Lew Wallace High School in Gary left school in the middle of the day to smoke marijuana and drink wine. Wanting money to play video games at a local arcade, the girls—all African-American—decided on a plan to rob Pelke, who was White and known to one of them as someone who offered Bible lessons to wayward youth. When they approached Pelke's home, asking her if she would teach them, the old woman invited the girls in, whereupon they attacked her. Cooper used a twelve-inch butcher knife to stab Pelke thirty-three times.[89] The teenagers then stole Pelke's car and ten dollars they found in a jar.[90]

The girls were apprehended and became the targets of public outrage. "People show more compassion for insects than she showed for Mrs. Pelke," said the Lake County prosecutor, Jack Crawford, referring to Cooper. Despite their youth, Crawford planned to ask for the death penalty for all four. Denise Thomas, who was fourteen at the time, was pregnant. In the end, she was convicted of felony murder and sentenced to twenty-five years in prison. April Beverly, fifteen, who had stood lookout for the other three, received twenty-five years in prison. Karen Corder, who was sixteen, had a two-year-old child. She pleaded guilty and was sentenced to sixty years in prison; while Corder had not done the stabbing, she had held the knife in Pelke's chest while the old woman, reciting the Lord's Prayer, died.

Cooper also pleaded guilty—she hoped that might prompt the judge, James Kimbrough Jr., who was known to be opposed to capital punishment, to spare her life. In a hearing on her sentencing, Cooper's public defender asked that the judge consider her tough background, citing Cooper as a frequent runaway who had spent time in foster care and juvenile centers. She came from a home, he said, where her father had beaten her with belts and extension cords. Cooper's mother once tried to commit suicide by sitting in a running car in a garage, with Paula and her sister by her side. But

Kimbrough was unimpressed. "We would not want our children to be beaten with extension cords," he said from the bench, "but we would not expect them to go out and kill little old ladies because of it." The judge then pronounced Cooper's crime to be a special one. Despite his opposition to the death penalty, he declared, "the wantonness and brutality" of her actions justified a sentence of death by electric chair. The prosecutor called the decision "courageous."

The last time that a female minor had been executed for a crime in the United States was 1912, when Virginia Christian, sixteen, a mentally disabled African-American maid, killed her employer, an elderly White Virginia aristocrat, in a fight by stuffing a towel down her throat.[91] So naturally, when news of Cooper's sentence was broadcast around the world, it created an outcry. The idea that a civilized nation would put a sixteen-year-old defendant to death struck many as barbaric. In fact, Indiana statutes at the time allowed for children as young as ten to be sentenced to death.

Cooper was assigned to the Indiana Women's Prison while her case underwent the requisite appeals. While there, she was sexually abused by prison guards. Meanwhile, the international movement objecting to her sentence gained steam. A petition asking for reconsideration received more than two million signatures. From the Vatican, Pope John Paul II asked for clemency. The victim's grandson, Bill Pelke, announced that while he had originally approved of the sentence, a religious epiphany prompted him to forgive Cooper. It was his feeling, he said, that his grandmother would not have wanted her to die for the crime.

In 1987, the Indiana state legislature, responding in part to the clamor over Paula Cooper's fate, passed a bill preventing the state from executing defendants under the age of sixteen, but, ironically, the law did not apply to Cooper herself,[92] whose conviction predated the new law. Nonetheless, in 1989, in a review of her case, the Indiana Supreme Court commuted Cooper's sentence to sixty years. The justices cited the state legislature's change of heart as well as a recent decision in the United States Supreme Court, which found unconstitutional the pending execution of a juvenile for a crime committed when he was fifteen years old.[93] The court also cited "evolving standards of decency that mark the progress of a maturing society." With no other Western nation allowing for such juvenile executions, one has to wonder why the maturation of America's "standards of decency" had taken so long.

After rebelling in prison and spending the equivalent of three years in solitary confinement, Cooper became, by all accounts, a model inmate. She earned a college degree, managed the prison kitchen, tutored other inmates, and expressed remorse for her crime. Then, in 2013, after twenty-eight years behind bars, Paula Cooper was released from prison. She found a job at a Five Guys Burgers and Fries restaurant, cooking hamburgers. She was engaged to be married. She shared her story and the lessons she had learned by speaking to community groups. Eventually, she landed a job as a legal assistant to Monica Foster, the chief federal defender for the Southern District of Indiana, who, as a fervent opponent of the death penalty, had helped Cooper's cause in the months after her initial sentencing.[94] Foster praised Cooper's "sunny personality" and her fierce advocacy on behalf of Foster's clients.[95] She was, in many ways, the embodiment of the good intentions that had animated prison reformers from the earliest days of the nation: humbled by her crime, she had been rehabilitated. Still, decades of trauma, guilt, and neglect had left her with deep psychological scars. Though she was no longer behind bars, Paula Cooper was not free. Early in the morning of May 26, 2015, she drove her black Toyota Corolla to an Indianapolis parking lot in the 9500 block of Angola Court. Raising a Bryco .380-caliber handgun to her head,[96] Paula Cooper did to herself what the State had wanted done to her thirty years before. She was forty-five years old.

VI.

Emergency

F lint, Michigan, is a city of roughly one hundred thousand people located in Genesee County, just sixty miles north of Detroit. In the middle of the twentieth century, Flint was at the heart of the nation's thriving car industry—a past admired by its residents, as seen in the "Vehicle City" sign on the arch that spans Saginaw Street, the city's main artery. Statues mounted here honor some of America's greatest auto pioneers: Louis Chevrolet, David Dunbar Buick, Albert Champion, and William C. "Billy" Durant. It was in Flint where Durant, determined to unite early car manufacturers, founded General Motors. While he eventually went bankrupt, Alfred P. Sloan first emerged to steer GM to success, making it the largest corporation in the world by 1953. The people of Flint—and there were twice as many of them back then as there are now[1]—were prosperous beneficiaries of this growth. At one point, it could be said that Flint was so tied to GM that 80 percent of its population participated in the company's success.[2]

Today, however, that rosy history is little more than a memory. Beginning in the 1980s, GM fell on hard times. Facing stiff competition from manufacturers in the Far East, the company, which once inspired the slogan "As General Motors goes, so goes the nation," evolved into more of a financial-services operation than a carmaker.[3] Commanding a smaller share of the auto market and desperate to cut labor costs, GM soon began shuttering many of its Michigan operations. By 1987, this drawdown included "Fisher One," the imposing GM body plant, site of the historic 1937 sit-down strike that established the United Auto Workers as a formidable management foe.[4]

As GM went, so went the city of Flint, which entered into an economic decline that persists to this day. In 1989, Flint native Michael Moore scored big with *Roger and Me*, a wry documentary built around his unsuccessful efforts to meet with then GM chairman Roger Smith and make him answer for the effects of layoffs on Flint's residents. Moore reprised his visit to Flint for his 2004 film *Fahrenheit 9/11*, in which, in addition to mocking the saber-rattling of George W. Bush's "War on Terror," he trailed Marine recruiters as they approached out-of-work Flint teens, most of them Black, and unsuccessfully tried to get them to join the fight.[5]

At the time of *Roger and Me*, GM employed approximately fifty thousand workers, down from eighty thousand at its peak. Today it has 7,200.[6] About 40 percent of Flint's residents now live below the poverty line, and the unemployment rate, which peaked at 20 percent during the financial and auto industry crises of 2008, has made only a modest recovery, hovering stubbornly around 10 percent throughout 2015.[7] While GM recently declared an investment of $877 million in its sole remaining Flint assembly plant, it was greeted here as a hollow victory since the company also said that their investment would add *no new jobs*.[8]

The vicissitudes of the modern, global, postindustrial economy certainly contributed to Flint's woes (more on that later). Yet, more importantly, a city heavily dependent upon one industry cannot protect its tax base, and Flint is a case in point. As the auto industry left, "Vehicle City" began to accumulate so much debt that, in 2002, it went into receivership, a state of financial emergency in which a manager is appointed to oversee operations.[9] Recovering a few years later, it continued to hobble along until it went into a state of financial emergency again. In 2011, with Flint running a $7.3 million deficit,[10] the state's Republican governor, Rick Snyder, who once had a career as an accountant,[11] appointed an emergency manager to take control. Under Michigan law, emergency managers have virtually total and unchecked power. They can sell municipal assets, initiate bankruptcy proceedings, adjust budget priorities, and even break union contracts, all in the interest of bringing the finances of distressed cities under control.[12] Over the past fifteen years or so, receivership arrangements have become fairly common in economically plagued Michigan. At the same time that Flint was being run by an emergency manager, several other municipalities in the state, such as Detroit, Pontiac, and Highland Park—all one-time car towns and all, like Flint, majority Black—were also being run by emergency managers. At one point in 2014, nearly half of the Black population of Michigan was governed not by its elected leaders but by a manager appointed by its Republican governor.[13]

That same year, Detroit's receivership position became part of Flint's problem. For fifty years, Flint had bought its water from the Detroit Water and Sewerage Department (DWSD),[14] but with Detroit looking hard for cash to face down its own debts (it declared bankruptcy in 2013, the largest American city ever to do so),[15] Flint was increasingly being asked to pay higher rates for water. From 2004 to 2013, the price Flint paid Detroit for water had doubled, and more rate hikes appeared to be in the offing.[16] Encouraged by its emergency manager,[17] who claimed that the move would save

Flint four million dollars a year,[18] the city decided to join other municipalities in a new pipeline venture that would bypass Detroit and bring water directly from Lake Huron.

The Flint city council approved the manager's plan by a vote of 7–1, though, critically, its vote was not required for the emergency manager to act. Detroit, now looking at a loss of revenue, responded with bitterness; the city charged that with its decision, Flint had "launched the greatest water war in Michigan's history."[19] It announced that it would end its existing arrangement with Flint, forcing the emergency manager to find another source for water until the proposed new pipeline was finished.[20] This is when the story went from sad to tragic.

On April 25, 2014, Flint mayor Dayne Walling joined emergency manager Darnell Earley at a ceremony marking the closing of the Detroit pipeline and the beginning of a temporary arrangement to pump water from the Flint River.[21] Blame for choosing that river, which had a history as a depository for industrial waste, has not been attributed to any one person. But almost immediately after the switch was made, Flint residents discovered that their drinking water tasted different, looked different, and had a distinct odor.

Had the authorities actually listened to Flint's residents, the crisis could have ended after a few weeks. For while the river water contains high levels of chlorides[22] that can cause corrosion in metal pipes—levels eight times higher than the water in Lake Huron—there were at least some corrective measures that could have been employed to stanch the bleeding. For example, the water could have been treated with an anticorrosion agent like the one that Detroit had long used.[23] It was also possible for the emergency manager to open emergency negotiations to reconnect with Detroit, something that a democratically elected (rather than privately appointed) official would likely have considered essential in her role as the people's representative. But, by definition, the emergency manager works for the State, not the public; her priority is not the people's safety and welfare but fiscal discipline. And so, while public officials were focused on measuring Flint's savings and deflecting complaints from worried residents, the people of Flint continued to drink, bathe, clean, and play in water that carried toxins into their bloodstreams on a daily basis.

Flint issued the first of a series of "boil water" advisories to its residents in August of 2014, after reports that coliform bacteria were found in the water. That October, Flint's GM plant announced that it would stop using the Flint River water because it was rusting its auto parts. But while the company arranged to get cleaner water from a different source, Flint residents were told to continue drinking from the Flint River.[24] In January 2015, Flint water showed alarmingly high levels of total trihalomethanes (TTHM), a chlorination by-product, in violation of the Clean Water Act. Notices to residents from the city acknowledged that excessive amounts of TTHM over a prolonged period could result in central nervous system problems and an increased risk for cancer. Still, authorities insisted that the water was safe to drink.[25] Recognizing that a true emergency was at hand, Detroit officials offered to reconnect Flint to their pipeline, even agreeing to waive the four-million-dollar reconnection fee. But Flint's emergency manager declined.[26]

Around this time, LeeAnne Walters, a concerned mother of four who had pressed to have her family's water tested—the rust color had made it look nearly opaque—discovered that, in addition to everything else that it was carrying, the water contained massive amounts of lead that had likely leeched from the walls of the old lead pipes carrying the water into her home. That, at least, may have explained why her kids had developed body rashes and her entire family was losing hair.[27] Exposure to lead can result in severe and lifelong neurological complications; it can also lead to miscarriages. But state and local officials minimized Walters's sampling as insignificant—believing at the time that hers was the only house that was affected—and continued not to act. Walters pushed on, getting researchers from Virginia Tech to confirm the earlier lead-contamination findings. They found lead levels at 13,200 parts per billion (ppb) in one sample, while the acceptable level by the EPA's standards is just 15 ppb.[28] "Even after twenty minutes of flushing," said the head Virginia Tech engineer of the sample, "it never got below 300 ppb."

A pediatrician at Flint's Hurley Medical Center, Dr. Mona Hanna-Attisha, then stepped into the fray. Through her research, Hanna-Attisha had noticed a pattern of alarming levels of lead in the blood of local children. She brought her concerns to the public, insisting that it was her "professional obligation" to do so. "Lead poisoning is irreversible," she said.[29] At first, state officials dismissed her worries as "near-hysteria." Then, only a month later, they reversed themselves and acknowledged that they had been wrong. And just like that, a year and a half after the Flint River had been adopted as the city's prime water supply, the colossal scale of the injustice done to Flint's people was exposed to the world. "If you were going to put something in a population to keep them down for generations to come," said Dr. Hanna-Attisha, "it would be lead."

While Flint was reconnected to Detroit's water supply by October 2015, the damage to the pipes and to the people of Flint, in particular to its 8,567 children,[30] was permanent. Officials estimate that the cost of replacing Flint's water pipes could run as high as $1.5 billion.[31] The city must also gird itself for decades of aftereffects, including children with learning disabilities, difficulty in fine motor skills, problems with memory and speech articulation, and who develop a greater tendency toward violence.[32] At the same time, the city's vulnerable must cope with the nagging sentiment that none of this would have happened if the people of Flint had been residents of tony Grosse Pointe, an affluent Michigan suburb just an hour away. If they had dwelled in a place of means, one with economic and political clout, perhaps there would have been a greater sense of urgency in addressing their concerns. Unfortunately, they were from a working-class city that, like the water, had long ago been left to rot.

IMAGINE A COMMUNITY FILLED with the people you have met in this book: Michael Brown, Sandra Bland, Eric Garner, Dorian Johnson, Walter Scott, Paula Cooper, Freddie Gray, Jordan Davis, Trayvon Martin, Ramsey Orta, and Kathryn Johnston. If you could bring them all together and join them in a single space of urban geography, that place would look a lot like Flint. Today's Flint resembles Eric Garner's Staten Island, Michael Brown's St. Louis, and Freddie Gray's Baltimore, all of them once great American cities where today too many citizens—White and Black—live lives of desperation under the thumb of nameless authorities, held back in the "land of opportunity."

Anyone looking for the telltale signs of urban decay and disorder, those "broken windows" discussed in Chapter 2, will find them in Flint. Nearly a third of the 56,000 homes in Flint are abandoned or in an essentially unlivable state.[33] When so many homes are unattended, arson is inevitably a popular crime; Flint has hundreds of cases each year, ranking among cities with the highest per-capita incidence of arson. And because the city can afford only one arson investigator, most of these crimes go unsolved.[34] Blame for the arsons can be attributed to gang wars or building owners looking for insurance money on a property that is otherwise nothing more than a tax drain. Some cases, a few theorize, are the work of neighbors fed up with the eyesores that greet them out the window every day.[35] They know that if they torch an abandoned home, the city will move it to an emergency list for demolition, which is preferable to leaving it as an attraction for drug dealers and thieves.

Drugs and violence, lots of violence, also plague the city. In 2012, an eighty-seven-year-old woman was raped in broad daylight as she carried groceries home.[36] A twelve-year-old boy was killed by his cousin in 2015.[37] That same year, a one-year-old and her seventy-year-old caregiver were shot and killed in the caregiver's home in the middle of the night, while seven other children also under her watch slept nearby. Due to crimes like these—thousands of them—Flint has earned the ignoble distinction of being among the most violent cities in America.[38] It topped the list from 2010 to 2012, and dropped to number two, behind Oakland, California, in 2013.[39, 40] In 2015, it fell off the list, not because life suddenly improved but precisely because it didn't: things got so bad in Flint that more people moved out, dipping the population below the one-hundred-thousand-resident threshold needed to qualify for the FBI's "Most Violent City" list.[41]

Not only is the government in Flint wracked with debt, so are the schools. To address a $21.5 million budget deficit, in 2015, Flint closed three elementary schools, bringing the number of empty school buildings to more than two dozen.[42, 43] The city's beloved Flint Central High School, built in 1928, is among those now abandoned.[44] When it closed in 2009, many imagined that it would soon reopen. But instead it remains closed, a behemoth in center city, a brick-and-mortar reminder of Flint's better days.

In addition to adequate schools, clean water, and general safety, Flint also lacks access to food. The Kroger grocery store on Davison

Road closed in 2015.[45] That followed the closing of the Meijer supermarket on Pierson Road,[46] which followed the closing of the
Kroger on Pierson Road[47] as well. In fact, there are now so few grocery stores in Flint that the city has added a bus line to take people
thirty minutes away to shop at a Walmart outside Flint,[48] and that is
a problem that goes beyond mere convenience.[49] Calcium- and iron-
rich foods are recommended as a way of counterbalancing the effects
of lead poisoning, but without easy access to fresh vegetables and
fruits, Flint residents can't enhance their diets to get that nutrition.

"Food deserts," as these needy areas without access to affordable
or high-quality foods are called, are hardly exclusive to Flint. Poorer
neighborhoods in Baltimore, New York City, and in many rural
areas face the same dilemmas around food insecurity.[50, 51] Notably,
Flint's problems are shared by countless American cities, especially
those with similar profiles. Youngstown, Ohio, was once a thriving
center of the steel industry, but with steel production moving to the
Far East, Youngstown Sheet and Tube abruptly closed in 1977 on a
day still known locally as "Black Monday." Like Flint, Youngstown
had not diversified its industry base. Since 1977, the city has lost 60
percent of its population, leaving thousands of vacant homes and an
arson problem as troubling as Flint's.[52]

Camden, New Jersey, was once a shipbuilding capital and headquarters of RCA—at one time the world's largest manufacturer of
radios—but that is all gone, and the city has lost 40 percent of its
population since the 1950s.[53, 54] The city has no hotels, no movie
theaters, and just one bookstore, the Barnes and Noble that services
Rutgers University–Camden. Camden's biggest industries these days
are the illicit drug trade, the processing of waste (fifty-eight million
gallons of the area's sewage per day is moved through a forty-acre
waterfront plant built in 1972), and the shredding of scrap metal.[55]

A million tons of crushed aluminum, copper, and steel—made from discarded autos, appliances, and worksite overruns—is shipped out of the Beckett Street Terminal[56] each year, most of it on the way to China and India, where it is melted down and repurposed for new appliances, autos, and worksite materials that will be sold back to American consumers.[57] A significant part of Camden's economy is animated by homeless drug addicts forced to ransack abandoned buildings for copper tubing, which they sell to the scrap yards for drug money, while the whole scene is perfumed by the stench of South Jersey's sewage runoff.[58, 59]

There is something darkly poetic in Flint having to deal with a lead problem. After all, the detrimental effects of lead poisoning only came to light after a series of studies by the EPA in the early 1970s showed that lead additives in gasoline were poisoning the American public. It was General Motors, the primary employer of Flint's citizens, along with a few other corporations, that had deliberately engineered the wide use of lead in automobile fuels. By the 1970s, lead was being phased out of gasoline and paint products before being formally banned in the 1980s. Yet even today, Flint is far from the only poor postindustrial city that has had to cope with a lead problem. In March of 2016, as I write this book, Newark, New Jersey, school officials have found heightened levels of lead in their water supply.[60] Lead paint, peeling from the walls of older buildings, is likely responsible for most of the two thousand cases of lead poisoning each year in Cuyahoga County, Ohio, home to Cleveland.[61] The state of Pennsylvania recently found that 8.5 percent of its children under the age of six had excessive levels of lead in their blood.[62] High rates of lead-paint poisoning have been found in Washington, Philadelphia, Camden, and Baltimore, where both

Freddie Gray and William G. Porter, one of the policemen charged in Gray's death, were victims of lead poisoning.[63]

Like post-Hurricane Katrina New Orleans, Flint and other cities are plagued by a public health crisis now deemed worthy of national attention and emergency intervention.[64] But lead poisoning is but an extravagant example of a far more fundamental and unwieldy set of structural problems. It would be too simplistic to merely attribute Flint's current condition to corruption, incompetence, indifference, or outright racial animus, though all these things are certainly factors. Instead, we must examine the ways in which many American cities have lived in a state of economic emergency for decades. Since long before the levees broke in New Orleans or the water was poisoned in Flint, these cities have been plagued by an increasingly contradictory set of economic relations, shifting modes of production, and a yawning gap between America's have-gots and have-nots.

OVER THE PAST FEW years, the subject of inequality has become a more prominent talking point in American political discourse. The rise of the Occupy movement in 2011 is largely responsible, along with the 2013 publication of French economist Thomas Piketty's wildly popular book *Capital in the Twenty-First Century*, giving the idea resonance within the intellectual mainstream. It is no surprise, then, that both Republicans and Democrats have relied on various forms of economic populism throughout the 2016 presidential campaign season; there has been nearly a national acceptance of the fact that the wealthiest 1 percent of Americans controls a disproportionate part of the economy. More important, there is a growing consensus that this arrangement of capital is a grave problem.

Though nuanced and thorough, Piketty's primary thesis can be summed up quite simply: economic growth of the kind that the United States enjoyed in the industrial heyday of the late nineteenth century and the first two-thirds of the twentieth century is an outlier. During those years, the economy—driven by an unprecedented (and, to date, unmatched) age of invention that brought us electricity, the internal combustion engine, time-saving home appliances, and new communications and entertainment media—ran at a rate that sustained real wage increases and established a prosperous middle class. Even with the significant interregnum of the Great Depression, these were economic boom years, and they marked the transformation of the United States from an agricultural economy to a robust industrial one.

But starting around 1970, the underlying mechanisms of capitalism that had created alarming economic disparities in the Gilded Age began to reclaim their place.[65] Growth slowed, and wages became stagnant. The result is what we have today: an era in which capital—that is, real property, bonds, stocks, and other assets—is growing at a rate significantly greater than the economy itself, making the rich richer and the poor poorer. The Dow Jones Industrial Average breaks 17,000, a signpost of increased economic recovery and strength, while household incomes shrink, with unskilled workers enduring the brunt of the blow. In the forty years from 1971 to 2011, the median-age male blue-collar worker—the very sort of laborer who once supported a family in Flint—saw his annual earnings decline by 28 percent, yet the incomes of the "1 percent" touched the stratosphere. The historian T. J. Jackson Lears remarked that the disparities of the Gilded Age were the product of a "galloping conscienceless capitalism"[66]—a description apt for our own day.

There are many reasons for this. Technological advances have erased the need for many manufacturing and administrative jobs; labor unions have lost much of their membership and, in turn, their clout; cheaper labor markets have opened up and been exploited overseas; and foreign-produced goods are competing at price levels no American-produced goods can match. In the 1980s, America amended decades of progressive taxation with a cut in the marginal rate from 70 to 28 percent, producing a short-term recovery, and the 1990s economy rode a substantial tech boom. But these interruptions only masked underlying structural problems while also serving to support a mythical notion of capitalism that simply cannot be sustained unless it is on the backs of the working class. Whatever one may choose to highlight as the cause, it now appears that the "Great Compression," as economists sometimes refer to the era of rampant shared prosperity in the post–World War II years, is not only over, but that nothing quite like it will ever happen again. "The general evolution is clear," writes Piketty. "Bubbles aside, what we are witnessing is . . . the emergence of a new patrimonial capitalism."[67]

While Piketty's book caused a sensation, his analysis is not far from that of many of his contemporaries. Consider, for instance, the work of Robert J. Gordon, who, like Piketty, sees the years of rapid growth as an anomaly—he calls the period from 1870 to 1970 "the Special Century"—and, to make the point, reminds his readers that there was "virtually no economic growth for millennia before 1770." Why, then, he asks, should we presume that economies would grow at a steady pace now, generation after generation? Maybe the "normal" pattern for capitalism is what happened before, and, now, after the "Special Century." Similarly, economist Paul Krugman has coined the term "Great Divergence" for the period after 1970, when the fortunes of a few began their journey one way while those of the many went the other.[68]

As an illustration of the excesses of our time, all three men point to the gross inflation of executive compensation, which was 20 times an average worker's pay in 1973 and is roughly 260 times an average worker's salary today.[69] And they assert the obvious yet compelling fact that an economy in which capital earns significantly higher returns than wage income will only perpetuate itself; that is, the rich will continue to use their money to grow more money, which they will pass to the next generation. To add insult to injury, those earning their income from wages must, under the current tax code, pay a *higher* percentage of their wages to the government than those who earn their income from dividends and capital gains.

If there seems to be something un-American about all this, consider how the great masses felt in 1870 when Mark Twain published *The Gilded Age: A Tale of Today*, using an image Twain chose precisely because a "gild" is nothing more than a thin, shiny exterior. To Twain, who coined the term "gilded age," and many others who became increasingly vocal during that time, the grotesqueries of wealth in their day concealed a brutal truth[70] that would be discovered in "wage slavery," corrupt business practices, dangerous if not deadly workplaces, and the exploitation of natural resources. Fifty or so years later, the historian Matthew Josephson popularized the phrase "robber baron"[71] to describe the titans of industry who assumed the airs of royalty while concealing their often criminal means of gaining wealth, but he was only describing what the have-nots of that day knew all too well and against which they eventually rebelled. Violent clashes between management and labor were also part of the Gilded Age, as unskilled workers pushed back against the forces that were claiming corporate control over national life.

What our current age is hiding is equally troubling. No matter how many politicians try optimistically to mask the fact, manufacturing, as we have long known it, is over. In nervous conversations about the future, one sometimes hears the euphemistic term *"advanced* manufacturing," a category that values the efficiencies created by using robots over the inefficiencies of working with people.[72] But old-fashioned smokestack manufacturing—the kind that involves unskilled laborers producing something tangible that is then sold in the marketplace—for Americans, at least, is essentially finished. However fragile the recovery from the 2008 economic debacle has been, it is, as some have called it, a "jobless recovery," a phrase with the ring of an oxymoron, like "jumbo shrimp." When you measure the pace of recovery, a mere six hundred thousand of the six million manufacturing sector jobs lost from 2000 to 2009 have been recouped.[73] In the final analysis, this may be as good as it gets.

The few jobs that do remain in the industrial sector make a mockery of the gains achieved by labor unions in the twentieth century. Consider that a Volkswagen plant that opened in Chattanooga, Tennessee, in 2011 pays assembly-line workers just $14.50 an hour,[74] when the same worker at a GM union plant would have been paid twice that wage ten years ago.

Notably, Tennessee is known as a "Right to Work" state, which, despite having the ring of a guaranteed job, is a phrase that refers to laws that ensure workers are not required to pay union fees as a condition of their employment. The "Right to Work" movement was initiated in Southern states as a way of weakening union control and, in doing so, luring factory jobs from the Rust Belt. Studies have shown that workers in "Right to Work" states tend to have lower wages, inferior health insurance, and inferior pension programs when compared to workers in states that do not have "Right to Work" laws.[75] But in the present environment, for those who need jobs, the pressure to have any manufacturing job wins out over the pressure to demand a good one, even in the Rust Belt. In 2012, Michigan, despite vocal objection from the United Auto Workers, passed a "Right to Work" law, the twenty-fourth state to do so.[76, 77] More recently, Wisconsin and West Virginia became the twenty-fifth and twenty-sixth such states.[78, 79]

Still, "Right to Work" laws are disturbingly reminiscent of the "liberty of contract" notion pushed by free-market champions a hundred years ago, when the Supreme Court, in its 1905 *Lochner v. New York* decision, famously struck down a New York state statute limiting the hours that bakers could work. For the next thirty years, the court continued to identify with the capitalist class, challenging Progressive Era and then New Deal legislation that supported the interests of workers, all based on the specious notion that there was an individual liberty at stake. In truth, the "liberty of contract" (a term never mentioned in the Constitution) was little more than a way for management to break unions and resist costly regulation in the form of child-labor laws, minimum-wage laws, and other workplace rules. This era, derisively known as the "*Lochner* Court," has long been seen by both Republicans and Democrats as an embarrassing illustration of judges legislating from the bench—until now. Kentucky senator Rand Paul, for instance, spoke out in favor of the decision when addressing the Cato Institute in 2013. In 2015, conservative columnist George Will attacked Chief Justice Roberts—no liberal himself—when Roberts referenced the decision as a regrettable example of judicial activism.[80]

At this point, the real question is not whether American manufacturing is over; rather, it is whether anyone other than those who actually need these jobs cares that it is done. A key societal value of the Great Compression was that the general interest was valued over private interest. If General Motors made substantial amounts of money, its management and shareholders weren't the only ones that benefitted; so too did the assembly-line worker in Flint. There was a pact—often explicit (generous UAW contracts, for instance), but also implicit (a national understanding that we were all in this together)—that said that this was precisely what was supposed to happen. But this is no longer the case. When capital grows faster than the economy, private interest reigns over the general.

It makes sense within the logic of capitalism. When the only real money is being made on property rather than from hourly and salaried income, what solidarity does the capitalist have with the wage earner? When cheap foreign workers and technological advancements lead to sustained or even greater productivity, what reason is there to care about the worker who has been abandoned by it all? It's fitting that two bestselling books during the Gilded Age were entitled *Progress and Poverty* and *Wealth Against Commonwealth*, for it now appears that our future will sustain prosperity for the few while a large, permanent class of people will live lives of destitution. Who will speak up for them? The sense that we all occupy the same community has been eroded, and in its place we witness the gross exaltation of the individual, the discrediting of social welfare as nothing more than a "nanny State," the "privatization of risk," and a message that if you are living on the underside of the American economy, it is no one's fault but your own.

ZUCCOTTI PARK IS A thirty-thousand-some square foot outdoor plaza in lower Manhattan named for a former New York City deputy mayor, John Zuccotti. While known as a familiar urban open space reserved for pedestrians, relaxation, chess playing, and public sculpture, Zuccotti is, in fact, a POPS, or "privately owned public space," a category of real estate that carries its own neoliberal contradictions. These public-private partnerships, which were conceived in the 1960s,[81] represent a bargain of sorts: in exchange for providing community space, developers are granted concessions to build higher or wider, or, in the case of New York, to stretch the rules on setbacks that were adopted to ensure that the streets still get sunlight and pedestrians are not engulfed in a cavern of overlapping shadows.

There are dozens of POPSs in New York and in many other cities these days, the most famous one being the atrium at 725 Fifth Avenue, more commonly known as Trump Tower. The developer-turned-politician Donald Trump constructed the building in 1980 on the site of the long-treasured department store Bonwit Teller, destroying the former building's historic sculptural façade with his jackhammers even though he had promised to donate that very facade to the Metropolitan Museum of Art. Voicing outrage, the *New York Times* editorial board accused Trump of valuing "cash flow calculations" over "public sensibilities."[82] But, in all honesty, what did they expect? In what should be no surprise, Trump has treated Trump Tower's POPSs status the same way: the aspects of the space that were intended to solidify it as a public arena—benches, twenty-four-hour access, trees—have been either ignored or subsumed by this self-aggrandizing monument. Indeed, throughout the 2016 presidential campaign, in which Trump emerged as the GOP front-runner, the atrium featured a kiosk that sold Trump campaign merchandise. The store replaced a mandated public bench.[83]

Zuccotti Park, of course, has had a different history. The manufacturing giant US Steel built the park, which abuts a fifty-four-story office tower,[84] in 1968. Much of the park, which was known as Liberty Plaza until just a few years ago, was destroyed during the

9/11 terror attacks. Not destroyed, however, was J. Seward Johnson's kitschy sculpture of a businessman sitting on a bench, his briefcase open while he does a double check of its contents. The *Double Check* sculpture—and Zuccotti Park—can be seen in iconic photographs from that awful day, in which it appears covered in a fine gray limestone dust, rubble shards strewn around it like a wreath.[85]

The fact that *Double Check* survived more or less intact was seen by some as a testament to the durability of the American businessman. Others, including Johnson himself, came to see his creation as a representation of all those who did not make it home after the attacks. Still, from the perspective of fifteen years after, it is hard not to compare the fate of *Double Check* to the fate of the "Dust Lady," a woman named Marcy Borders. Borders was one month into a new position with Bank of America, working on the eighty-first floor of the North Tower, when the terrorists' planes struck.[86] As she made her way out of the tower, she was overcome with smoke and fell to her hands and knees. A strange, shirtless man pulled her to safety inside a neighboring building.[87] There were others there, including veteran photojournalist Stan Honda. "A woman came in completely covered in gray dust," Honda later recounted. "You could tell she was nicely dressed for work and for a second she stood in the lobby. I took one shot of her before the police officer started to direct people up a set of stairs."[88]

That picture, which soon became famous the world over, has a ghostly quality to it. The dust on Borders is so dense her black skin appears to be white, perhaps even formed of plaster. In the picture, she is a sculpture in her own right, frozen mid-gesture, her left hand outstretched as if she were pleading to the cameraman for help. Borders was lucky to get out alive that day, but the then twenty-eight-year-old native of Bayonne, New Jersey, did not truly survive 9/11.

Anxiety and depression dogged her. She abused alcohol and began using crack. After recovering from her addictions, Borders was diagnosed with stomach cancer. She had no job and no health insurance. In 2015, Marcy Borders died. She was forty-two years old.[89] In many ways, the different outcomes of *Double Check* and the "Dust Lady" are a metaphor for the current socioeconomic moment.

Today, Zuccotti Park is owned by Brookfield Office Properties. It was the latter company that faced the 2011 encampment there of the Occupy Wall Street movement, a protest that the organizers billed as America's own "Tahrir Square."[90] The Tahrir Square reference alludes to the popular revolution in Egypt earlier that same year that situated itself in the main public plaza in downtown Cairo as it successfully pushed for the downfall of the entrenched and corrupt regime of Hosni Mubarak. After installing itself at Zuccotti, the Occupy Wall Street movement aimed its rage at what its members believed were the root causes of America's chronic economic disparities, concentrating blame for these on big financial institutions, multinational corporations, political corruption, and an unjust tax code. The encampment, which went on for months, grabbed the world's attention. As a political movement, Occupy had surprising staying power, which years later was most visibly carried forward in the impressive 2016 presidential campaign of Senator Bernie Sanders of Vermont and the introduction of the phrase "the 1 percent" into everyday political parlance.

One of the most important achievements of Occupy activists was that, in the face of an epidemic of privatization and corporatization, they staked a symbolic claim to public property. The privatization of government responsibility has run rampant in recent years, urged on by cries that it is time to "make government run like a business."[91] Businesspeople—in 2012, it was former Massachusetts

governor Mitt Romney, in 2016, Donald Trump—ran for president
on the claim that government needed the kind of fiscal management
and deal-making savvy that only a man of business knows. Until
Flint, Michigan governor Rick Snyder—the former accountant and
successful venture capitalist with no previous government experience—was considered a rising star in the Republican Party.

There is plenty of reason to debate the central premise of privatization—that business always does it better—but we don't have to
go there to find this idea objectionable. In the way that privatization
separates government responsibilities from democratic accountability, the notion is flawed from its very conception. Businesses are not
made to function for the public good. They are made to function
for the *good of profit*. There is nothing inherently evil in that. In most
cases, the profit motive will almost certainly lead to a more efficient
and orderly execution of tasks. But it does not necessarily lead to
an *equitable* execution of tasks; indeed, it quite naturally resists an
equitable execution of tasks. Furthermore, by injecting moneymak-
ing into the relationship between a citizen and the basic services
of life—water, roads, electricity, and education—privatization dis-
torts the social contract. People need to know that the decisions of
governments are being made with the common good as a priority.
Anything else is not government; it is commerce. One only needs to
look back at Michigan to see this idea manifested because the crisis
in Flint, as Henry Giroux has written, is what happens when the
State is "remade in the image of the corporation."[92]

Roughly twenty years ago, the Harvard sociologist Robert
Putnam published an essay titled "Bowling Alone: America's Declining Social Capital," in which he bemoaned the nation's growing
indifference to civic engagement. "Bowling" was the image that
captured his title, but that was merely a particularization of Putnam's

wider theme. Putnam's research showed that Americans were simply doing less together; whether it was the family dinner, the Elks club, public meetings, or church, fewer people were spending time around other people. In one of Putnam's more clever lines, he declared that people seemed to be more interested in watching the popular 1990s television sitcom *Friends* than in actually having friends.

This was not simply an issue of generational preference. Putnam saw membership drop in well-established organizations like the NAACP and the Veterans of Foreign Wars, but no new groups of younger people were luring members away from them. Instead, he saw a turning inward. People were joining gyms more than they were playing sports. They were listening to music (usually on inward-focusing headphones) more than they were making music in local bands or church choirs. People were still bowling, but they were not bowling in leagues or as members of teams; they were, in fact, bowling alone. It wasn't so much the end of bowling leagues that concerned Putnam as it was what people traditionally did as they participated in bowling leagues, played softball, walked home together after a town meeting, or sat in the sun for a summer church social. For it was in these moments that social barriers were loosened, commonalities were discovered, and bonds were formed.

Of course, Putnam's misty-eyed nostalgia needs qualification. His analysis seemed to ignore the ways in which the public sphere has never been fully available to Blacks, women, the working poor, and LGBTQ populations. Putnam also overlooks the fact that many such associations were built around rigid and divisive interests that reinforced bigotry and class antagonism. But to Putnam, the value of being in social organizations was not so much in what people were getting together to do as that they were getting together at all. The mind, when isolated from other minds, can become rigid and intolerant, a caricature of itself, but ideas—often good ideas—grow and develop in the presence of others. This "social capital," Putnam argued, is every bit as important for the successful functioning of a modern democracy as financial capital, and any society that ignores it does so at its own peril.

Putnam's essay was published twenty years ago, and a lot has happened since then. In many ways, we have become even more isolated from one another. New technologies have made it possible to access the world through computers we wear on our wrists, fit into our coat pockets, or wear strapped around our heads. There is no need to check out a book from a library and no need to even telephone a friend, much less see her, since so-called social media makes it possible to connect through the glow of the screen and do so without ever having to risk the obligation attached to a more formal interaction. The term itself—social *media*—speaks to the distance we set between us. We use electronics as a go-between, as an agency, as a separator.

These shifting social and cultural dynamics are the perfect complement to the current neoliberal economic moment. At the same time that market logic promotes the private interest over the public good, everything else in our society has become increasingly fractured, fragmented, and individualized. Mainstream churches are promoting individual wealth building over communal notions of love and justice. Activism is being taken up through symbolic social-media gestures rather than engaged, on-the-ground struggles. Education is being assessed through individual accountability measures rather than a collective sense of intellectual engagement. Individual philanthropy rather than sound public policy has become the proposed solution to our social problems. And, tragically, those who are unable to survive America's war on the vulnerable are blamed exclusively for their own failures.

One of the more painful aspects of America's war on the vulnerable is that so many of its casualties—Michael Brown, Jordan Davis, Trayvon Martin—have been children. Add to that the children of Flint; the story of seventeen-year-old Laquan McDonald, killed by Chicago police in 2014; and the story of Tamir Rice, the twelve-year-old Cleveland boy who, in 2014, while playing with a pellet gun in a recreation center—a public park, if you will—was gunned down by a police officer within two seconds of encountering him. Together these figures paint a tragic picture of a nation that is also at war with its young or, to be more precise, with the young that it deems disposable.

It would be easy, given the logic of the current moment, to individualize this crisis. We could say that our problems are the work of a few bad apples and that the great majority of police, prosecutors, politicians, corporations—indeed the great majority of the nation—frowns on the exploitation of the vulnerable. But, as I have tried to show throughout this book, such an argument is both untrue and largely irrelevant. Regardless of our individual or collective intentions, we are nonetheless bound up in a state of emergency in this nation. In order to repair the damage that has been done, we must craft a new set of frameworks for our economy, for our schools, for our justice system, for public housing. We must resist the power and persuasion of market values. We must reinvest in communities. We must imagine the world that is not yet.

VII.

Somebody

This book has told the stories of those marked as Nobody in America. By spotlighting the social, cultural, and economic conditions that undermine the lives of the vulnerable, I hope to have offered a thicker analysis of the current crisis. At the same time, this analysis does not tell the full story of the moment. Since the death of Michael Brown on August 9, 2014, we have also witnessed the birth of a twenty-first-century resistance movement organized, led, and engaged by those very Nobodies.

All around the country, people are engaging in profound acts of civil disobedience. On South Carolina's statehouse grounds, activist Bree Newsome made a courageous climb up a flagpole to take down the confederate flag, America's version of the swastika. In cities like Ferguson and Baltimore, citizens rejected State-imposed curfews, subjecting themselves to arrest and imprisonment to demand justice for those killed by law enforcement. From Los Angeles to New York, protestors of all ages have blocked highways, overtaken government buildings, and shut down presidential campaign speeches in order to assert the value of Black life and call for principled action from the State. These actions reflect an ethic of risk that is crucial for effecting radical social change.

University campuses are once again becoming sites of radical protest. A hunger strike and football team boycott compelled the University of Missouri to address campus racism and force the resignations of both the Chancellor and school system president. Students at schools like Morehouse College and Columbia University have challenged their institutions to develop proactive and humane policies surrounding sexual violence. Campus activists are partnering with community groups to resist the ruthless gentrification of surrounding neighborhoods. College- and university-based unions are beginning to grow in response to the increasing casualization of faculty labor, dismantling of tenure, and exploitation of graduate students.

We have also witnessed the Black Church articulate a renewed sense of purpose and possibility. At a moment when neoliberal gospels of prosperity have moved from the margins to the center of American religious life, leaders like Osagyefo Sekou, Michael McBride, and Starsky Wilson have helped reclaim the spirit of the Black prophetic tradition. Events like "Moral Mondays" have created opportunities for the church to link the revolutionary love ethic of Jesus to a radical engagement with the unjust laws of the modern day. In cities around the country, clergy have abandoned their safe sanctuaries and stood in the streets in direct confrontation with State power. In the process, they have challenged the modern church to reassess its own internal politics around race, gender, sexuality, and empire.

As the Internet becomes an increasingly central part of everyday life, a new generation of activists has also made social media a key component of the resistance movement. When Fox News reported that police were hurling smoke bombs at Ferguson activists as a "warning," people on the ground tweeted that they were actually being blinded by tear gas. At the same time, residents of the West Bank and Gaza tweeted messages of support and used Instagram to offer tips for cleaning their eyes and creating makeshift gas masks. When Sandra Bland's death became public, Internet campaigns like #SayHerName and #IfIDieInPoliceCustody raised awareness about her case and created space for dialogues about State violence against the many cisgender and transgender women who had been ignored by mainstream media and Black activist movements. Although there is nothing inherently radical about corporatized social media outlets, a new generation of activists is actively refashioning them into spaces of critical dialogue, political education, and global solidarity.

The story of the current moment is not merely one of courageous activism but also committed organizing. In recent years, organizations like Black Lives Matter, Dream Defenders, Black Youth Project 100, Hands Up United, Millennial Activists United, and Lost Voices have emerged as valuable leaders of the current struggle. These groups have not only engaged in mass protests but also developed sustainable long-term strategies and effective programs for social justice. Pushing aside civil rights–era orthodoxies, these groups have embraced queer, trans, female, and shared leadership, rejected rigid respectability politics, and resisted (to varying degrees of success) the temptation of co-optation by the dominant power structure. As a result of their efforts, issues of social and economic justice have been forced into the national conversation.

Contrary to the claims of critics, the current generation of Freedom Fighters has done more than produce public spectacles and garner media attention. Through their efforts, the value of Black lives has become a key talking point in the 2016 presidential elections. The deaths of citizens at the hands of the State have been subjected to increased scrutiny by the media and government institutions.

Terms like "body cameras," "stop and frisk," and "citizen review boards" are not only part of the criminal justice lexicon but also concrete demands made by voting blocs. At a more fundamental level, everyday citizens are beginning to question the legitimacy of unfettered capitalism, mass incarceration, and State power.

It should not be surprising that such movements are developing against the backdrop of State violence, economic injustice, and social misery. At every moment in history, oppression has been met with resistance. In every instance in which the State has consigned the vulnerable to the status of Nobody, The People have asserted that they are, in fact, Somebody. In doing so, they offer hope that another world is indeed possible, that empires eventually fall, and that freedom is closer than we think.

Acknowledgments

I give thanks to the Creator for the many mercies and blessings that allow this project, and me, to exist.

I am grateful to all of our beloved ancestors, whose battles for freedom have allowed us the opportunity to share in this beautiful struggle.

I am eternally thankful to my parents, Hallean and Leon Hill, for their love, support, and abiding faith. I hope to make you proud.

Since I was seventeen years old, Michael Eric Dyson has been my example for what engaged public scholarship looks like. This book, and perhaps my career, would not exist if not for his example, mentorship, money, prayers, advice, and friendship. There are simply no words.

The intellectual fingerprints of my departed friend and mentor Greg Dimitriadis can be seen throughout this text. His intellectual adventurousness and deep love of ideas are my biggest inspirations. I only wish that he could have lived to read this book.

Although she is too humble to admit it, Katherine Schultz is probably the only reason I got into graduate school. Once I got there, her generous advice, rigorous feedback, and unwavering belief in my ability (even when I didn't share it) pushed me to my limits in the best ways imaginable. That support continues to sustain me to this day.

Although the ideas herein are mine, I could not have written this book without the help of a brilliant and loving community. R. L'Heureux Lewis-McCoy listened to all of my ideas (good, bad, and really bad), recommended key texts, and offered indispensable sociological insights. Treva B. Lindsey encouraged me in my journey as a fake historian (smile) and forced me to consider ways of making the writing more accessible to a broad audience. Melissa Harris-Perry, as always, forced me to recognize my intellectual blind spots and challenged me to think about politics, gender, and race in new and interesting ways. Eddie S. Glaude constantly inspired me to deploy my "radical imagination" as I worked through the text and offered key insights for making the manuscript more cohesive throughout. Imani Perry continues to model principled and engaged scholarship. Our conversations on activism, gender, and class have made the book significantly better. Melissa Valle served as an intellectual sounding board and provided invaluable advice on various dimensions of the project. Todd Brewster offered a wonderful foreword and gave indispensable guidance, editorial support, and practical advice throughout the process. Phillip Atiba Goff directed me to key criminal justice research and offered lifesaving feedback. Vinay Harpalani helped me make sense of legal scholarship and its critical nuances. India Arie ordered me to stop writing another book and focus on what my "spirit was saying to write." Johnetta Elzie, Stephanie Keene, and Cherrell Brown read significant portions of the book and offered key insights on protest politics, gender, and my own location in the text. Mary Moore offered timely research, introduced me to significant figures, and answered all my random questions. Mychal

Denzel Smith read the full manuscript and helped me hammer home key insights. He also served as a sounding board as we navigated this trade book publishing world together.

My siblings Darrell, Debbie, Leonard, and Anthony continue to offer unconditional support, laughter, and commitment to keeping me as humble as possible. My line brother Paul Thomas is one of the most loyal, loving, and dependable people I've ever met. James Downs has been there since Day One, creating space for me to laugh and escape from the world while keeping my confidence high as I destroy him in video-game basketball. LeShawna Coleman is not only the ideal co-parent but also a treasured friend. This book couldn't have happened without her generosity and sacrifices. A million thank-yous! My daughter, Anya, is my inspiration to continue writing, and fighting, for a better world. I love you more than words can convey.

My colleagues and students at Morehouse College have given me a rigorous intellectual environment and a wonderful family. Special thanks to John Wilson, Garikai Campbell, Sam Livingston, Jamila Lyn, David Wall Rice, Avery Jackson, and Laketha Hudson for making the House feel like a home.

Thank you to my family at BET (especially Debra Lee, Stephen Hill, Connie Orlando, Candi Carter, Stacey Muhammad, and Angela Chambers) and CNN for supporting and enhancing my time in Ferguson, Baltimore, and Flint.

I'm grateful to my literary agent, George Greenfield, and my editor, Todd Hunter, for trusting my voice and vision and riding with me for every moment of this journey. My assistant, Shunta Wilborn, controls every aspect of my life, and does so with humor, southern charm, and masterful skill.

And to the rest of my crew: AAA, Ahmad, Aisha, Akiba, Alicia,

Angela, Aquil, Asha, Ashlee, Beenz, Bianca, Biany, Camika, Cassandra, Chad, Chris, Cindy, Damon, Ed, Elon, FEW, Flume, George, Greg, Guy, Halcyon, James, Jamila, Jamilah, Jasmine, Jeff, Joan, John, Jonathan, Josanne, Justin, Keisha, Kiese, Kris, Lamont, MAN, Mela, Melissa, Miko, Milos, Mumia, Mychal, Rafael, Reagen, Shaun, Shonte, Stacey, Star, Tarana, Tauheedah, Umi, and Rev. Waller. I love you all.

Notes

PREFACE

1. Eddie Glaude, *Democracy in Black: How Race Still Enslaves the American Soul* (New York: Crown, 2016).
2. See Kimberle Crenshaw's foundational essay "Demarginalizing the Intersection of Race and Sex: A Black Feminist Critique of Antidiscrimination Doctrine, Feminist Theory and Antiracist Politics," *University of Chicago Legal Forum* 1989, no. 1: 129–67.

I. NOBODY

1. Jessica Bock, "State Votes to Strip Normandy Schools of Accreditation," *St. Louis Post-Dispatch*, September 18, 2012, http://www.stltoday.com/news/local /education/state-votes-to-strip-normandy-schools-of-accreditation/article _d5a11724-01a4-11e2-87a5-0019bb30f31a.html.
2. Elisa Crouch, "Normandy High: The Most Dangerous School in the Area," *St. Louis Post-Dispatch*, May 5, 2013, http://www.stltoday.com/news/local/ education/normandy-high-the-most-dangerous-school-in-the-area/article _49a1b882-cd74-5cc4-8096-fcb1405d8380.html.
3. While the widespread media exposure of the Brown shooting has made the Normandy School District part of the national education debate, it has been part of the statewide conversation for years. For an example of the conservative argument, see James V. Shuls's op-ed, "School Choice Must Be an Option," in the *St. Louis American*, May 27, 2015, http://www.stlamerican.com/news/ editorials/article_c1e39f38-04e2-11e5-bde2-3b8a2d8949e9.html.
4. Jessica Lussenhop, "Family of Michael Brown, Teenager Shot to Death by Ferguson Police, Talks About His Life," *Riverfront Times*, August 10, 2014, http:// www.riverfronttimes.com/newsblog/2014/08/10/family-of-michael-brown- teenager-shot-to-death-by-ferguson-police-talks-about-his-life.

5. Catherine E. Shoichet, "Missouri Teen Shot by Police Was Two Days Away from Starting College," CNN.com, August 13, 2014, http://www.cnn.com /2014/08/11/justice/michael-brown-missouri-teen-shot/index.html.

6. Paul Hampel, "Ferguson Market and Liquor," *St. Louis Post-Dispatch*, August 3, 2015, http://www.stltoday.com/news/special-reports/multimedia/ferguson -market-liquor/article_ead8b0f8-e91c-507c-a45f-7a53c574b75f.html.

7. Gore Perry Reporting and Video, transcript of grand jury hearing in *State of Missouri v. Darren Wilson*, vol. 4, September 10, 2014, 19, http://www .documentcloud.org/documents/1370541-grand-jury-volume-4.html.

8. Ibid., 36.

9. Ibid., 38.

10. Ibid, vol. 5, September 16, 2014, https://www.documentcloud.org/documents /1370494-grand-jury-volume-5.html.

11. Gore Perry, transcript of grand jury, vol. 4, 45.

12. According to a March 2015 Department of Justice memorandum: "When pressed by federal prosecutors, Wilson denied using profane language, explaining that he was on his way to meet his fiancée for lunch, and did not want to antagonize the two subjects. Witness 101 responded to Wilson that he was almost to his destination, and Wilson replied, 'What's wrong with the sidewalk?'" United States Department of Justice, "Department of Justice Report Regarding the Criminal Investigation into the Shooting Death of Michael Brown by Ferguson, Missouri Police Officer Darren Wilson," March 4, 2015, 12, http://www.justice.gov/sites/default/files/opa/press-releases/attachments /2015/03/04/doj_report_on_shooting_of_michael_brown_1.pdf.

13. Kevin Horrigan, "At Last, the 90-Municipality Protest Song We've Craved," *St. Louis Post-Dispatch*, June 13, 2015, http://www.stltoday.com/news/opinion /columns/kevin-horrigan/horrigan-at-last-the—municipality-protest-song -we-ve/article_af3647ff-3d8f-5b3f-acce-74b6589b8051.html.

14. McDonald released a statement decrying racism and stressing the need for investigating the disproportionate killing of Black suspects by law enforcement. Chris Payne, "Read Ferguson Native Michael Mc-Donald's Take on Violence, Race, and Michael Brown," *Billboard*, August 19, 2014, http://www.billboard.com/articles/news/6221894/ michael-mcdonald-michael-brown-ferguson-missouri.

15. Jackie Robinson as told to Alfred Duckett, *I Never Had It Made: An Autobiography of Jackie Robinson* (New York: Ecco, 2013). Kindle edition. "In late August we played the St. Louis Cardinals. In one of the last games, Enos Slaughter, a Cards outfielder, hit a ground ball. As I took the throw at first from the infielder, Slaughter deliberately went for my leg instead of the base and spiked me rather severely. It was an act that unified the Dodger team. Teammates such as Hugh Casey of the poker game incident came charging out on the field to protest. The team had always been close to first place in the pennant race, but the spirit shown after the

Slaughter incident strengthened our resolve and made us go on to win the pennant. The next time we played the Cards, we won two of the three games."

16. See Colin Gordon's *Mapping Decline: St. Louis and the Fate of the American City,* Politics and Culture in Modern America (Philadelphia: University of Pennsylvania Press, 2009). Kindle edition. Gordon's website allows you to hover over maps and see various developments: http://mappingdecline.lib.uiowa.edu/map/.

17. During the 1964 presidential campaign, a racial covenant was discovered in the deed for a piece of real estate owned by Lyndon B. Johnson and briefly became a campaign issue; see Gladwin Hill, "Johnson Deed with Race Clause Traced in Austin," *New York Times,* September 24, 1964, http://www.nytimes.com/1964/09/24/johnson-deed-with-race-clause-traced-in-austin.html.

18. Editorial, "The Death of Michael Brown: Racial History Behind the Ferguson Protests," *New York Times,* August 12, 2014, http://www.nytimes.com/2014/08/13/opinion/racial-history-behind-the-ferguson-protests.html.

19. Elwood Street, "Community Organization in Greater St. Louis," *Social Forces* 6, no. 2 (1927): 249, cited in Gordon, *Mapping Decline.*

20. United States Census Bureau, "Missouri—Race and Hispanic Origin for Selected Large Cities and Other Places: Earliest Census to 1990," July 13, 2005, http://www.census.gov/population/www/documentation/twps0076/MOtab.pdf.

21. Henry Louis Gates Jr., "New Negroes, Migration, and Cultural Exchange," in *Jacob Lawrence: The Migration Series,* ed. Elizabeth Hutton Turner (Washington, DC: Rappahannock Press, 1993), 17–21.

22. Malcolm McLaughlin, "Reconsidering the East St. Louis Race Riot of 1917," *International Review of Social History* 47, no. 2 (August 2002): 187–212, http://condemnationofblackness.voices.wooster.edu/files/2013/08/McLaughlin_Malcolm_Reconsidering-the-East-St.-Louis-Race-Riot-of-1917.pdf.

23. Cameron McWhirter writes of the riot: "Thousands of Whites had attacked black neighborhoods of the factory town known with derision as 'the Hoboken of St. Louis.' An estimated 6,000 blacks fled across the Mississippi River to St. Louis as White mobs burned and ransacked black homes and businesses. Future international entertainer Josephine Baker, then an eleven-year-old living in St. Louis, likened it to the Apocalypse. 'The entire black community appeared to be fleeing,' she recalled. At least forty blacks and eight Whites were killed." See McWhirter, *Red Summer: The Summer of 1919 and the Awakening of Black America* (New York: Henry Holt and Co., 2011). Kindle edition.

24. James N. Gregory, *The Southern Diaspora: How the Great Migrations of Black and White Southerners Transformed America* (Chapel Hill: University of North Carolina Press, 2005), 48.

25. Gordon, *Mapping Decline,* Kindle edition.

26. Ibid.

27. "Emerson Electric Co.," *St Louis Post-Dispatch,* November 27, 2013, http://www.stltoday.com/news/multimedia/emerson-electric-co/image

_cfb7cb3d-bb38-5bf8-87a9-dea1da4c6424.html; Tim O'Neil, "A Look Back: Emerson Factory Turns Out Turrets for Bombers During World War II," *St. Louis Post-Dispatch*, December 1, 2013, http://www.stltoday.com/news/local/metro/look-back/a-look-back-emerson-factory-turns-out-turrets-for-bombers/article_22ab79fd-20fe-5629-a76e-41c593dbeaa9.html.

28. Emerson was also known for tensions between labor and management. But in the 1940s, under the leadership of future Missouri senator and presidential candidate Stuart Symington, the company mended ways with the workforce, established a Black grievance committee, and maintained an integrated cafeteria (the bathrooms remained segregated). See Eric Pace, "Stuart Symington, 4-Term Senator Who Ran for President, Dies at 87," *New York Times*, December 15, 1988, http://www.nytimes.com/1988/12/15/obituaries/stuart-symington-4-term-senator-who-ran-for-president-dies-at-87.html.

29. Lisa Beilfuss, "Emerson Electric Profit Drops 23% as Revenue Slides," *Wall Street Journal*, August 4, 2015, http://www.wsj.com/articles/emerson-electric-profit-drops-23-as-revenue-slides-1438687836.

30. There's no manufacturing at the Ferguson campus today, but, as Emerson Electric headquarters, it is "home to many key operations and functions at corporate and business level," according to company spokesman Mark Polzin. About 1,300 Emerson employees work in Ferguson compared to more than 30,000 total US employees and 110,000 around the world. Benjamin Snyder, "Amid Unrest, It's Business as Usual for Ferguson's Emerson Electric," *Fortune*, August 18, 2014, http://fortune.com/2014/08/18/ferguson-emerson-electric/.

31. Brian Feldt, "Why Emerson's CEO David Farr Makes More Than You," *St. Louis Business Journal*, January 17, 2014, http://www.bizjournals.com/stlouis/print-edition/2014/01/17/why-emersons-ceo-david-farr-makes.html.

32. From the DOJ memorandum summarizing its findings: "Wilson and other witnesses stated that Brown then reached into the SUV through the open driver's window and punched and grabbed Wilson. This is corroborated by bruising on Wilson's jaw and scratches on his neck, the presence of Brown's DNA on Wilson's collar, shirt, and pants, and Wilson's DNA on Brown's palm. While there are other individuals who stated that Wilson reached out of the SUV and grabbed Brown by the neck, prosecutors could not credit their accounts because they were inconsistent with physical and forensic evidence, as detailed throughout this report." United States Department of Justice, "Department of Justice Report Regarding the Criminal Investigation into the Shooting Death of Michael Brown," 6.

33. Erik Eckholm, "Witnesses Told Grand Jury That Michael Brown Charged at Darren Wilson, Prosecutor Says," *New York Times*, November 24, 2014, http://www.nytimes.com/2014/11/25/us/witnesses-told-grand-jury-that-michael-brown-charged-at-darren-wilson-prosecutor-says.html.

34. Missouri Rev. Statues, Ann. § 563.046.1 (Missouri General Assembly 2015), http://www.moga.mo.gov/mostatutes/stathtml/56300000461.html.

35. See Imani Perry, *More Beautiful and More Terrible: The Embrace and Transcendence of Racial Inequality in the United States* (New York: New York University Press, 2011).

36. Wilson's beliefs on these topics were made clear in Jake Halpern's article in the August 10 & 17, 2015, issue of the *New Yorker*, "The Man Who Shot Michael Brown." In it, Wilson argues that Black people lack initiative to find jobs. While he acknowledges the scarcity of employment, he adds, "There's also lack of initiative to get a job. You can lead a horse to water, but you can't make it drink." He also discusses parenting, attitudes toward police, and other issues in the Black community. The article is viewable at http://www.newyorker.com/magazine/2015/08/10/the-cop.

37. This lack of shock stands in contrast to the narratives of surprise and sentiments suggesting that "This shouldn't happen here" that accompany tragedies in majority-White areas. For an examination of such narratives, see Marc Lamont Hill, "This Shouldn't Happen Here: Sandy Hook, Race, and the Pedagogy of Normalcy," *Journal of Curriculum and Pedagogy* 10, no. 2 (2013): 109–12.

38. Steve Almasy and Holly Yan, "Protestors Fill Streets Across Country as Ferguson Protests Spread Coast to Coast," CNN.com, November 26, 2014, http://www.cnn.com/2014/11/25/us/national-ferguson-protests/index.html.

39. It is disputable whether Wilson was referring to Brown when using the term "it." Some argue that he was referring to his gun, while others suggest "it" referred to Brown's head, which is also referenced in the transcript. After careful reading of the text, however, I strongly believe that Wilson was referring to Brown. This is also supported by other statements made by Wilson, in which he describes Brown as subhuman in his response to being shot.

40. Rachel Clarke and Mariano Castillo, "Michael Brown Shooting: What Darren Wilson Told the Ferguson Grand Jury," CNN.com, November 26, 2014, http://www.cnn.com/2014/11/25/justice/ferguson-grand-jury-documents/index.html; Juliet Lapidos, "How Darren Wilson Saw Michael Brown," nytimes.com, November 25, 2014, http://takingnote.blogs.nytimes.com/2014/11/25/how-darren-wilson-saw-michael-brown-in-ferguson/.

41. Nancy J. Parezo and Don D. Fowler, *Anthropology Goes to the Fair: The 1904 Louisiana Purchase Exposition* (Lincoln: University of Nebraska Press, 2007).

42. Robert W. Rydell, *All the World's a Fair: Visions of Empire at American International Expositions, 1876–1916* (Chicago: University of Chicago Press, 2013). Kindle edition.

43. Ibid.

44. Ibid. For another important analysis of the relationships among anthropology, World's Fairs, and America's racial logic, see Lee D. Baker's *From Savage to Negro: Anthropology and the Construction of Race, 1896–1954* (Berkeley: University of California Press, 1998).

45. Bill Cotter, *The 1939–1940 New York World's Fair*, Images of America(Charleston, SC: Arcadia Publishing, 2009). Kindle edition.

46. Many of these displays were mounted by corporations, including the popular Futurama, General Motors's take on the "World of Tomorrow," the fair's overall theme. Its centerpiece, "Democracity," was a vision of urban life that came straight out of the controlling imagination of the modernist architect, complete with overlapping highways and massive high-rise buildings. As the narration accompanying the exhibit proudly proclaimed, the city of the future would no longer be "a plan-less jumble of slum and grime and smoke, but town and country joined for work and play and sunlight and good air." Visitors toured the miniature model of the metropolis on a moving carpet, listening to the exhibit's theme music, "A Rising Tide"—composed on commission by William Grant Still, an African-American composer chosen in a blind competition. It was "the first time," Still later reflected, "that a colored man has ever been asked to write something that is extremely important that does not necessarily have to be Negroid." See Catherine Parsons Smith's *William Grant Still*, (Champaign: University of Illinois Press, 2008), 64.

47. For an analysis of Le Corbusier's theory of urban planning and its relationship to contemporary housing issues, see John Joe Schlichtman, John Patch, and Marc Lamont Hill, *Gentrifier* (Toronto: University of Toronto Press, forthcoming). In this text, the authors link these urban housing issues to a broader set of political, sociocultural, and ethical dilemmas that must be confronted by gentrifiers.

48. City of St. Louis City Plan Commission, "Comprehensive City Plan 1947," January 14, 1947, https://www.stlouis-mo.gov/archive/1947-comprehensive-plan/introduction.shtml.

49. See Gordon, *Mapping Decline*, Kindle edition. "As local planners and federal funds transformed the city's transportation infrastructure, they also called attention to the deteriorating neighborhoods found at each off-ramp and bisected by the new expressways. '17,000 vehicles a day traverse these streets through this blighted area, transporting the public from the residential district to the downtown,' the city's Anti-Slum Commission noted in 1948, adding that 'this experience has a devastating effect upon the morale of the citizens.'"

50. George B. Nesbitt, "Relocating Negroes from Urban Slum Clearance Sites," *Land Economics* 25, no. 3 (August 1949): 275–288.

51. Henry Ford as quoted in Kenneth T. Jackson's *Crabgrass Frontier: The Suburbanization of the United States* (New York: Oxford University Press, 1987). Kindle edition.

52. "Mill Creek Valley," University of Missouri St. Louis, accessed November 12, 2015. http://www.umsl.edu/virtualstl/phase2/1950/mapandguide/millcreeknode.html.

53. Harland Bartholomew as quoted in Gordon, *Mapping Decline*, Kindle edition. "Early on, local planners hoped that public housing in the central city would

slow the spread of Black occupancy or, as Harland Bartholomew put it, 'reduce their migration [to] other portions of the city that would not welcome them.'"

54. Ibid.

55. "From the beginning, the Saint Louis Housing Authority intended to demolish all but a few structures on the large site and to replace all the homes of the 3,200 families (or 11,200 people) with new residences." Alexander Von Hoffman, "Why They Built Pruitt-Igoe," in *From Tenements to the Taylor Homes: In Search of an Urban Housing Policy in Twentieth-Century America*, eds. John F. Bauman, Roger Biles, and Kristin M. Szylvian (University Park: Penn State University Press, 2000). Kindle edition.

56. See Bauman, Biles, and Szylvian, eds., *From Tenements to the Taylor Homes*, Kindle edition.

57. Katharine G. Bristol, "The Pruitt-Igoe Myth," *Journal of Architectural Education* 44, no. 3 (1991): 163–71.

58. See Edward G. Goetz, *New Deal Ruins: Race, Economic Justice, and Public Housing Policy* (Ithaca, NY: Cornell University Press, 2013). Kindle edition.

59. Ibid.

60. Jackson, *Crabgrass Frontier*, Kindle edition.

61. Bauman, Biles, and Szylvian, eds., *From Tenements to the Taylor Homes*, Kindle edition.

62. Jackson, *Crabgrass Frontier*, Kindle edition.

63. Robert Hughes, *The Shock of the New: The Hundred-Year History of Modern Art, Its Rise, Its Dazzling Achievement, Its Fall* (New York: Alfred A. Knopf, 2013). Kindle edition.

64 . Occupancy levels in 1957, at their peak, were 91 percent; by 1960, 84 percent; and by 1970, a stunning 35 percent. See Bauman, Biles, and Szylvian, *From Tenements to the Taylor Homes*, Kindle edition.

65. Ibid.

66. This quotation comes from Thomas P. Costello, acting director of the St. Louis Housing Authority, in the *New York Times*: John Herbers, "The Case History of a Housing Failure," *New York Times*, November 2, 1970, http://query.nytimes.com/mem/archive/pdf?res=9902E7DF143BEE34BC4A53DFB767838B669EDE.

67. These accounts are found in *The Pruitt-Igoe Myth*, directed by Chad Freidrichs (2011; New York: First Run Features, 2012), DVD.

68. Michael R. Allen and Nora Wendl, "The Unmentioned Modern Landscape," Pruitt-Igoe Now, accessed November 12, 2015, http://www.pruittigoenow.org/the-unmentioned-modern-landscape/.

69. *The Avenue* (blog of the Brookings Institution); "On Ferguson, Fragmentation, and Fiscal Disparities," blog entry by Bruce Katz and Elizabeth Kneebone, April 2, 2015, http://www.brookings.edu/blogs/the-avenue/posts/2015/04/02-ferguson-fragmentation-fiscal-disparities-katz-kneebone; see also Alana

Semuels, "Suburbs and the New American Poverty," *Atlantic*, January 7, 2015, http://www.theatlantic.com/business/archive/2015/01/suburbs-and-the-new-american-poverty/384259/. For a more detailed analysis of the experiences of African-Americans in the suburbs, as well as the material consequences of such populartion shifts, see R. L'Heureux Lewis-McCoy's *Inequality in the Promised Land: Race, Resources, and Suburban Schooling* (Palo Alto, CA: Stanford University Press, 2014).

70. Paulina Firozi, "5 Things to Know About Ferguson Police Department," USA Today Network, August 19, 2014, http://www.usatoday.com/story/news/nation-now/2014/08/14/ferguson-police-department-details/14064451/.

71. All quoted materials are taken directly from the DOJ report: United States Department of Justice, Civil Rights Division, "Investigation of the Ferguson Police Department," March 4, 2015. You can read the entire DOJ report at http://www.justice.gov/sites/default/files/opa/press-releases/attachments/2015/03/04/ferguson_police_department_report.pdf.

72. Ibid.

73. Radley Balko, "How Municipalities in St. Louis County, Mo., Profit from Poverty," *Washington Post*, September 3, 2014, https://www.washingtonpost.com/news/the-watch/wp/2014/09/03/how-st-louis-county-missouri-profits-from-poverty/.

74. For an excellent conceptual and empirical analysis, see Matthew Desmond and Nicol Valdez, "Unpolicing the Urban Poor: Consequences of Third-Party Policing for Inner-City Women," *American Sociological Review* 78, no. 1 (2003): 117–41. See also Cari Fais, "Denying Access to Justice: The Cost of Applying Chronic Nuisance Laws to Domestic Violence," *Columbia Law Review* 108, no. 5 (2008):1181–225.

75. Forward Through Ferguson, "This Report," http://forwardthroughferguson.org/report/executive-summary/clarifying-our-terms/.

76. Wesley Lowery, "Missouri Commission Formed After Ferguson Concludes: 'Make No Mistake. This Is About Race,'" *Washington Post*, September 14, 2015, https://www.washingtonpost.com/news/post-nation/wp/2015/09/14/missouri-commission-formed-after-ferguson-concludes-make-no-mistake-this-is-about-race/.

77. Mitch Smith, "Two Reviews of Tamir Rice Shooting in Cleveland Are Seen as Shielding Police," *New York Times*, October 11, 2015, http://www.nytimes.com/2015/10/12/us/tamir-rice-outside-reviews-cleveland-police-charges.html?_r=0.

78. Richard Pérez-Peña, "University of Cincinnati Officer Indicted in Shooting Death of Samuel Dubose," *New York Times*, July 29, 2015, http://www.nytimes.com/2015/07/30/us/university-of-cincinnati-officer-indicted-in-shooting-death-of-motorist.html.

79. Charles M. Blow, "The DuBose Family: Grieving, But Determined," *New York Times*, July 30, 2015, http://www.nytimes.com/2015/07/31/opinion/charles-blow-the-dubose-family-grieving-but-determined.html.

80. Michael S. Schmidt and Matt Apuzzo, "South Carolina Officer Is Charged with Murder of Walter Scott," *New York Times*, April 7, 2015, http://www .nytimes.com/2015/04/08/us/south-carolina-officer-is-charged-with-murder-in-black-mans-death.html.

81. Alan Blinder and Manny Fernandez, "North Charleston Prepares for Mourning and Protest in Walter Scott Shooting," *New York Times*, April 10, 2015, http://www.nytimes.com/2015/04/11/us/north-charleston-prepares-for-weekend-of-mourning-and-protest-in-walter-scott-shooting.html?_r=2.

82. Katie Rogers, "The Death of Sandra Bland: Questions and Answers," *New York Times*, July 23, 2015, http://www.nytimes.com/interactive/2015/07/23/us/23blandlisty.html.

83. "A week later, at a news conference about health care, President Obama was asked about the incident and he said that Skip Gates was a friend and that the Cambridge police had 'acted stupidly' in arresting somebody who had proven that he was in his own home. The uproar that followed led Obama to invite both Gates and Crowley to the White House for guy talk and trouser hitching as they drank beer. Obama seemed to be scrambling to defend his image as the national reconciler, while having to absorb the warning implicit in the protests of policemen's unions that white America was made uneasy by the nation's first black president speaking as a black man or identifying with the black man's point of view." See Darryl Pinckney, "Invisible Black America," *New York Review of Books*, March 11, 2010, http://www.nybooks.com/articles/archives /2011/mar/10/invisible-black-america/.

84. See Charles Ogletree, *The Presumption of Guilt: The Arrest of Henry Louis Gates, Jr. and Race, Class and Crime in America* (New York: St. Martin's Press, 2012). Kindle edition.

85. Xuan Thai and Ted Barrett, "Biden's Description of Obama Draws Scrutiny," CNN. Com, February 9, 2007, http://www.cnn.com/2007/POLITICS/01/31 /biden.obama/.

86. I borrow the term "respectability politics" from Evelyn Brooks Higginbotham, whose conceptualization of "politics of respectability" is often cited and frequently misrepresented. In this instance, Brown's behavior in the store compromised his moral authority in the eyes of many observers. This moral authority is necessary in order to present Brown, and the broader Black community, as being worthy of respect in the eyes of the general public. As Higginbotham has recently argued, the term "politics of respectability" has been wrongly associated with passivity, class arrogance, and an antiresistance posture. For a full explication of Higginbotham's idea, see *Righteous Discontent: The Women's Movement in the Black Baptist Church, 1880–1920* (Cambridge, MA: Harvard University Press, 1993). For a more recent analysis of the idea in light of the Black Lives Matter movement, see Higginbotham's interview with the feminist website *For Harriet*: Kimberly Foster, "Wrestling with

Respectability in the Age of #BlackLivesMatter: A Dialogue," *For Harriet*, October 2015, http://www.forharriet.com/2015/10/wrestling-with-respect-ability-in-age-of.html#axzz3ve5FZd4s.

87. I use the term "formal" to stress the ways in which de facto poll taxes, in the form of voter ID laws, continue to obstruct access to full voting rights for people of color and poor people. For a thorough examination of this issue, read Judge Richard Posner's dissenting opinion on the issue in *Ruthelle Frank et al. v. Scott Walker, Governor of Wisconsin et al.*, and *League of United Latin American Citizens (LULAC) of Wisconsin et al., v. David G. Deininger, Member, Government Accountability Board et al.*, Nos. 14-2058 & 14-2059, 2014 US App (4th Cir. October 10, 2014): https://s3.amazonaws.com/s3.documentcloud.org/documents/1312285/posner.pdf.

88. See Henry A. Giroux, "Barbarians at the Gates: Authoritarianism and the Assault on Public Education," *Truthout*, December 30, 2014, http://www.truth-out.org/news/item/28272-barbarians-at-the-gates-authoritarianism-and-the-assault-on-public-education. Giroux argues: "What unites all of these disparate issues is a growing threat of authoritarianism—or what might be otherwise called totalitarianism with elections. Neoliberal societies embrace elections because they 'exclude and alienate most people from political power' and thus provide a kind of magical defense for the authoritarian project of depoliticizing the public while removing all obstacles to their goal of defending massive inequities in power, wealth and the accumulation of capital. It is impossible to understand the current assault on public education without coming to grips with the project of neoliberalism and its devaluation of the social, critical agency and informed thinking as part of its attempt to consolidate class power in the hands of a largely white financial and corporate elite."

89. Throughout the book, I use the term "neoliberal" to describe not only the liberalization of the market but the accompanying processes of privatization, austerity, deregulation, and "free" trade. In addition to its economic dimensions, neoliberal ideology promotes the fragmentation of community, hyperindividualism, a conflation of citizenship with consumerism, and an obsession with market values at the expense of deeper and more democratic moral, ethical, and social commitments. For a deeper analysis of neoliberalism, see David Harvey's *A Brief History of Neoliberalism* (New York: Oxford University Press, 2005) and Wendy Brown's *Undoing the Demos: Neoliberalism's Stealth Revolution* (Brooklyn, NY: Zone Books, 2015).

II. BROKEN

1. Soraya Nadia McDonald, "Friends: Eric Garner Was a 'Gentle Giant,'" *Washington Post*, December 4, 2014, https://www.washingtonpost.com/news/morning-mix/wp/2014/12/04/friends-eric-garner-was-a-gentle-giant/.

2. Saki Knafo, "The Death and Life of Eric Garner," *Atlantic*, August 8, 2015,

http://www.theatlantic.com/politics/archive/2015/08/the-tragic-roots-of-remembrance-day/400574/.

3. Aaron Smith, "60% of Cigarettes Sold in New York Are Smuggled: Report," CNN Money, January 10, 2013, http://money.cnn.com/2013/01/10/news/companies/cigarette-tax-new-york/index.html.

4. John Marzulli, Rocco Parascandola, and Thomas Tracy, "NYPD No. 3's Order to Crack Down on Selling Loose Cigarettes Led to Chokehold Death of Eric Garner," New York Daily News, August 7, 2014, http://www.nydailynews.com/new-york/nyc-crime/wife-man-filmed-chokehold-arrested-article-1.1893790.

5. "The video shared widely last summer left out roughly two minutes of conversation before the physical confrontation, including attempts to handcuff Mr. Garner." See Ford Fessenden, "New Perspective on Eric Garner's Death," New York Times, updated June 13, 2015, http://www.nytimes.com/interactive/2014/12/03/us/2014-12-03-garner-video.html.

6. Zak Koeske, "NYPD Officer Stripped of His Gun, Badge Over Chokehold of Eric Garner, Police Say," Staten Island Advance, July 19, 2014, http://www.silive.com/news/index.ssf/2014/07/nypd_officer_who_chokeheld_gar.html.

7. "Original Eric Garner Fatal Arrest Video," YouTube video, 2:55, posted by New York Daily News, December 30, 2014, https://www.youtube.com/watch?v=LfXqYwyzQpM.

8. Fessenden, "New Perspective on Eric Garner's Death."

9. Giri Nathan, "Eric Garner Died from Chokehold While in Police Custody," Time, August 1, 2014, http://time.com/3071288/eric-garner-chokehold-death-nypd-medical-examiner/.

10. Lucy McCalmont, "Rep. King: Health Issues Lead to Death," Politico, December 4, 2014, http://www.politico.com/story/2014/12/peter-king-eric-garner-reaction-113319.

11. According to NYPD officials, such as Chief John Timoney in 1993, choke holds became common during this period because crack made it more difficult to subdue suspects being brought into custody; see Ian Fisher, "Kelly Bans Choke Holds by Officers," New York Times, November 24, 1993, http://www.nytimes.com/1993/11/24/nyregion/kelly-bans-choke-holds-by-officers.html. Such claims are a product of 1980s and '90s mythologies around drugs in general and crack in particular, which were used to justify draconian and racially disparate drug war policies. For a thorough examination of such myths, see Dr. Carl Hart's High Price: A Neuroscientist's Journey of Self-Discovery That Challenges Everything You Know About Drugs and Society (New York: Harper Perennial, 2014).

12. City of Los Angeles v. Lyons, 461 U.S. 95 (1983). The court's decision is available at http://caselaw.findlaw.com/us-supreme-court/461/95.html.

13. Ian Millhiser, "How the Supreme Court Helped Make It Possible for Police to Kill by Chokehold," ThinkProgress, December 4, 2014, http://thinkprogress

.org/justice/2014/12/04/3599605/how-the-supreme-court-helped-make-it-possible-for-police-to-kill-by-chokehold/.

14. The Warren Court era, which I discuss in greater detail in chapter 3, refers to the period from 1953–1969 in which Earl Warren served as chief justice of the United States Supreme Court. The Burger Court era was from 1969–1986.

15. 461 U.S. at 137.

16. This quotation is from Burger's dissent in *Bivens v. Six Unknown Fed. Narcotics Agents*, 403 U.S. 388 (1971); viewable at https://www.law.cornell.edu/supremecourt/text/403/388.

17. 461 U.S. at 137.

18. It is worth noting that the facts of the case are not in dispute. As was reported at the time, "Both the Baez family and the police agree on what led to the arrest of Mr. Baez Dec. 22 at 1:43 A.M. Mr. Baez was throwing a football with two brothers when two throws within minutes of each other hit two separate parked police patrol cars near the corner of Cameron Place and Jerome Avenue in the University Heights section of the Bronx. Neither the Police Department nor the family has suggested that the ball was thrown at the cars intentionally." Clifford Krauss, "Clash Over a Football Ends with a Death in Police Custody," *New York Times*, December 30, 1994, http://www.nytimes.com/1994/12/30/nyregion/clash-over-a-football-ends-with-a-death-in-police-custody.html.

19. "Deeper Failures in the Livoti Case," *New York Times*, October 15, 1998, http://www.nytimes.com/1998/10/15/opinion/deeper-failures-in-the-livoti-case.html.

20. David M. Herszenhorn, "Judge Assails But Acquits Officer in Man's Choking Death in Bronx," *New York Times*, October 8, 1996, http://www.nytimes.com/1996/10/08/nyregion/judge-assails-but-acquits-officer-in-man-s-choking-death-in-bronx.html.

21. Ibid.

22. Specific demographic information, racial and otherwise, about the jurors has been kept secret. For all available information, see http://www.cnn.com/2014/08/22/us/missouri-teen-shooting/.

23. Rich Schapiro and Thomas Tracy, "Eric Garner's Unmarked Grave in New Jersey Cemetery Goes Largely Unnoticed and Unvisited," *New York Daily News*, July 13, 2015, http://www.nydailynews.com/new-york/eric-garner-unmarked-grave-largely-unnoticed-unvisited-article-1.2291042.

24. J. David Goodman, "Eric Garner Case Is Settled by New York City for $5.9 Million," *New York Times*, July 13, 2015, http://www.nytimes.com/2015/07/14/nyregion/eric-garner-case-is-settled-by-new-york-city-for-5-9-million.html.

25. The database can be searched at http://comptroller.nyc.gov/reports/claimstat/.

26. Although the majority of these claims are not due to police brutality or even misconduct—the number includes claims against schools, sanitation workers,

et cetera—they nonetheless comprise a substantial portion of claims. Further, while the trend is downward throughout most of the city, it is on the rise in central Brooklyn and the South Bronx, two of the city's poorest areas. "Executive Summary," Office of the Comptroller, accessed February 17, 2016, http://comptroller.nyc.gov/reports/claimstat/.

27. George L. Kelling and James Q. Wilson, "Broken Windows," *Atlantic*, March 1982, http://www.theatlantic.com/magazine/archive/1982/03/broken-windows/304465/.

28. Ibid.

29. "Boston in Transit War Against Uneasy Riding," *New York Times*, March 23, 1986, http://www.nytimes.com/1986/03/23/us/boston-in-transit-war-against-uneasy-riding.html.

30. Calvin Sims, "Transit Police to Eject Subway Panhandlers," *New York Times*, May 31, 1990, http://www.nytimes.com/1990/05/31/nyregion/transit-police-to-eject-subway-panhandlers.html.

31. "An estimated 170,000 people a day were entering the system, by one route or another, without paying a token." In Malcolm Gladwell, *The Tipping Point: How Little Things Can Make a Big Difference* (New York: Little, Brown and Company, 2006). Kindle edition.

32. One out of seven arrestees had an outstanding warrant for a previous crime, and one out of twenty was carrying a weapon of some sort. Ibid, Kindle edition.

33. From William Bratton's essay, "Crime Is Down in New York City: Blame the Police" *in Zero Tolerance: Policing a Free Society* by Ray Mallon et al. (London: Institute of Economic Affairs, 1997).

34. In William Bratton with Peter Knobler, *The Turnaround: How America's Top Cop Reversed the Crime Epidemic* (New York: Random House, 2009). Kindle edition.

35. Mark Chiusano, "Beyond Broken Windows," *Atlantic*, November 12, 2014, http://www.theatlantic.com/national/archive/2014/11/joe-fox-broken-windows/382668/.

36. Sheryl Gay Stolberg, "Fragile Baltimore Struggles to Heal After Deadly Police Encounter," *New York Times*, October 20, 2015, http://www.nytimes.com/2015/10/21/us/a-fragile-baltimore-struggles-to-heal-itself.html?_r=0.

37. "The city has had a slight increase in murders, to 340 as of Sunday, but is still near the low of 333 recorded at the end of last year." J. David Goodman, "New York Police Commissioner and Predecessor Spar Over Accuracy of Crime Data," *New York Times*, December 29, 2015, http://www.nytimes.com/2015/12/30/nyregion/bratton-rebukes-kelly-for-questioning-new-york-crime-data-shame-on-him.html?ref=topics.

38. J. David Goodman, "Bratton to Lead New York Police for Second Time," *New York Times*, December 5, 2013, http://www.nytimes.com/2013/12/06/nyregion/william-bratton-new-york-city-police-commissioner.html.

39. The notion of a causal relationship between disorder and crime has remained largely unproven through empirical studies. See Bernard E. Harcourt and Jens Ludwig's article, "Broken Windows: New Evidence From New York City and a Five-City Social Experiment," *University of Chicago Law Review* 73 (2006): 271–320. The authors refute George Kelling and William Sousa's 2001 study of New York City crime statistics, which argues that broken-windows policing has caused a drop in crime. Also see Robert J. Sampson and Stephen W. Raudenbush's article, "Systematic Social Observation of Public Spaces: A New Look at Disorder in Urban Neighborhoods," *American Journal of Sociology* 105, no. 3, (November 1999): 603–51.

40. This speaks to a deeper methodological problem within broken-windows studies. Many studies wrongly presume that the exogenous variable (disorder) is a different construct than the outcome variable (crime). Such a presumption is countered by scholars like John Worrall, who found the two constructs to be empirically indistinguishable. While some scholars (such as Skogan, 1990 and Xu, Fielder, and Flaming, 2005) find the two to be different constructs, this is largely due to yet another design flaw in broken-windows studies. Specifically, scholars were relying upon both official (i.e., "objective" and predetermined) and observational measures of disorder and crime, despite the fact that the original broken-windows thesis was based entirely on how citizens subjectively perceived disorder and crime. For a more detailed explanation, see Jacinta M. Gau and Travis C. Pratt's study, "Broken Windows or Window Dressing? Citizens' (In)Ability to tell the Difference Between Disorder and Crime," *Criminology & Public Policy* 7: 163–94; Wesley G. Skogan's 1990 text *Disorder and Decline: Crime and the Spiral of Decay in American Neighborhoods* (Berkeley: University of California Press, 1990); and Yili Xu, Mora L. Fielder, and Karl H. Flaming, "Discovering the Impact of Community Policing: The Broken Windows Thesis, Collective Efficacy, and Citizens' Judgment," *Journal of Research in Crime and Delinquency* 42 (2005):147–86.

41. See Sampson and Raudenbush, "Systematic Social Observation."

42. See Robert J. Sampson's and Stephen Raudenbush's article, "Seeing Disorder: Neighborhood Stigma and the Social Construction of 'Broken Windows,'" *Social Psychology Quarterly* 67, no. 4 (2004): 319–42. Also see psychologist Courtney Bonam's 2010 Stanford University doctoral dissertation, "Devaluing Black Space: Black Locations as Targets of Housing and Environmental Discrimination." In it, she argues that individuals understand spaces in racial terms and engage those spaces based on their ostensible "race."

43. See Peter K. B. St. Jean's *Pockets of Crime: Broken Windows, Collective Efficacy, and the Criminal Point of View* (Chicago: University of Chicago Press, 2007).

44. "Many large cities—including Boston, Houston, Los Angeles, St. Louis, San Diego, San Antonio, San Francisco, and Washington, D.C.—have experienced significant declines in crime, in some cases proportionately larger than New

York City's." Bernard E. Harcourt, *Illusion of Order: The False Promise of Broken Windows Policing*, (Cambridge, MA: Harvard University Press, 2009), 9.

45. "A 2001 survey found that more than one-third of the nation's 515 largest police departments had implemented Compstat in some form." *City Room* (*New York Times* blog); "Why Did Crime Fall in New York City?" blog entry by Sewell Chan, August 13, 2007, http://cityroom.blogs.nytimes.com/2007/08/13/why-did-crime-fall-in-new-york-city/.

46. Harvey A. Silverglate, *Three Felonies a Day: How the Feds Target the Innocent* (New York: Encounter Books, 2009).

47. Adam Liptak, "Right and Left Join Forces on Criminal Justice," *New York Times*, November 23, 2009, http://www.nytimes.com/2009/11/24/us/24crime.html.

48. The *New York Times* story above quotes the number as 4400, but the Heritage Foundation's ebook, *USA vs You: The Flood of Criminal Laws Threatening Your Liberty* (Washington, DC: Heritage Foundation, 2013) says the number is 4500. (The ebook can be downloaded free of charge at http://www.heritage.org/usavsyou/download.html.)

49. Heritage Foundation, *USA vs You*.

50. Thomas Stackpole, "Rand Paul's Strange Obsession with an Obscure, Century-Old Trading Act," *New Republic*, May 4, 2012, https://newrepublic.com/article/101328/rand-paul-lacey-focus-shoenwetter.

51. Robert H. Jackson as quoted in Antonin Scalia, *Scalia Dissents: Writings of the Supreme Court's Wittiest, Most Outspoken Justice* (Washington, DC: Regnery Publishing, 2004).

52. Ulysses S. Grant: "Proclamation 204—Suspending the Writ of Habeas Corpus in the County of Union, South Carolina," November 10, 1871. Online by Gerhard Peters and John T. Woolley, *The American Presidency Project*, http://www.presidency.ucsb.edu/ws/?pid=70261.

53. Robert A. Caro, *Master of the Senate: The Years of Lyndon Johnson III* (New York: Alfred A. Knopf, 2009). Kindle edition.

54. Anna Bruzgulis, "Confederate Flag Wasn't Flown at South Carolina State-house Until 1961, Pundit Claims," *PunditFact*, June 22, 2015, http://www.politifact.com/punditfact/statements/2015/jun/22/eugene-robinson/confederate-flag-wasnt-flown-south-carolina-state-/.

55. "Walter Scott Shooting—Dashcam Video Shows the Moments Before the Shooting," YouTube video, 3:01, posted by Elite NWO Agenda, April 9, 2015, https://www.youtube.com/watch?v=HLRwAcyljSg.

56. Holly Yan, "Police Shoot Man in Back: Who Was Walter Scott?" CNN.com, April 9, 2015, http://www.cnn.com/2015/04/08/us/south-carolina-who-was-walter-scott/index.html.

57. "Walter Scott Shooting Footage Synced with Police Scanner Audio—Video," video, 3:14, *Guardian* (London), April 8, 2015, http://www.theguardian.com/

us-news/video/2015/apr/09/north-charleston-shooting-police-scanner-video; "Walter Scott Shooting," video, 3:13, *Post and Courier* (Charleston, SC), exact date unavailable, https://vimeo.com/124336782.

58. David A. Graham, "The Shockingly Familiar Killing of Walter Scott," *Atlantic,* April 8, 2015, http://www.theatlantic.com/national/archive/2015/04/the-shockingly-familiar-killing-of-walter-scott/390006/.

59. Yan, "Police Shoot Man in Back."

60. Harry Houck, interview by Anderson Cooper, *Anderson Cooper 360,* CNN, April 9, 2015. A transcript of the interview is available at http://transcripts.cnn.com/TRANSCRIPTS/1504/09/acd.01.html.

61. Refer to the map of the district at http://www.scstatehouse.gov/maps/senate/Sen45.pdf.

62. Pinckney's speech as seen in the video posted alongside Adam Geller and Seanna Adcox, Associated Press, "Charleston Shooting Victim Clementa Pinckney's Chilling Speech About Walter Scott," *The Grio,* June 18, 2015, http://thegrio.com/2015/06/18/clementa-pinckney-victim-walter-scott/.

63. Yamiche Alcindor and Doug Stanglin, "Affidavits Spell Out Chilling Case Against Dylann Roof," *USA Today,* June 19, 2015, http://www.usatoday.com/story/news/nation/2015/06/19/dylann-roof-charleston-police-charged—murder-black-church/28975573/.

64. Sam Roberts, "Author of 'Broken Windows' Policing Defends His Theory," *New York Times,* August 10, 2014, http://www.nytimes.com/2014/08/11/nyregion/author-of-broken-windows-policing-defends-his-theory.html?_r=0.

65. "When Mayor Rudolph Giuliani appointed Bratton to be his police commissioner in 1994, to implement the theory in New York, he took to calling it 'zero tolerance,' a phrase Bratton rejected because it implied 'zealotry and a lack of cop discretion.' But zero tolerance was an accurate description of the practice, as arrests for the most minor infractions began to soar." See Michael Greenberg, "'Broken Windows' and the New York Police," *New York Review of Books,* November 6, 2014, http://www.nybooks.com/articles/2014/11/06/broken-windows-and-new-york-police/.

66. Sheryl Gay Stolberg and Ron Nixon, "Freddie Gray: Another City, Another Death in the Public Eye," *New York Times,* April 21, 2015, http://www.nytimes.com/2015/04/22/us/another-mans-death-another-round-of-questions-for-the-police-in-baltimore.html?_r=0.

67. Kelling and Wilson, "Broken Windows."

68. Sarah Ryley, Laura Bult, Dareh Gregorian, "Exclusive: *Daily News* Analysis Finds Racial Disparities in Summonses for Minor Violations in 'Broken Windows' Policing," *New York Daily News,* August 4, 2014, http://www.nydailynews.com/new-york/summons-broken-windows-racial-disparity-garner-article-1.1890567.

69. Brent Staples, "The Human Cost of 'Zero Tolerance,'" *New York Times*, April 28. 2012, http://www.nytimes.com/2012/04/29/opinion/sunday/the-cost-of-zero-tolerance.html.

70. "'My neighborhood is like it's under martial law. We got all these rookie officers on each corner. These officers, they just run around and ask you for any excuse to ask you for your ID and write you a summons,' said Angel Garcia, 34, of East Harlem, waiting in line at summons court in lower Manhattan last month." Quoted in Ryley, Bult, and Gregorian, "Exclusive: *Daily News Analysis.*"

71. "They reveal that precinct bosses threaten street cops if they don't make their quotas of arrests and stop-and-frisks, but also tell them not to take certain robbery reports in order to manipulate crime statistics. The tapes also refer to command officers calling crime victims directly to intimidate them about their complaints." Graham Rayman, "The NYPD Tapes: Inside Bed Stuy's 81st Precinct," *Village Voice*, May 4, 2010, http://www.villagevoice.com/news/the-nypd-tapes-inside-bed-stuys-81st-precinct-6429434.

72. Ibid. "Three weeks after his meeting with QAD investigators, on October 31, Schoolcraft felt sick and went home from work. Hours later, a dozen police supervisors came to his house and demanded that he return to work. He declined, on health grounds. Eventually, Deputy Chief Michael Marino, the commander of Patrol Borough Brooklyn North, which covers 10 precincts, ordered that Schoolcraft be dragged from his apartment in handcuffs and forcibly placed in a Queens mental ward for six days." Also see Jim Dwyer, "For Detained Whistle-Blower, a Hospital Bill, Not an Apology," *New York Times*, March 15, 2012, http://www.nytimes.com/2012/03/16/nyregion/officer-adrian-schoolcraft-forcibly-hospitalized-got-no-apology-just-a-bill.html.

73. Wendy Ruderman, "Crime Report Manipulation Is Common Among New York Police, Study Finds," *New York Times*, June 28, 2012, http://www.nytimes.com/2012/06/29/nyregion/new-york-police-department-manipulates-crime-reports-study-finds.html.

74. J. David Goodman, "Officer Who Disclosed Police Misconduct Settles Suit," *New York Times*, September 29, 2015, http://www.nytimes.com/2015/09/30/nyregion/officer-who-disclosed-police-misconduct-settles-suit.html.

75. John Marzulli, Stephen Rex Brown, "Cop Sues NYPD, Claims Locker Vandalized After Blowing Whistle on Quotas," *New York Daily News*, September 1, 2015, http://www.nydailynews.com/new-york/nypd-quota-system-impacts-minority-officers-suit-article-1.2344608.

76. See J. L. Eberhardt, P. A. Goff, V. J. Purdie, and P. G. Davies, "Seeing Black: Race, Crime, and Visual Processing," *Journal of Personality and Social Psychology* 87, no. 6 (2004): 876–93.

77. *Terry v. Ohio*, 392 U.S. 1 (1968) at 16–17.

78. From an opinion in *Terry*: "Each case of this sort will, of course, have to be

decided on its own facts. We merely hold today that where a police officer observes unusual conduct which leads him reasonably to conclude in light of his experience that criminal activity may be afoot and that the persons with whom he is dealing may be armed and presently dangerous, where in the course of investigating this behavior he identifies himself as a policeman and makes reasonable inquiries, and where nothing in the initial stages of the encounter serves to dispel his reasonable fear for his own or others' safety, he is entitled for the protection of himself and others in the area to conduct a carefully limited search of the outer clothing of such persons in an attempt to discover weapons which might be used to assault him. Such a search is a reasonable search under the Fourth Amendment, and any weapons seized may properly be introduced in evidence against the person from whom they were taken." Ibid., 31; see http://caselaw.findlaw.com/us-supreme-court/392 /1.html.

79. See William J. Stuntz, "Local Policing After the Terror," 111 *Yale Law Journal* (2002): 2137–94. His footnote there: "(47.) In *Terry*, the suspected crime was robbery. 392 U.S. at 28. On the application of *Terry*'s analysis to suspected drug crime, see, for example, *Alabama v. White*, 496 U.S. 325 (1990). On its application to minor crimes, see *Delaware v. Prouse*, 440 U.S. 648, 663 (1979), where the Court states that a reasonable suspicion that a driver is driving with an expired license would justify a stop." (The ruling in *Delaware v. Prouse* reads in part: "Accordingly, we hold that, except in those situations in which there is at least articulable and reasonable suspicion that a motorist is unlicensed or that an automobile is not registered, or that either the vehicle or an occupant is otherwise subject to seizure for violation of law, stopping an automobile and detaining the driver in order to check his driver's license and the registration of the automobile are unreasonable under the Fourth Amendment.")

80. *United States v. Lopez*, 321 Fed. App'x 65, 67 (2d Cir. 2009), quoting *Arizona v. Johnson*, 555 U.S. 323 at 326–327 (2009).

81. "Video Exposes Philadelphia's Abusive Stop and Frisk Tactics," *Police State USA*, October 13, 2013, http://www.policestateusa.com/2013/ video-exposes-philadelphias-abusive-stop-frisk-tactics/.

82. "Detroit Police Are Training to 'Stop and Frisk' the Public Without Probable Cause," *Police State USA*, August 20, 2013, http://www.policestateusa.com /2013/detroit-police-are-training-to-stop-frisk-the-public-without-probable -cause/.

83. Christine Kraly, "STOP Team Anti-crime Approach 'Like Fishing,'" *Northwest Indiana Times*, August 28, 2013, http://www.nwitimes.com/news/local/stop- team-anti-crime-approach-like-fishing/article_99424026-0107-5810-819c-c2 8ceb466936.html.

84. *United States v. Broomfield*, 417 F.3d 654, 655 (7th Cir. 2005) (Posner, R.)

85. "The LAPD: Chief Bratton," Official Site of the Los Angeles Police

Department, accessed March 1, 2016, http://www.lapdonline.org
/history_of_the_lapd/content_basic_view/1120; "The Life and Times
of Incoming NYPD Commissioner Bill Bratton," *New York Daily
News*, December 5, 2013, http://www.nydailynews.com/news/politics/
timeline-new-nypd-commissioner-bratton-article-1.1538689.

86. Jennifer Fermino, "Bill Bratton Expanded Stop and Frisk When He Ran
Los Angeles Police Department," *New York Daily News*, November 24,
2013, http://www.nydailynews.com/new-york/bratton-article-1.1527258;
Michael Goodwin, "De Blasio Is to Blame for the Bratton-Kelly Feud,"
New York Post, December 31, 2015, http://nypost.com/2015/12/31/
how-de-blasio-started-this-unfortunate-bratton-kelly-feud/.

87. Leslie Casimir, "In Waller, Racial Segregation Stays Alive in Graves," *Houston
Chronicle*, July 15, 2008, http://www.chron.com/news/houston-texas/article/
In-Waller-racial-segregation-stays-alive-in-1756666.php.

88. Tom Dart, "The Texas County Where Sandra Bland Died: There's 'Racism
from Cradle to Grave,'" *Guardian*, July 17, 2015, http://www.theguardian
.com/us-news/2015/jul/17/sandra-bland-alleged-suicide-waller-county-texas
-racism.

89. John R. Ross, "Lynching," *Handbook of Texas Online*, Texas State Historical
Association, last modified August 26, 2013, https://tshaonline.org/handbook/
online/articles/jgl01.

90. "Enrollment Statistics," Prairie View A&M University, accessed April 1, 2016,
https://www.pvamu.edu/ir/pvamu-data/enrollment-statistics/.

91. Geoff Ziezulewicz, Bill Bird, and Lolly Bowean, "Family Wary After Naper-
ville Woman's Death in Texas Jail; Grand Jury to Inquire," *Chicago Tribune*,
July 16, 2015, http://www.chicagotribune.com/news/local/breaking/ct-
sandra-bland-texas-jail-death-met-0717-20150717-story.html.

92. The short version of the video is available online: "Sandra Bland Dashcam
Video Released," YouTube video, 10:08, posted by Police Center—News &
Pursuits, July 21, 2015, https://www.youtube.com/watch?v=jpSEemvwOn4.
A longer version of the video was released earlier, but it appeared to have some
glitches and to have been edited, raising suspicions. The Texas Department
of Public Safety then released the shorter version. The longer version—which
is also on YouTube—begins earlier than the shorter version and shows Bland
making her lane change without signaling.

93. See Ryan Grim, "The Transcript of Sandra Bland's Arrest Is as Revealing as
the Video," *Huffington Post*, July 23, 2015, http://www.huffingtonpost.com/
entry/sandra-bland-arrest-transcript_55b03a88e4b0a9b94853b1f1 for a full
transcript of their exchange.

94. "Sandra Bland's Arrest," YouTube video, 1:37, posted by Shazzam1294, July
15, 2015, https://www.youtube.com/watch?v=IYim6pDZV0Y.

95. A link to the full autopsy report can be found in Tasneem Nashrullah and

Amanda Chicago Lewis, "Texas Officials Release Full Sandra Bland Autopsy, Results Show No Signs of Homicide," *Buzzfeed*, July 23, 2015, http://www .buzzfeed.com/tasneemnashrulla/texas-officials-detail-sandra-blands-autopsy-results#.cxKKlB2Gj2.

96. "In addition, the authorities late on Wednesday released the 15-page jail-booking screening form, which included questions about Ms. Bland's mental health. On the form, the 'yes' box was checked in response to the question, 'Have you ever been depressed?' On whether she had ever attempted suicide, the form noted 'yes,' in 2014, by using 'pills' because of a 'lost baby.'" David Montgomery and Michael Wines, "Dispute Over Sandra Bland's Mental State Follows Death in a Texas Jail," *New York Times*, July 22, 2015, http://www.nytimes.com/2015/07/23/us/sandra-blands-family-says-video-sheds-no-light-on-reason-for-her-arrest.html?_r=0.

97. Ibid.

98. "No one was indicted in relation to the jailhouse death, but a grand jury did not believe Encinia's statement that he removed Bland from the car she was driving so he could conduct a safer traffic investigation." Tina Burnside and Joshua Burlinger, "Trooper Who Arrested Sandra Bland Formally Fired," CNN, March 3, 2016, http://www.cnn.com/2016/03/03/us/sandra-bland-officer-fired/.

99. Brittney Cooper, "I Could Have Been Sandra Bland: Black America's Terrifying Truth," *Salon*, July 23, 2015, http://www.salon.com/2015/07/23/black _americas_terrifying_truth_any_of_us_could_have_been_sandra_bland/.

100. This quote is from the report "The Sexual Abuse To Prison Pipeline: The Girl's Story," by Malika Saada Saar, Rebecca Epstein, Lindsay Rosenthal, and Yasmin Vafa; http://rights4girls.org/wp-content/uploads/r4g/2015/02/2015 _COP_sexual-abuse_layout_web-1.pdf.

101. I emphasize both women and girls to underscore the ways in which the criminalization of Black female bodies operates not only in American jails and prisons but also in the juvenile "justice" system. See Jyoti Nanda, "Blind Discretion: Girls of Color and Delinquency in the Juvenile Justice System," *UCLA Law Review* 59 (2012): 1502, 1529–30; Tina L. Freiburger and Alison S. Burke, "Status Offenders in the Juvenile Court: The Effects of Gender, Race, and Ethnicity on the Adjudication Decision," *Youth Violence and Juvenile Justice* 9 (2011): 352–65.

102. For a definitive treatment of the "controlling images" that govern our understanding of Black female identity, see Patricia Hill Collins's now-classic *Black Feminist Thought* (New York: Routledge, 1990).

103. For example, Brittney Cooper argued, "I do not believe that Sandra Bland hanged herself just a few hours before her sister was set to come and pay the $500 bail it would have taken to get her out of jail. I do not believe Sandra Bland hanged herself two days before taking her dream job at her alma

mater. I do not believe Sandra Bland hanged herself. No one with good sense believes that. And I challenge the sense of anyone who is willing to contort themselves into intellectual knots to make such a ridiculous story seem remotely plausible." Brittney Cooper, "'If I Die in Police Custody': Why Sandra Bland's Death Is Just the Latest Evidence that Black America Is Under Attack," *Salon*, July 22, 2015, http://www.salon.com/2015/07/22/if_i_die _in_police_custody_why_sandra_blands_death_is_just_the_latest_evidence _that_black_america_is_under_attack/.

104. For an excellent analysis of Black womanhood, mental health, and shame, see Melissa Harris-Perry's *Sister Citizen: Shame, Stereotypes, and Black Women in America* (New Haven, CT: Yale University Press, 2011).

105. Thomas H. Cohen and Brian A. Reaves, "Pretrial Release of Felony Defendants in State Courts," Bureau of Justice Statistics special report, US Department of Justice Office of Justice Programs, November 2007, http://www.bjs .gov/content/pub/pdf/prfdsc.pdf.

106. Dana Liebelson and Nick Wing, "A Texas Jail Failed Sandra Bland, Even If It's Telling the Truth About Her Death," *Huffington Post*, July 22, 2015, http://www.huffingtonpost.com/entry/sandra-bland-jail-death_us _55ae9f12e4b07af29d569875.

107. Ibid.

108. Breanna Edwards, "At Least 5 Black Women Have Died in Police Custody in July; WTF?!" *Root*, July 30, 2015, http://www.theroot.com/articles/news /2015/07/at_least_5_black_women_have_died_in_police_custody_in_july _wtf.html.

III. BARGAINED

1. Sheryl Gay Stolberg and Alan Blinder, "Marilyn Mosby, Prosecutor in Freddie Gray Case, Takes a Stand and Calms a Troubled City," *New York Times*, May 1, 2015, http://www.nytimes.com/2015/05/02/us/marilyn-mosby-prosecutor- in-freddie-gray-case-seen-as-tough-on-police-misconduct.html.

2. "Mosby won the Democratic nomination for the post in the June 24 primary when she defeated incumbent State's Attorney Gregg L. Bernstein. No Republican is running." Kevin Rector and Ian Duncan, "Neverdon Loses Again as He Strives for Place on November Ballot," *Baltimore Sun*, September 9, 2014, http://www.baltimoresun.com/news/maryland/baltimore-city/bs-md- ci-neverdon-loses-appeal-20140909-story.html.

3. "Mosby made tackling violent crime a key theme of her primary campaign. But she will take office in January with high expectations that she will root out corruption in the police department and prosecute officers for brutality." Ian Duncan, "Mosby Is Next Baltimore State's Attorney," *Baltimore Sun*, November 4, 2014, http://www.baltimoresun.com/news/maryland/politics/ campaign-2014/bs-md-ci-city-races-20141104-story.html.

4. Aside from the fact that Freddie Gray's switchblade was not illegal, it also was not in his possession at the time he entered the police van. Thus, he was unarmed at the time of his death.

5. "It's been 78 days since Michael Brown was shot in the street by a police officer," Ms. Mosby said in October at her alma mater, Alabama's Tuskegee University. "It's been 101 days since Eric Garner was choked to death in New York by a police officer, and 54 days since the New York City medical examiner ruled that incident a homicide. Neither has resulted in an indictment." Stolberg and Blinder, "Marilyn Mosby Takes a Stand."

6. "HABC—Over 75 Years of Rich History," Housing Authority of Baltimore City, accessed March 17, 2016, http://www.baltimorehousing.org/75th _timeline.

7. Associated Press, "Maryland: Suit Alleges Sex Was Extorted for Repairs," *New York Times*, September 28, 2015, http://www.nytimes.com/2015/09/29/us/ maryland-suit-alleges-sex-was-extorted-for-repairs.html.

8. "Why Freddie Gray Ran," *Baltimore Sun*, April 25, 2015, http://www .baltimoresun.com/news/opinion/editorial/bs-ed-freddie-gray-20150425- story.html.

9. Michael A. Fletcher, "Freddie Gray and William Porter: Two Sons of Baltimore Whose Lives Collided," *Washington Post*, September 3, 2015, https:// www.washingtonpost.com/local/freddie-gray-and-william-porter-two-sons- of-baltimore-whose-lives-collided/2015/09/03/a6273e5c-4a66-11e5-846d- 02792f854297_story.html.

10. "In Sumer, public slaves were referred to as *iginu'du*, meaning 'not raising their eyes,' which apparently they were forbidden to do as a symbol of their degradation and social death—and probably to prevent their eyes from looking at nonslave women. Some slaves were branded with the same mark as livestock." In David Brion Davis, *Inhuman Bondage: The Rise and Fall of Slavery in the New World* (New York: Oxford University Press, 2006). Kindle edition.

11. "Unwritten Rules . . . Unwritten Legacy," WNET/PBS, accessed March 17, 2016. http://www.pbs.org/wnet/jimcrow/tools_unwritten.html.

12. Those mourning Freddie Gray picked up on the symbolism of this moment. In his eulogy, Reverend Jamal Bryant said: "On April 12 at 8:39 in the morning, four officers on bicycles saw your son. And your son, in a subtlety of revolutionary stance, did something black men were trained to know not to do. He looked police in the eye. And when he looked the police in the eye, they knew that there was a threat, because they're used to black men with their head bowed down low, with their spirit broken. He was a threat simply because he was man enough to look somebody in authority in the eye. I want to tell this grieving mother . . . you are not burying a boy, you are burying a grown man. He knew that one of the principles of being a man is looking somebody in the eye." See Stacia L. Brown, "Looking While Black,"

New Republic, April 30. 2015, https://newrepublic.com/article/121682/
freddie-grays-eye-contact-police-led-chase-death.

13. Ray Sanchez, "Freddie Gray Case: Actions That Led to Charges Against Six,"
CNN, May 6, 2015, http://www.cnn.com/2015/05/01/us/freddie-gray-officers-actions/index.html.

14. Catherine Rentz, "Videographer: Freddie Gray Was Folded Like 'Origami,'"
Baltimore Sun, April 23, 2015, http://www.baltimoresun.com/news/maryland/
baltimore-city/bs-md-gray-video-moore-20150423-story.html.

15. Alan Blinder and Richard Pérez-Peña, "6 Baltimore Police Officers Charged in
Freddie Gray Death," *New York Times*, May 1, 2015, http://www.nytimes.com/2015
/05/02/us/freddie-gray-autopsy-report-given-to-baltimore-prosecutors.html.

16. The use of vehicle transport as a means of extrajudicial punishment, and torture, is a longstanding practice within the American criminal justice system.
In addition to the "rough rides" given to criminal suspects, convicted prisoners are subjected to "diesel therapy," in which unduly long and painful trips
in prison transportation vehicles causes physical and psychological damage to
inmates. See Seth M. Ferranti, "Diesel Therapy: Torturing Prisoners Legally
Takes the Bus," *Vice*, February 2004, http://www.november.org/stayinfo/
breaking2/Ferranti.html; also see Stevin Hoover's *Mark Whitacre Against All
Odds: How "The Informant" and His Family Turned Defeat into Triumph*, (Bloom-
ington, IN: Xlibris, 2009).

17. Jean Marbella, "Six Baltimore Police Officers Charged in Freddie Gray's
Death," *Baltimore Sun*, May 2, 2015, http://www.baltimoresun.com/news/
maryland/freddie-gray/bs-md-freddie-gray-mainbar-20150501-story.html.

18. "Marilyn Mosby Getz the Angela Davis Black Power Award," *Moor-
bey'z Blog*, May 7, 2015, https://moorbey.wordpress.com/2015/05/07/
marilyn-mosby-getz-the-angela-davis-black-power-award/.

19. William J. Stuntz, *The Collapse of American Criminal Justice* (Cambridge, MA:
Harvard University Press, 2011). Kindle edition.

20. U.S. Const. amend XIV, §1.

21. "Criminal Cases," United States Courts, accessed May 11, 2016, http://www
.uscourts.gov/about-federal-courts/types-cases/criminal-cases.

22. Erica Goode, "Stronger Hand for Judges in the 'Bazaar' of Plea Deals," *New
York Times*, March 22, 2012, http://www.nytimes.com/2012/03/23/us/stronger
-hand-for-judges-after-rulings-on-plea-deals.html.

23. *Lafler v. Cooper*, 132 S.Ct. 1376, 1388 (2012).

24. Lucian E. Dervan, "Bargained Justice: Plea Bargaining's Innocence Problem
and the Brady Safety-Valve," *Utah Law Review* 51 (2012). Available online from
the Social Science Research Network: http://ssrn.com/abstract=1664620.

25. *Santobello v. New York*, 404 U.S. 257 (1971) at 260, http://caselaw.findlaw.com/
us-supreme-court/404/257.html.

26. Editorial, "A Broader Right to Counsel," *New York Times*, March 22, 2012,

http://www.nytimes.com/2012/03/23/opinion/a-broader-right-to-counsel. html?_r=0.

27. "Every state that penned a constitution between 1775 and 1789 featured at least one express affirmation of jury trial, typically celebrating the jury with one or more of the following words: 'ancient,' 'sacred,' 'inviolate,' 'great,' and 'inestimable.' The Northwest Ordinance also affirmed 'trial by Jury' and, in a separate provision, a man's right not to be deprived of his liberty or property in the absence of 'the judgment of his peers, or the law of the land.'" In Akhil Reed Amar, *America's Constitution: A Biography* (New York: Random House, 2012). Kindle edition.

28. This origin story is covered in Stuntz, *The Collapse of American Criminal Justice*. It is worth noting that while I agree with Stuntz's general analysis of the problem, I disagree strongly with some of his proposed solutions. In particular, Stuntz argues that expanding city police forces would discourage crime and ultimately contribute to greater and more effective mechanisms of justice. I find such a solution shortsighted, as it ignores the ways in which an expansive police presence functions as an occupying and destabilizing force within vulnerable communities.

29. Drug Policy Alliance, "The Drug War, Mass Incarceration and Race," http://www.drugpolicy.org/sites/default/files/DPA Fact Sheet_Drug War Mass Incarceration and Race_(Feb. 2016).pdf.

30. Stuntz, *The Collapse of American Criminal Justice*, Kindle edition.

31. Angela J. Davis, *Arbitrary Justice: The Power of the American Prosecutor* (New York: Oxford University Press, 2006). Kindle edition.

32. "Profile: Robert P. McCulloch," St. Louis County Office of the Prosecuting Attorney, accessed May 12, 2016, http://www.stlouiscopa.com/Extras.aspx ?ID=191.

33. Joe Garofoli, "Lack of Black Prosecutors Poses Criminal Justice Problem," *San Francisco Chronicle*, December 27, 2014, http://www.sfgate.com/news/article/ Lack-of-black-prosecutors-poses-criminal-justice-5981413.php.

34. Editorial, "A Jury Draws a Line," *New York Times*, June 1, 2012, http://www .nytimes.com/2012/06/02/opinion/a-jury-draws-a-line-on-sentencing.html.

35. "What Are Mandatory Minimums," Families Against Mandatory Minimums, http://famm.org/mandatory-minimums/.

36. Anti–Drug Abuse Act of 1986, Pub. L. No. 99-570, 100 Stat. 3207 (1986), https://www.congress.gov/bill/99th-congress/house-bill/5484.

37. "Cracks in the System: 20 Years of the Unjust Federal Crack Cocaine Law," American Civil Liberties Union, accessed May 12, 2016, https://www.aclu.org /cracks-system-20-years-unjust-federal-crack-cocaine-law.

38. Sentencing Memoranda: *United States v. Green*, No. 02-10054 (D. Mass. June 18, 2004), http://www.cjpc.org/Judge%20Young's%20Opinion.pdf.

39. This conception of the criminal justice system, and the prison more

specifically, as a space to express contrition was one of the organizing principles behind the American prison. This origin story is covered extensively in
chapter 5.

40. See *Berthoff v. United States*, 140 F. Supp. 2d 50 (D. Mass. 2001), in which "fact
bargaining" is defined as "the knowing abandonment by the government of
a material fact developed by law-enforcement authorities or from a witness
expected to testify in order to induce a guilty plea."

41. "Prosecutors negotiate plea deals without having interviewed the victims or
witnesses; instead they rely on a few details scribbled in a police report and
hope the defense lawyers will overlook any inaccuracies. Amy Bach, *Ordinary
Injustice: How America Holds Court* (New York: Henry Holt and Co., 2010).
Kindle edition.

42. "Surrency had taken only fourteen cases to trial out of 1,493; he won five. The
rest of the cases he managed during that period—more than 99 percent—he
plea-bargained. In this particular session no cases went to trial. People either
pleaded guilty or had their cases rescheduled, a drill that took only two days.
There were 142 defendants on the court calendar and 89 were Surrency's. In
a flash, it seemed, forty-eight of his clients rose from the rickety dark wooden
benches, one after the other, to plead guilty. After the first day I spent in court
observing him, he announced, 'We have successfully done a ten-page calendar
in one day!' For Surrency, speed meant success." Ibid.

43. Ibid.; emphasis added.

44. Amar, *America's Constitution*, Kindle edition.

45. This value of openness was understood by the framers to be righteous in and
of itself. "[O]pen examination of witnesses viva voce [by word of mouth], in
the presence of all mankind," wrote eighteenth-century English jurist William
Blackstone, "is much more conducive to the clearing up of truth, than the
private and secret examination taken down in writing before an officer, or his
clerk . . . for a witness may frequently depose that in private, which he will be
ashamed to testify in public." William Blackstone, *Commentaries on the Laws of
England: All Books* (Waxkeep Publishing, 2013). Kindle edition.

46. Catherine Rentz, "Freddie Gray Remembered as Jokester Who Struggled
to Leave Drug Trade," *Baltimore Sun*, November 22, 2015, http://www
.baltimoresun.com/news/maryland/freddie-gray/bal-freddie-gray-remembered-
as-jokester-who-struggled-to-leave-drug-trade-20151120-story.html.

47. Holly Yan and Ashley Fantz, "Freddie Gray Funeral Draws White House Officials, Eric Garner's Family," CNN, April 29, 2015, http://www.cnn.com/2015
/04/27/us/baltimore-freddie-gray-funeral/index.html.

48. Ray Sanchez, "Baltimore Riots: Catalyst for Rebuilding Burned
Down," CNN, April 29, 2015, http://www.cnn.com/2015/04/28/us/
baltimore-community-center-fire/.

49. Jeffrey Gettleman, "In Baltimore, Slogan Collides with Reality," *New York*

Times, September 2, 2003, http://www.nytimes.com/2003/09/02/us/in-baltimore-slogan-collides-with-reality.html?ref=topics&pagewanted=2.

50. Melody Simmons, "Home Where Family Died Is Now Safe Haven," April 8, 2007, http://www.nytimes.com/2007/04/08/us/08baltimore.html.

51. David Simon, *Homicide: A Year on the Killing Streets* (New York: Henry Holt and Co., 2006).

52. "Detective Edward Norris," HBO, accessed February 12, 2016, http://www.hbo.com/the-wire/cast-and-crew/edward-norris/index.html.

53. Shaila K. Dewan, "New York's Gospel of Policing by Data Spreads Across U.S.," April 28, 2004, http://www.nytimes.com/2004/04/28/nyregion/new-york-s-gospel-of-policing-by-data-spreads-across-us.html.

54. "Crime Rate in Baltimore, Maryland (MD)," City-Data.com, http://www.city-data.com/crime/crime-Baltimore-Maryland.html.

55. Sheryl Gay Stolberg, "Fragile Baltimore Struggles." Baltimore's population is 623,000; New York City's is 8.4 million.

56. Justin Fenton, Mayah Collins, and Christine Jedra, "The Victims of July's Violence," *Baltimore Sun*, August 29, 2015, http://www.baltimoresun.com/news/maryland/investigations/bal-remembering-the-victims-of-homicides-in-july-20150827-htmlstory.html#anchor-0.

57. Justin Fenton, Christina Jedra, and Mayah Collins, "45 Murders in 31 Days: Looking Back at Baltimore's Deadliest Month," *Baltimore Sun*, August 29, 2015, http://www.baltimoresun.com/news/maryland/investigations/bs-md-ci-july-homicide-victims-20150829-story.html.

58. Bill Keller, "David Simon on Baltimore's Anguish," Marshall Project, April 29, 2015, https://www.themarshallproject.org/2015/04/29/david-simon-on-baltimore-s-anguish.

59. Justin Fenton, "With Fewer Arrests in Baltimore, Fewer Cases That Don't Stick," *Baltimore Sun*, July 3, 2011, http://articles.baltimoresun.com/2011-07-03/news/bs-md-ci-released-without-charges-20110703_1_fewer-arrests-drug-dealers-city-police.

60. Theo Emery, "Baltimore Police Scandal Spotlights Leader's Fight to Root Out Corruption," May 8, 2012, http://www.nytimes.com/2012/05/09/us/baltimore-police-corruption-case-tests-commissioner.html.

61. Tricia Bishop, "Baltimore Officer Convicted of Drug Dealing," *Baltimore Sun*, March 16, 2012, http://www.baltimoresun.com/news/breaking/bs-md-ci-redd-rearraignment-20120315-story.html.

62. For a more nuanced analysis of the "Stop Snitchin'" movement and its broader relationship to the criminal justice system and the Black community, see Marc Lamont Hill, "Damned If You Do. Damned If You Don't," *Pop Matters*, accessed February 12, 2016, http://www.popmatters.com/column/hill060224-1/.

63. "The U.S. Department of Justice is conducting a separate review of complaints

about Baltimore's Police Department at Batts' request. That request followed a *Baltimore Sun* investigation that found taxpayers had paid nearly $6 million since 2011 to settle more than 100 lawsuits alleging police brutality and other misconduct." Natalie Sherman, Chris Kaltenbach, and Colin Campbell, "Freddie Gray Dies a Week After Being Injured During Arrest," *Baltimore Sun*, April 19, 2015, http://www.baltimoresun.com/news/maryland/crime/blog/bs-md-freddie-gray-20150419-story.html#page=1.

64. Mark Puente, "Undue Force," *Baltimore Sun*, September 28, 2014, http://data.baltimoresun.com/news/police-settlements/.

65. Mark Puente, "As Homicides Soar in Baltimore, Police Commissioner Looks to Reform Department," *Baltimore Sun*, December 5, 2015, http://www.baltimoresun.com/news/maryland/baltimore-city/bs-md-bpd-kevin-davis-interview-20151205-story.html.

66. Keith L. Alexander, "Baltimore Reaches $6.4 million settlement with Freddie Gray's Family," *Washington Post*, September 8, 2015, https://www.washingtonpost.com/local/crime/baltimore-reaches-64-million-settlement-with-freddie-grays-family/2015/09/08/80b2c092-5196-11e5-8c19-0b6825aa4a3a_story.html.

67. Josh Feldman, "Alan Dershowitz Rips Charges Against Baltimore Cops: 'Sad Day for Justice,'" *Mediaite*, May 1, 2015, http://www.mediaite.com/tv/alan-dershowitz-rips-charges-against-baltimore-cops-sad-day-for-justice/.

68. Stolberg, "Fragile Baltimore Struggles."

69. Anthony Lewis, *Gideon's Trumpet* (New York: Vintage Books, 2011). Kindle edition.

70. The defendant was Haywood Patterson. See James Goodman's *Stories of Scottsboro* (New York: Pantheon Books, 1994).

71. This was not the only gross violation of criminal procedure and basic decency in the case. Among other insults, Black jurors were not permitted to serve on the trial. This led to another Supreme Court case, *Norris v. Alabama* (1935), in which the court found due process to be denied when Black jurors are excluded from the trials of Black defendants.

72. *Miranda v. Arizona*, 384 U.S. 436 (1966), https://www.law.cornell.edu/supremecourt/text/384/436.

73. For an analysis of the complicated legacy of *Brown*, see James T. Patterson's Brown v. Board of Education: *A Civil Rights Milestone and Its Troubled Legacy*, Pivotal Moments in American History (New York: Oxford University Press, 2001). See also the special issue of the *Journal of Negro Education* 83, no. 3 (Summer 2014), "60 Years After *Brown v. Board of Education of Topeka Kansas*: Educational Opportunities, Disparities, Policies, and Legal Actions."

74. American Bar Association Standing Committee on Legal Aid and Indigent Defendants, Gideon's *Broken Promise: America's Continuing Quest for Equal Justice* (Chicago: American Bar Association, 2004). The report may be viewed

at http://www.americanbar.org/content/dam/aba/administrative/legal_aid
_indigent_defendants/ls_sclaid_def_bp_right_to_counsel_in_criminal
_proceedings.authcheckdam.pdf.

75. Ibid.; emphasis added.

76. National News Briefs, "Let Sleeping Lawyers Counsel, Court Says," *New York Times*, October 28, 2000, http://www.nytimes.com/2000/10/28/us/ national-news-briefs-let-sleeping-lawyers-counsel-court-says.html. This article references the decision of a three-judge panel of the Fifth Circuit. When the full court took up the case en banc, they affirmed the decision of the lower court, which had said that the lawyer's sleeping constituted denial of effective counsel.

77. Lise Olsen, "Slow Paperwork in Death Row Cases Ends Final Appeals for 9," *Houston Chronicle*, March 21, 2009, http://www.chron.com/ news/houston-texas/article/Slow-paperwork-in-death-row-cases-ends-final-1736308.php.

78. Bach, *Ordinary Injustice*, Kindle edition.

79. Ibid.

80. "'People often know that they are guilty and want to hear what the offer is' from the source itself, she said, adding that 'a lot of people know' her and her credible reputation. Also, at every juncture before someone pleaded guilty she would ask, 'Are you sure this is what you are going to do?' Whether it was a credit to her or a rebuke to the public defender, almost half of the people picked the peppy, wide-eyed Fachini over the uninviting defense attorney. Many ended up pleading guilty without a lawyer." Ibid.

81. In addition to the fifty states, Guam, Puerto Rico, and multiple territories also have their own systems.

82. "State Indigent Defense Systems," Sixth Amendment Center, accessed March 15, 2016, http://sixthamendment.org/the-right-to-counsel/ state-indigent-defense-systems/.

83. To be clear, there are sixteen states whose counties' public-defender systems have no state oversight. The four listed here are those that have both no oversight and no state funding. See ibid.

84. Stephanie Chen, "Pennsylvania Rocked by 'Jailing Kids for Cash' Scandal," CNN, February 24, 2009, http://www.cnn.com/2009/CRIME/02/23 /pennsylvania.corrupt.judges/.

85. See the piece by David Carroll, director of the Sixth Amendment Center, entitled "Gideon's Despair: Four Things the Next Attorney General Needs to Know About America's Indigent Defense Crisis," Marshall Project, January 2, 2015, https://www.themarshallproject.org/2015/01/02/four-things-the-next-attorney-general-needs-to-know-about-america-s-indigent-defense-crisis.

86. Joe Watson, "States Create Special Commissions to Study Flat-Fee Indigent Defense," *Prison Legal News*, December 15, 2012, https://www.prisonlegalnews

.org/news/2012/dec/15/states-create-special-commissions-to-study-flat-fee-indigent-defense/.

IV. ARMED

1. Dunn lived with Rouer at 250 Ocean Residence Court in Satellite Beach, Florida. You can hear Rouer reference this address at roughly the seven-minute mark in the video of her testimony: "Michael Dunn Trial. Day 3. Part 5. Rhonda Rouer, Michael Dunn Fiance [*sic*] Takes Stand," YouTube video, 1:13:10, posted by TheTawniDilly, February 8, 2014, https://www.youtube .com/watch?v=ur_z2KJePIE.

2. The wedding was in Orange Park, Florida, a suburb of Jacksonville. Dunn mentions Orange Park in his testimony, at approximately the 6:00 mark: "Michael Dunn Trial. Day 5. Part 3. Michael Dunn Takes Stand," YouTube video, 2:38:59, posted by TheTawniDilly, February 11, 2014, https://www.youtube .com/watch?v=HxBAIbVTPxs.

3. Rouer later recalled that she had two drinks and Dunn had three or four. "Michael Dunn's Girlfriend: 'I Heard Pop, Pop, Pop,'" HLN, February 10, 2014, http://www.hlntv.com/article/2014/02/08/ michael-dunn-trial-jordan-davis-saturday.

4. Julia Dahl, "Day 2 of 'Loud Music' Trial Deliberation Ends, No Verdict," CBS News, February 13, 2014, http://www.cbsnews.com/news/ jurors-in-loud-music-murder-trial-watch-surveillance-video/.

5. "Friends Describe Moments Before Jordan Davis Died," HLN, February 7, 2014, http://www.hlntv.com/article/2014/02/07/michael-dunn-jordan-davis-friends-tevin-leland.

6. "Song Played in Jordan Davis Shooting Revealed," First Coast News, February 8, 2014, http://legacy.firstcoastnews.com/story/news/crime/2014/02/08/ beef-lil-reese-jordan-davis-song-michael-dunn/5314323/.

7. He may have called Dunn a "cracker" and even threatened him by saying "I am going to kill you." At least Dunn claimed that Davis did, though the other teens insisted that he did not.

8. "Friends Describe Moments," HLN, February 7, 2014.

9. "Uncut: Tevin Thompson Testimony," online video, 57:54, News 4 Jacksonville, February 7, 2014, http://www.news4jax.com/news/uncut-tevin-thompson-testimony. See Tevin Thompson's testimony at 12:40.

10. In Rouer's testimony, she describes seeing Dunn's driver's side door opened as he held the gun. See "Michael Dunn Trial. Day 3. Part 5," YouTube, at roughly the 19:30 mark.

11. "The jury did convict Mr. Dunn, 47, on three counts of second-degree attempted murder, one for each surviving teenager in the car. Jurors agreed that Mr. Dunn was trying to kill the teenagers—not to defend himself—when he got out of his car, crouched and shot several more bullets into the truck as it drove away." Lizette

Alvarez, "Florida Self-Defense Law Complicated Jury's Job in Michael Dunn Trial," *New York Times*, February 16, 2014, http://www.nytimes.com/2014/02/17/us/florida-self-defense-law-hung-over-jury-in-michael-dunn-trial.html.

12. "Michael Dunn Trial. Day 3. Part 5," YouTube. This reference to "pop, pop" comes at roughly 18:00.

13. Ibid. At roughly 32:00, the prosecutor plays the surveillance video from the Gate gas station. You can hear the clerk speaking.

14. Ibid., at 35:15. Note that the phrases "good guy with a gun" and "protect you" are offered by Dunn's lawyer to Rouer, who then agrees with that statement.

15. Ibid., at 20:30.

16. Ibid., at 21:25.

17. Ibid., at 26:25.

18. See the prosecutor's opening statement: "Uncut: Prosecutor John Guy's Opening Statement," News 4 Jacksonville, February 12, 2014, http://www.news4jax.com/news/uncut-prosecutor-john-guy-opening-statement.

19. Ben Kenigsberg, "Review: '3 ½ Minutes, Ten Bullets' Explores a Gas Station Slaying in Florida," *New York Times*, June 18, 2015, http://www.nytimes.com/2015/06/19/movies/review-3-minutes-ten-bullets-explores-a-gas-station-slaying-in-florida.html?_r=0.

20. "NOW homicide, or the killing of any human creature, is of three kinds; justifiable, excusable, and felonious. The first has no share of guilt at all; the second very little; but the third is the highest crime against the law of nature, that man is capable of committing." In Blackstone, *Commentaries*, Kindle edition.

21. "Wherefore, to excuse homicide by the plea of self-defense, it must appear that the slayer had no other possible means of escaping from his assailant." Ibid.

22. Ibid.; emphasis added.

23. Ibid.

24. Ibid.

25. "Semayne's Case Definition," Duhaime's Law Dictionary, accessed March 4, 2016, http://www.duhaime.org/LegalDictionary/S/SemaynesCase.aspx; Sir Edward Coke, *The Selected Writings and Speeches of Sir Edward Coke*, ed. Steve Sheppard (Indianapolis: Liberty Fund, 2003). Vol. 1. The text of this volume is available online at http://oll.libertyfund.org/titles/911.

26. See Adam Gopnik's interesting essay on Lincoln and the American passion for gun violence, "Abraham Lincoln and the Birth of Stand Your Ground," *New Yorker*, July 18, 2013, http://www.newyorker.com/news/daily-comment/abraham-lincoln-and-the-birth-of-stand-your-ground.

27. *Brown v. United States*, 256 U.S. 335 (1921), https://www.law.cornell.edu/supremecourt/text/150/93.

28. Holmes to Laski as quoted in Richard Maxwell Brown, *No Duty to Retreat: Violence and Values in American History and Society* (Norman: University of Oklahoma Press, 1994).

29. *Beard v. United States*, 158 U.S. 550 (1895), http://caselaw.findlaw.com/us-supreme-court/158/550.html.

30. For an excellent discussion of the relationship between American violence and masculinity, see bell hooks's *The Will to Change: Men, Masculinity, and Love* (New York: Atria Books, 2004).

31. Abby Goodnough, "Florida Expands Right to Use Deadly Force in Self-Defense," *New York Times*, April 27, 2005, http://www.nytimes.com/2005/04/27/us/florida-expands-right-to-use-deadly-force-in-selfdefense.html.

32. Ibid.

33. Ibid.

34. The National Rifle Association lobbied hard for the bill's passage, and Wayne LaPierre, the group's executive vice president, said it would use the victory to push for similar measures elsewhere. The bill's sponsor, Representative Dennis K. Baxley of Ocala, said it would curb violent crime and make citizens feel safer. Ibid.

35. "ALEC Castle Doctrine," ALEC Exposed, accessed March 3, 2016, http://www.alecexposed.org/wiki/ALEC_Castle_Doctrine#cite_ref-2.

36. Lisa Graves, "ALEC exposed: The Koch Connection," *Nation*, July 12, 2011, http://www.thenation.com/article/alec-exposed-koch-connection/.

37. Steven Jansen and M. Elaine Nugent-Borakove, "Expansions to the Castle Doctrine: Implications for Policy and Practice," http://www.ndaa.org/pdf/Castle%20Doctrine.pdf.

38. "'It's a clear position that we will stand with victims of violent attacks when the law is in their favor,' said Mr. Baxley, a Republican. 'People want to know we stand on the side of victims of crime instead of the side of criminals.'" Goodnough, "Florida Expands Right."

39. Susan Ferriss, "NRA Pushed 'Stand Your Ground' Laws Across the Nation," Center for Public Integrity, March 26, 2012, http://www.publicintegrity.org/2012/03/26/8508/nra-pushed-stand-your-ground-laws-across-nation.

40. John F. Timony, "Florida's Disastrous Self-Defense Law," op-ed, *New York Times*, March 23, 2012, http://www.nytimes.com/2012/03/24/opinion/floridas-disastrous-self-defense-law.html.

41. US Const. amend II.

42. *District of Columbia v. Heller*, 554 U.S. 570 (2008), https://www.law.cornell.edu/supct/html/07-290.ZS.html.

43. US Const. amend I.

44. Warren Burger as quoted in John Paul Stevens's op-ed "The Five Extra Words That Can Fix the Second Amendment," *Washington Post*, April 11, 2014, https://www.washingtonpost.com/opinions/the-five-extra-words-that-can-fix-the-second-amendment/2014/04/11/f8a19578-b8fa-11e3-96ae-f2c36d2b1245_story.html.

45. Stephanie Brown, "Dunn's Attorney Reveals Why No 'Stand Your Ground'

Immunity Sought," News 104.5 WOKV, February 13, 2014, http://www
.wokv.com/news/news/local/dunns-attorney-reveals-why-no-stand-your-
ground-im/ndNXF/.

46. Lizette Alvarez, "Florida Man Is Convicted of Murdering Teenager in Dispute
Over Loud Music," *New York Times*, October 1, 2014, http://www.nytimes
.com/2014/10/02/us/verdict-reached-in-death-of-florida-youth-in-loud-
music-dispute.html.

47. "No duty to retreat. § 776.013(5), Fla. Stat. See *Novak v. State*, 974 So. 2d 520
(Fla. 4th DCA 2008) regarding unlawful activity. There is no duty to retreat
where the defendant was not engaged in any unlawful activity other than the
crime(s) for which the defendant asserts the justification.

"If the defendant [was not engaged in an unlawful activity and] was attacked in any place where [he] [she] had a right to be, [he] [she] had no duty
to retreat and had the right to stand [his] [her] ground and meet force with
force, including deadly force, if [he] [she] reasonably believed that it was
necessary to do so to prevent death or great bodily harm to [himself] [her-
self] [another] or to prevent the commission of a forcible felony." In "Justifiable Use of Non-Deadly Force Jury Instruction," *Florida Bar News*, July
1, 2013, https://www.floridabar.org/DIVCOM/JN/jnnews01.nsf/Articles/
ED8018FC340175F285257B89006CE898.

48. Nicole Flatow, "Juror: Some On Panel Though the Killing of Unarmed
Teen Jordan Davis Was 'Justified,'" *ThinkProgress*, February 20, 2014, http://
thinkprogress.org/justice/2014/02/20/3312751/juror-panel-believed-michael
-dunn-justified-shooting-jordan-davis/.

49. The intellectual work of Nina Sun Eidsheim is foundational here, as she talks
about the significance of "sonic blackness," or the way in which particular
sounds are perceived to be coming from Black bodies. See Nina Sun Eidsheim,
"Marian Anderson and 'Sonic Blackness' in American Opera," *American Quarterly* 63, no. 3 (September 2011): 641–71. Regina Bradley extends this conception of sonic Blackness by exploring how these racialized conceptions of music
and sound enter spaces (such as White suburbs) that are otherwise resistant to
the presence of Black people. As Bradley explains, "The centrality of sound in
the deaths of Trayvon Martin, Renisha McBride, Jordan Davis, and Jonathan
Ferrell—i.e. 911 tapes and banging on house doors—is critical in identifying
race and space. Sonic markers of racial anxiety in their deaths devastatingly
reemphasize the connection of race and sound in White privilege spaces. . . .
The negative connotations of hip hop as 'thug music' and Davis' mere presence as a young black man trigger a devastating response to the disruption
of White privileged space." In Regina N. Bradley, "Fear of a Black (in the)
Suburb," *Sounding Out!*, February 17, 2014, http://soundstudiesblog.com/tag/
sonic-blackness/.

50. Associated Press, "Loud Music Shooting: Michael Dunn Guilty of Attempted

Murder," CBC News, February 15, 2014, http://www.cbc.ca/news/world/ loud-music-shooting-michael-dunn-guilty-of-attempted-murder-1.2539034.

51. Wayne LaPierre, "Is Chaos at Our Door?" NRA, October 15, 2014, http://www.americas1stfreedom.org/articles/2014/10/15/is-chaos-at-our-door/.

52. "Trayvon Martin Shooting Fast Facts," CNN, February 7, 2016, http://www .cnn.com/2013/06/05/us/trayvon-martin-shooting-fast-facts/index.html.

53. Zimmerman call transcript, http://www.documentcloud.org/documents /326700-full-transcript-zimmerman.html.

54. "Lawyer: Trayvon Martin's Girlfriend Heard Altercation," ClickOrlando.com, March 20, 2012, http://www.clickorlando.com/news/local/ lawyer-trayvon-martins-girlfriend-heard-altercation.

55. Seni Tienabeso and Matt Gutman, "George Zimmerman Witness Can't Say Who Threw First Punch," ABC News, June 27, 2013, http://abcnews.go.com /US/george-zimmerman-witness-threw-punch/story?id=19504826.

56. Editorial, "Trashing Trayvon," *New York Daily News*, July 13, 2013, http:// www.nydailynews.com/opinion/trashing-trayvon-article-1.1397657.

57. "Listen to Trayvon Martin/George Zimmerman 911 Calls," Axiom Amnesia, http://trayvon.axiomamnesia.com/trayvon-martin-911-calls-audio/.

58. Amy Davidson, "What Trayvon Martin and George Zimmerman Heard," *New Yorker*, May 18, 2012, http://www.newyorker.com/news/amy-davidson/ what-trayvon-martin-and-george-zimmerman-heard.

59. Madison Gray, "George Zimmerman's Gun: A Popular Choice for Concealed Carry," *Time*, March 28, 2012, http://newsfeed.time.com/2012/03/28/ george-zimmermans-gun-a-popular-choice-for-concealed-carry/.

60. Erin Donaghue, "George Zimmerman Trial: In Closing Arguments, Defense Attorney Asks Jury Not to 'Fill In Gaps' in State's Case," CBS News, July 12, 2013, http://www.cbsnews.com/news/george-zimmerman-trial-in-closing-arguments-defense-attorney-asks-jury-not-to-fill-in-gaps-in-states-case/.

61. Charles M. Blow, "The Whole System Failed Trayvon Martin," op-ed, *New York Times*, July 15, 2013, http://www.nytimes.com/2013/07/16/opinion/the-whole-system-failed.html.

62. Zimmerman said he also carries a semiautomatic handgun for added safety. Caitlin Dineen, "At Lake Mary Gun Show, Zimmerman Details What Life Is Like," *Orlando Sentinel*, September 20, 2014, http://www.orlandosentinel.com/ news/trayvon-martin-george-zimmerman/os-george-zimmerman-lake-mary-gunshow-20140920-story.html.

63. Radley Balko, *Rise of the Warrior Cop: The Militarization of America's Police Forces* (New York: PublicAffairs, 2013). Kindle edition.

64. See Jeffrey Haas's *The Assassination of Fred Hampton: How the FBI and the Chicago Police Murdered a Black Panther* (Chicago: Chicago Review Press, 2011).

65. "'Special Weapons Attack Teams.' Davis blinked at me. 'No.' There was no way, he said dismissively, he would ever use the word 'attack.' I went out,

crestfallen, but a moment later I was back. 'Special Weapons and Tactics,' I said. 'Okay?' 'No problem. That's fine,' Davis said. And that was how SWAT was born. Balko, *Rise of the Warrior Cop*, Kindle edition.

66. For a brief discussion of the relationship between Blacks and the Second Amendment, and the historic pattern of disarming the vulnerable, see my *New York Daily News* op-ed in response to the Chicago decision. Marc Lamont Hill, "Strict Gun Laws Are Bad for Blacks: Why African-Americans Should Value Second Amendment Protections," *New York Daily News*, November 17, 2010, http://www.nydailynews.com/opinion/strict-gun-laws-bad-blacks-african-americans-amendment-protections-article-1.456730.

67. See Alexander DeConde, *Gun Violence in America: The Struggle for Control* (Boston: Northeastern University Press, 2001), 119. Adam Winkler, *Gunfight: The Battle Over the Right to Bear Arms in America* (New York: W. W. Norton & Company, 2011). Kindle Edition.

68. Adam Winkler, "The Secret History of Guns," *Atlantic*, September 2011, http://www.theatlantic.com/magazine/archive/2011/09/the-secret-history-of-guns/308608/.

69. "Armed Negroes Protest Gun Bill," *New York Times*, May 3, 1967, http://timesmachine.nytimes.com/timesmachine/1967/05/03/107188796.html?pageNumber=23.

70. "Francis knew Hanrahan was the prosecutor who had campaigned on the platform 'war on gangs.' He also knew Fred had repeatedly criticized Hanrahan in his speeches for using antigang rhetoric to carry out what Fred called 'a war on black youth.'" In Haas, *The Assassination of Fred Hampton*, Kindle edition.

71. "No Quarter for Wild Beasts," *Chicago Tribune*, November 15, 1969, http://archives.chicagotribune.com/1969/11/15/page/10/article/no-quarter-for-wild-beasts.

72. Balko, *Rise of the Warrior Cop*, Kindle edition.

73. "By 2005, at least 80 percent of towns with a population between 25,000 and 50,000 people had their own SWAT team. The number of raids conducted by local police SWAT teams has gone from 3,000 a year in the 1980s to over 50,000 a year today." In John Fund, "The United States of SWAT?" *National Review*, April 18, 2014, http://www.nationalreview.com/article/376053/united-states-swat-john-fund.

74. Anmargaret Warner, "Why Irvine, California Consistently Ranks as the Safest City in America," *Business Insider*, July 30, 2013, http://www.businessinsider.com/irvine-california-is-americas-safest-city-2013-7#ixzz2tFb3xrf3.

75. The BEAR is manufactured by Lenco Armored Vehicles: http://www.lencoarmor.com/.

76. Keegan Kyle and Christopher Earley, "In Irvine, 'America's Safest' City, Armored SWAT Truck Is Seldom Needed," *Orange County Register*, February 11, 2014, http://www.ocregister.com/taxdollars/irvine-601340-police-bear.html.

77. Fund, "The United States of SWAT?"

78. U.S. Const. amend IV.

79. "There was at least some opposition. Civil rights groups like the NAACP and the Congress of Racial Equality (CORE) held rallies in protest of both bills. The Association of the Bar of the City of New York protested the stop-and-frisk." Balko, *Rise of the Warrior Cop*, Kindle edition.

80. "Fruit of the Poisonous Tree," Legal Information Institute, accessed April 4, 2016, https://www.law.cornell.edu/wex/fruit_of_the_poisonous_tree.

81. *Weeks v. United States*, 232 U.S. 383 (1914) was the case that found this with respect to federal charges; *Mapp v. Ohio*, 367 U.S. 643 (1961) then applied the same rule on the states.

82. "The Court ruled that the exclusionary rule may be used only if there is an intentional or reckless violation of the Fourth Amendment or only if there are systemic police department violations with regard to searches and seizures. For the first time in history, the Court concluded that the exclusionary rule does not apply if the Fourth Amendment is violated by good-faith or even negligent police actions." In Erwin Chemerinsky, *The Conservative Assault on the Constitution* (New York: Simon & Schuster, 2010). Kindle edition.

83. "LatinoJustice Files Amicus Brief in Danbury 11 Case In Support of the Yale Law School Worker and Immigrant Rights Clinic," LatinoJustice, April 4, 2016, http://latinojustice.org/briefing_room/press_releases/latinojustice_files_amicus_brief_in_danbury_11_case_in_support_of_the_yale_law_school_worker_and_immigrant_rights_clinic/; Editorial, "Danbury Laborers Fight Unjust Arrests," *New York Times*, November 10, 2014, http://www.nytimes.com/2014/11/11/opinion/danbury-laborers-fight-unjust-arrests.html.

84. From the opinion: "Nor is there any other circumstance that can be fairly characterized as egregious. The group that was targeted was ostensibly assembled to offer themselves for day labor, an occupation that is one of the limited options for workers without documents. Bystanders and casual park visitors were excluded by no criteria other than self-selection. Nothing in Petitioners' account suggests that they were gathered by the authorities, let alone that they were selected by the authorities on the basis of race. They self-selected on the basis of their willingness to seek and accept day labor." *Maldonado v. Holder*, No. 10-3259 (2d Cir. 2014), http://caselaw.findlaw.com/us-2nd-circuit/1675614.html.

85. Keith Whitney, "The Bluff: Atlanta's Forgotten Community," NBC News, November 3, 2011, http://origin.11alive.com/news/article/211502/3/The-Bluff-Atlantas-forgotten-community.

86. Suzanne L. Baker, "Making a Difference on English Avenue," op-ed, *Atlanta Journal-Constitution*, November 17, 2015, http://www.myajc.com/news/news/opinion/making-a-difference-on-english-avenue/npPqH/?icmp=ajc_internallink_invitationbox_apr2013_ajcstubtomyajcpremium.

87. Brenda Goodman, "Police Kill Woman, 92, in Shootout at Her Home," *New*

York Times, November 23, 2006, http://www.nytimes.com/2006/11/23/us
/23atlanta.html?_r=1.

88. Jason Bronis, "Tapes Detail Shootout with Elderly Woman," *Washington Post*,
December 1, 2006, http://www.washingtonpost.com/wp-dyn/content/article
/2006/12/01/AR2006120101403.html.

89. Shaila Dewan and Brenda Goodman, "Anger Spills Over in Atlanta at Killing
of Aged Woman," *New York Times*, November 29, 2006, http://www.nytimes
.com/2006/11/29/us/29atlanta.html?ref=us&_r=0.

90. Shaila Dewan and Brenda Goodman, "Prosecutors Say Corruption in Atlanta
Police Dept. Is Widespread," *New York Times*, April 27, 2007, http://www
.nytimes.com/2007/04/27/us/27atlanta.html?fta=y.

91. Ted Conover, "A Snitch's Dilemma," *New York Times*, June 29, 2012, http://
www.nytimes.com/2012/07/01/magazine/alex-white-professional-snitch.html.

92. Rhonda Cook, "Atlanta Citizen Review Board Under Scrutiny," *Atlanta
Journal-Constitution*, May 27, 2012, http://www.ajc.com/news/news/local/
atlanta-citizen-review-board-under-scrutiny/nQT7W/.

93. Ibid.

94. The bill is Georgia's SB 159; its status can be tracked at http://openstates.org/
ga/bills/2015_16/SB159/.
Also see Kristina Torres, "Effort to Curb No-Knock Warrants in Georgia
May Be in Trouble," *Atlanta Journal-Constitution*, March 4, 2015, http://www
.myajc.com/news/news/state-regional-govt-politics/effort-to-curb-no-knock-
warrants-in-georgia-may-be/nkNyw/?icmp=ajc_internallink_invitationbox
_apr2013_ajcstubtomyajcpremium.

V. CAGED

1. The Bureau of Justice Statistics report for 2013 (issued in December of 2014)
calculates that there are 6,899,000 people under the supervision of America's
correctional systems, be they federal, state, or local. Of those, 2,220,300 are
actually incarcerated.

2. I've also found that Black men in their early thirties at the end of the 1990s
were more likely to have been to prison than to have graduated from college
with a four-year degree. See Bruce Western, *Punishment and Inequality in America* (New York: Russell Sage Foundation, 2006). Kindle edition; Becky Pettit
and Bruce Western, "Mass Imprisonment and the Life Course: Race and Class
Inequality in U.S. Incarceration," *American Sociological Review* 69 (April 2004):
151–69.

3. Lauren E. Glaze and Laura M. Maruschak, "Parents in Prison and Their
Minor Children," Bureau of Justice Statistics Special Report, US Department
of Justice Office of Justice Programs, revised March 30, 2010, http://www.bjs
.gov/content/pub/pdf/pptmc.pdf.

4. Eliana Dockterman, "How 'Sesame Street' Handles Tough Topics,"

Time, September 20, 2013, http://entertainment.time.com/2013/09/20/
how-sesame-street-handles-tough-topics/.

5. While Michelle Alexander is the latest, and perhaps the most celebrated,
   author on the subject, she is following a movement of scholars and activists
   who have linked mass incarceration to slavery. See Douglas A. Blackmon's
   Slavery by Another Name, (New York: Anchor Books, 2008); Dennis Childs's
   book *Slaves of the State: Black Incarceration from the Chain Gang to the Penitentiary*
   (Minneapolis: University of Minnesota Press, 2015); and Angela Davis's now
   classic text *Are Prisons Obsolete?* (New York: Seven Stories Press, 2003).

6. I use the term "ex-con" here to reflect the language deployed by the State to cate-
   gorize the formerly incarcerated community. Like many antiprison activists, I find
   such language problematic, as it marks individuals by what they have previously
   done rather than who they are as people. In practice, I advocate the use of more
   humane terms like "formerly incarcerated" or "people convicted of a crime."

7. Christopher Uggen, Sarah Shannon, and Jeff Manza, "State-Level Estimates
   of Felon Disenfranchisement in the United States, 2010," Sentencing Project, July 2012, http://sentencingproject.org/doc/publications/fd_State_Level
   _Estimates_of_Felon_Disen_2010.pdf.

8. See Brian C. Kalt, "The Exclusion of Felons from Jury Service," *American
   University Law Review* 53, no.1 (October 2003): 65–189.

9. Western, *Punishment and Inequality*, Kindle edition; Stuntz, *The Collapse of
   American Criminal Justice*, Kindle edition.

10. Michelle Alexander, *The New Jim Crow: Mass Incarceration in the Age of Color-
    blindness* (New York: The New Press, 2012). Kindle edition.

11. "Incarcerated Women and Girls," fact sheet, Sentencing Project, last updated
    November 2015, http://www.sentencingproject.org/doc/publications/cc
    _Incarcerated_Women_Factsheet_Sep24sp.pdf.

12. "Easy Access to the Census of Juveniles in Residential Placement: 1997–2013,"
    US Department of Justice Office of Juvenile Justice and Delinquency Preven-
    tion, http://www.ojjdp.gov/ojstatbb/ezacjrp/asp/display.asp.

13. "Trends in U.S. Corrections," fact sheet, Sentencing Project, last updated
    December 2015, http://sentencingproject.org/doc/publications/inc_Trends_in
    _Corrections_Fact_sheet.pdf.

14. Richard E. Redding, "Juvenile Transfer Laws: An Effective Deterrent to De-
    linquency?" *Juvenile Justice Bulletin*, June 2010, https://www.ncjrs.gov/pdffiles1/
    ojjdp/220595.pdf.

15. Jason Ziedenberg, "You're an Adult Now: Youth in Adult Criminal Justice
    Systems," US Department of Justice National Institute of Corrections, Decem-
    ber 2011, http://static.nicic.gov/Library/025555.pdf.

16. "From George Washington to The States, 8 June 1783," Founders Online,
    National Archives, http://founders.archives.gov/documents/Washington
    /99-01-02-11404.

17. David J. Rothman, *The Discovery of the Asylum: Social Order and Disorder in the New Republic*, New Lines in Criminology, revised edition (New Brunswick, ME: Aldine Transaction, 2002), xxvii.

18. Ibid., xxviii.

19. Ibid., 59.

20. See Paul Butler, "Racially Based Jury Nullification: Black Power in the Criminal Justice System," *Yale Law Journal* 105 (December 1995): 677–715.

21. "... that inmates would not be hardened criminals but 'good boys gone bad,' who after a period of corrective training would go on their way, not to return again." In Norval Morris and David J. Rothman, eds., *The Oxford History of the Prison: The Practice of Punishment in Western Society* (New York: Oxford University Press, 1995). Kindle edition.

22. See William Cohen, "Negro Involuntary Servitude in the South, 1865–1940: A Preliminary Analysis," *Journal of Southern History* 42, no. 1 (1976): 31–60; Randall Kennedy, *Race, Crime, and the Law* (New York: Vintage, 2012). Kindle edition. "Vagrancy, the offense of a person not being able to prove at a given moment that he or she is employed, was a new and flimsy concoction dredged up from legal obscurity at the end of the nineteenth century by the state legislatures of Alabama and other southern states. It was capriciously enforced by local sheriffs and constables, adjudicated by mayors and notaries public, recorded haphazardly or not at all in court records, and, most tellingly in a time of massive unemployment among all southern men, was reserved almost exclusively for black men." In Blackmon, *Slavery by Another Name*, Kindle edition.

23. "Neither slavery nor involuntary servitude, except as a punishment for crime whereof the party shall have been duly convicted, shall exist within the United States, or any place subject to their jurisdiction." U.S. Const. amend XIII § 1.

24. Alan Blinder, "South Carolina City Takes Steps to Evict Homeless from Downtown," *New York Times*, August 25, 2013, http://www.nytimes.com/2013/08/26/us/south-carolina-city-takes-steps-to-evict-homeless-from-downtown.html.

25. Gustave de Beaumont and Alexis de Tocqueville, *On the Penitentiary System in the United States, And Its Application in France; With An Appendix on Penal Colonies, And Also, Statistical Notes* (Philadelphia: Carey, Lea, and Blanchard, 1833).

26. Ibid.

27. Dickens later caricatured these flaws in his 1844 novel *Martin Chuzzlewit*.

28. "This is not the republic I came to see; this is not the republic of my imagination. I infinitely prefer a liberal monarchy—even with its sickening accompaniments of court circulars—to such a government as this. The more I think of its youth and strength, the poorer and more trifling in a thousand aspects it appears in my eyes. In everything of which it has made a boast—excepting its

education of the people and its care for poor children—it sinks immeasurably below the level I had placed it upon; and England, even England, bad and faulty as the old land is, and miserable as millions of her people are, rises in the comparison." Charles Dickens, *The Letters of Charles Dickens: Vol. 1, 1833–1856* eds. Mamie Dickens and Georgina Hogarth (London: Chapman and Hall, 1880). Kindle edition.

29. Fred Kaplan, *Dickens: A Biography* (New York: Open Road Media, 2013). Kindle edition.

30. Ibid.

31. Charles Dickens, *American Notes for General Circulation*, ed. Patricia Ingham (New York: Penguin Classics, 2001). Kindle edition.

32. Ibid.

33. This assessment is based on a study commissioned by the New York Prison Association and conducted by Enoch Cobb Wines and Theodore Dwight. "Their critical finding was that not one of the state prisons in the United States was seeking the reformation of its inmates as a primary goal or deploying efficient means to pursue reformation. More specifically, their pages were filled with a litany of shortcomings. They criticized the inadequacies of the physical plants, the lack of training of the staffs, and the absence of centralized state supervision of the systems. They strenuously objected to the regular reliance on corporal punishment for disciplinary purposes. Six of the states they investigated employed the punishment of the lash; New York used the yoke—putting inmates into a contraption that consisted of a heavy flat bar of iron five or six feet long with a center ring for the neck and wrist manacles." Morris and Rothman, eds., *The Oxford History of the Prison*, Kindle edition.

34. Michael Ignatieff, "State, Civil Society, and Total Institutions: A Critique of Recent Social Histories of Punishment," *Crime and Justice* 3 (1981): 153–92.

35. This is not to ignore the rigorous intellectual contributions of radical prison intellectuals like George Jackson, Angela Davis, Mumia Abu-Jamal, and the Critical Resistance movement, to name a few. For a rigorous analysis of this tradition, see Dylan Rodriguez's book *Forced Passages: Imprisoned Radical Intellectuals and the U.S. Prison Regime* (Minneapolis: University of Minnesota Press, 2006); also see Joy James's volume *Imprisoned Intellectuals: America's Political Prisoners Write on Life, Liberation, and Rebellion* (New York: Rowman and Littlefield Press, 2003).

36. "Crime in the United States 2012," Federal Bureau of Investigation Criminal Justice Information Services, accessed April 4, 2016 https://www.fbi.gov/about-us/cjis/ucr/crime-in-the-u.s/2012/crime-in-the-u.s.-2012/violent-crime/violent-crime.

37. Richard Norton Smith, *On His Own Terms: A Life of Nelson Rockefeller* (New York: Random House, 2014). Kindle edition.

38. "Confined in the Tombs Prison until September 10, when the court finally

approved his petition for bail, he put the time to excellent use by writing a short, self-absolving autobiography." In David Levering Lewis, *W. E. B. Du Bois, 1919–1963: The Fight for Equality and the American Century* (New York: Henry Holt and Co., 2001). Kindle edition.

39. In Smith, *On His Own Terms*, Kindle edition.

40. Quoted in Bill Berkowitz, "Cover-Up of Slaughter at Attica Prison Continues Decades Later," *Buzzflash*, September 10, 2014, http://truth-out.org /buzzflash/commentary/remembering-attica-critical-information-about-the-bloodiest-one-day-encounter-between-americans-since-the-civil-war-remains-hidden.

41. "As corrections officer Frank Kline felt the knife blade slash his throat, twice, inflicting wounds that would require fifty-two stitches to repair, gunfire erupted from all corners of the facility (more than two thousand rounds, by later count)." In Smith, *On His Own Terms*, Kindle edition.

42. Peter B. Flint, "Russell Oswald, 82, Prison Chief in New York During Attica Siege," *New York Times*, March 11, 1991, http://www.nytimes.com/1991/03 /11/obituaries/russell-oswald-82-prison-chief-in-new-york-during-attica-siege.html.

43. "A doctor from Genesee Memorial Hospital saw 'an inmate with large wounds around his rectum which were not from gunshot,' which the doctor later heard were caused by a broken bottle, Meyer wrote. The doctor also said he was refused permission to take a brain-damaged inmate to the hospital and a day later saw prisoners with untreated broken bones." Associated Press, "New Report on Attica Prison Riot Reveals Inmates Were Beaten," *Wall Street Journal*, May 21, 2015, http://www.wsj.com/articles/AP14469b94645b4ff9b9c95a 727d958adc?cb=logged0.17842178035473266.

44. Michael Muhammad Knight, *The Five Percenters: Islam, Hip-hop and the Gods of New York* (London: Oneworld Publications, 2007).

45. Major prison unrest in the late 1920s in upstate New York prompted the state to build the "ultimate prison." In Marie Gottschalk, *The Prison and the Gallows: The Politics of Mass Incarceration in America*, Cambridge Studies in Criminology (New York: Cambridge University Press, 2006) Kindle edition.

46. "1971: The Attica Prison Uprising," Libcom.org, accessed October 25, 2015, http://libcom.org/history/1971-the-attica-prison-uprising.

47. A thirty-foot wall, broken by fourteen gun towers, surrounded the prison's fifty-three acres. Its 2,243 inmates, a majority of them black, were housed in five cell blocks, overseen by a correctional staff of 398, all but one of whom was white." Smith, *On His Own Terms*, Kindle edition.

48. Flint, "Russell Oswald, 82."

49. "Frank Smith, an inmate who helped lead the revolt, told the *Post-Standard* of Syracuse in 1991 that Mr. Mancusi had ordered him to iron his shirts and clean the bed linens his wife sent, and paid him with a box of cigarettes for Christmas."

Douglas Martin, "Vincent Mancusi, Warden at Attica During Riot, Dies at 98," *New York Times,* July 21, 2012, http://www.nytimes.com/2012/07/21/nyregion/vincent-r-mancusi-attica-warden-during-riots-dies-at-98.html?_r=0.

50. Flint, "Russell Oswald, 82."

51. Russell G. Oswald, *Attica—My Story* (New York: Doubleday Books, 1972).

52. Tribune News Services, "Survivors of Attica Prison Riots Getting Payout for Injuries," *Chicago Tribune,* December 3, 2000, http://articles.chicagotribune.com/2000-12-03/news/0012030497_1_attica-inmates-attica-uprising-thirty-two-inmates.

53. Smith, *On His Own Terms,* Kindle edition.

54. Douglas Lipton, Robert Martinson, and Judith Wilks, *Effectiveness of Correctional Treatment: A Survey of Treatment Evaluation Studies* (New York: Praeger, 1983).

55. James Q. Wilson, *Thinking About Crime* (New York: Basic Books, 1983), 151.

56. Vernellia R. Randall, "Violence as a Public Health Issue," *St. Louis University Public Law Review* 15 (1996): 191–235. Text available at http://academic.udayton.edu/health/05bioethics/slavery04.htm; Fox Butterfield, "Dispute Threatens U.S. Plan on Violence," *New York Times,* October 23, 1992, http://www.nytimes.com/1992/10/23/us/dispute-threatens-us-plan-on-violence.html.

57. "Here is what we believe: America is now home to thickening ranks of juvenile 'superpredators'—radically impulsive, brutally remorseless youngsters, including ever more preteenage boys, who murder, assault, rape, rob, burglarize, deal deadly drugs, join gun-toting gangs and create serious communal disorders. They do not fear the stigma of arrest, the pains of imprisonment, or the pangs of conscience." In William Bennett, John DiIulio, and John P. Walters, *Body Count: Moral Poverty—and How to Win America's War Against Crime and Drugs* (New York: Simon & Schuster, 1996).

58. See chapter 1, "Superpredators and Other Myths About Juvenile Delinquency," in James C. Howell's *Preventing and Reducing Juvenile Delinquency: A Comprehensive Framework* (Thousand Oaks, CA: SAGE Publications, 2009). The text of the chapter is available at http://www.sagepub.com/sites/default/files/upm-binaries/27206_1.pdf.

59. Elizabeth Becker, "As Ex-Theorist on Young 'Superpredators,' Bush Aide Has Regrets," *New York Times,* February 9, 2001, http://www.nytimes.com/2001/02/09/us/as-ex-theorist-on-young-superpredators-bush-aide-has-regrets.html.

60. James321, "Hillary Clinton: Gangs of Kids Are 'Super Predators' with 'No Conscience, No Empathy,'" *Daily Kos,* January 8, 2016, http://www.dailykos.com/story/2016/1/8/1467336/-Hillary-Clinton-Gangs-of-kids-are-super-predators-with-no-conscience-no-empathy.

61. Sam Roberts, "Jerome G. Miller, 83, Dies; Emptied Reformatories to Better Juvenile Justice," *New York Times,* August 15, 2015, http://www.nytimes.com/2015/08/16/us/jerome-g-miller-who-reshaped-juvenile-justice-dies-at-83.html.

62. Oliver Roeder, Lauren-Brooke Eisen, Julia Bowling, "What Caused the Crime Decline?" Brennan Center for Justice, February 12, 2015, https://www.brennancenter.org/publication/what-caused-crime-decline.

63. Dana Goldstein, "10 (Not Entirely Crazy) Theories Explaining the Great Crime Decline," Marshall Project, November 24, 2014, https://www.themarshallproject.org/2014/11/24/10-not-entirely-crazy-theories-explaining-the-great-crime-decline.

64. *Roper v. Simmons*, 543 U.S. 551 (2005), https://www.law.cornell.edu/supct/html/03-633.ZS.html.

65. "Crime in the United States 2013," Federal Bureau of Investigation Criminal Justice Information Services, https://www.fbi.gov/about-us/cjis/ucr/crime-in-the-u.s./2013/crime-in-the-u.s.-2013/tables/table-38/table_38_arrests_by_age_2013.xls.

66. "Since 1990, the prison population over the age of 50 has increased by 550 percent, to 144,500 inmates. In part because of this aging population, the state and federal prison systems now spend some $4 billion annually on health care." Dana Goldstein, "Too Old to Commit Crime?" Marshall Project, March 20, 2015, https://www.themarshallproject.org/2015/03/20/too-old-to-commit-crime; Carrie Abner, "Graying Prisons: States Face Challenges of an Aging Inmate Population," *State News*, November/December 2006, http://www.csg.org/knowledgecenter/docs/sn0611GrayingPrisons.pdf.

67. Among other sources, this conclusion was drawn by the American Friends Service Committee, *Struggle for Justice: A Report on Crime and Punishment in America* (New York: Farrar, Straus & Giroux, 1971); the Twentieth Century Fund, *Fair and Certain Punishment: Report of the Twentieth Century Fund Task Force on Criminal Sentencing* (New York: McGraw-Hill, 1976); and Andrew Von Hirsch, *Doing Justice*, final report of the Field Foundation Committee for the Study of Incarceration (New York: Hill and Wang, 1976).

68. Gottschalk, *The Prison and the Gallows*, Kindle edition; Edward M. Kennedy, "Introduction to Symposium on Sentencing," *Hofstra Law Review* 7, nos. 1–9 (1978): 1–3.

69. Some of these issues related to mass incarceration have started to be redressed at the end of the Obama Administration. Using his bully pulpit, President Obama publicly called for prison reform, began investigation on the use of solitary confinement, and called for the restoration of voting rights to convicted felons. In addition, in July 2015, Obama commuted the sentences of forty-six nonviolent drug offenders, the most issued by a sitting president in more than forty years. With regard to the Pell Grant, Obama initiated the Second Chance Pell Pilot Program, a three-to-five year program that restores Pell benefits to prisoners who are eligible for release within five years. These moves evince not only the liberal (though certainly not radical) politics of President Obama but also the shifting tone of the national conversation on prison reform. For a detailed analysis of Obama's politics and policies related to mass incarceration,

see Michael Eric Dyson's *The Black Presidency: Barack Obama and the Politics of Race in America* (New York: Houghton Mifflin Harcourt, 2016).

70. Nicholas Fandos, "Joe Biden's Role in '90s Crime Law Could Haunt Any Presidential Bid," *New York Times*, August 21, 2015, http://www.nytimes.com /2015/08/22/us/politics/joe-bidens-role-in-90s-crime-law-could-haunt-any-presidential-bid.html.

71. Mark W. Bennett, "How Mandatory Minimums Forced Me to Send More Than 1,000 Nonviolent Drug Offenders to Federal Prison," *Nation*, October 24, 2012, http://www.thenation.com/article/how-mandatory-minimums-forced-me-send-more-1000-nonviolent-drug-offenders-federal-pri/.

72. Lawrence Van Gelder, "James Earl Ray, 70, Killer of Dr. King, Dies in Nashville," *New York Times*, April 24, 1998, http://www.nytimes.com/1998/04/24 /us/james-earl-ray-70-killer-of-dr-king-dies-in-nashville.html?pagewanted= print.

73. "Prison Tours," Missouri State Penitentiary, accessed October 25, 2015 http:// www.missouripentours.com/tours.php.

74. Mark Slavit, "Runners Pretend to Have a Prison Break," KCRG TV, September 6, 2014, http://krcgtv.com/news/neighborhood/runners-pretend-to-have-a-prison-break?id=1093301.

75. Tom Robbins, "A Brutal Beating Wakes Attica's Ghosts," *New York Times*, February 28, 2015, http://www.nytimes.com/2015/03/01/nyregion/attica-prison-infamous-for-bloodshed-faces-a-reckoning-as-guards-go-on-trial.html.

76. Greg Bishop, "After Protests, Prison Firm Pulls Donation," *New York Times*, April 2, 2015, http://www.nytimes.com/2013/04/03/sports/ncaafootball/ stadium-wont-be-named-for-private-prison-company.html?ref=topics.

77. Jana Friedman, "Inmate Population by Facility for Fiscal Year 2015–2016," Florida Department of Corrections, accessed October 25, 2015, http://www .dc.state.fl.us/pub/pop/facility/index.html.

78. "What Is the PIC? What Is Abolition?" Critical Resistance, accessed May 13, 2016. http://criticalresistance.org/about/not-so-common-language/.

79. "Comprehensive Annual Financial Report: Fiscal Year Ended June 30," City of Susanville, accessed October 25, 2015, http://www.cityofsusanville.net/ wp-content/uploads/documents/finance/CityofSusanvilleCAFR2014Final.pdf.

80. Even the prison economy itself isn't protected by the corporate profit motive. As detailed in the film *Prison Town, USA* (dir. Katie Galloway and Po Kutchins (2007; Los Angeles, CA: Docurama Films, 2008), DVD), the area prisons are attempting to bypass local businesses in search of more cost-effective solutions.

81. "Comprehensive Annual Financial Report," City of Susanville.

82. Dr. E. Fuller Torrey, "Ronald Reagan's Shameful Legacy: Violence, the Homeless, Mental Illness," *Salon*, September 29, 2013, http://www.salon .com/2013/09/29/ronald_reagans_shameful_legacy_violence_the_homeless _mental_illness/.

83. E. Fuller Torrey, MD, et al., "The Treatment of Persons with Mental Illness in Prisons and Jails: A State Survey," Treatment Advocacy Center, April 8, 2014, http://www.tacreports.org/treatment-behind-bars.

84. Loïc Wacquant, *Punishing the Poor: The Neoliberal Government of Social Insecurity* (Durham, NC: Duke University Press, 2009).

85. "Number of Executions by State and Region Since 1976," Death Penalty Information Center, last updated April 28, 2016, http://www.deathpenaltyinfo .org/number-executions-state-and-region-1976.

86. Deborah Fins, "Death Row U.S.A.," quarterly report by the Criminal Justice Project, NAACP Legal Defense and Educational Fund, Inc., Spring 2015, http://www.deathpenaltyinfo.org/documents/DRUSASpring2015.pdf; "National Statistics on the Death Penalty and Race," Death Penalty Information Center, last updated April 28, 2016, http://www.deathpenaltyinfo.org/race-death-row-inmates-executed-1976?scid=5&did=184#racestat.

87. "Between 1642 and 1973, 344 juveniles were executed in the United States, and at least thirty-nine of these offenders were between the ages of ten and fifteen at the time of their capital crimes. In the modern era of death-penalty jurisprudence, beginning with the landmark 1972 decision of *Furman v. Georgia*, twenty-two juvenile offenders have been executed. Thus, from 1642 through February 2005, at least 366 juveniles were executed out of about 20,000 confirmed executions in United States history." "Death Penalty for Minors," USLegal.com, accessed April 4, 2016, http://deathpenalty.uslegal .com/minors/death-penalty-for-minors/.

88. "U.S. Executions Since 1976," Office of the Clark County Prosecuting Attorney, http://www.clarkprosecutor.org/html/death/usexecute.htm.

89. "Ruth Pelke," National Organization of Victims of Juvenile Murderers, accessed October 25, 2015, http://www.teenkillers.org/index.php/memorials/ indiana-victims/ruth-pelke/.

90. "Paula Cooper Case Records, 1986–1989," Indiana Historical Society, accessed October 25, 2015, http://www.indianahistory.org/our-collections/ collection-guides/paula-cooper-case-records-1986-1989.pdf.

91. David V. Baker, "Black Female Executions in Historical Context." *Criminal Justice Review* 33, no. 1 (2008): 64–88.

92. *Cooper v. State*, 540 N.E.2d 1216 (1989), http://www.leagle.com/decision /19891756540NE2d1216_11695.xml/COOPER%20v.%20STATE.

93. *Thompson v. Oklahoma*, 487 U.S. 815 (1988), https://www.law.cornell.edu/ supremecourt/text/487/815.

94. Amy Linn, "Freedom, Finally, After a Life in Prison," *New York Times*, August 21, 2015, http://www.nytimes.com/2015/08/23/opinion/sunday/freedom-finally-after-a-life-in-prison.html?ref=topics.

95. "Paula Cooper Memorial," Indiana Federal Community Defenders,

June 14, 2015, http://www.indianafederaldefender.org/about-us/press/
paula-cooper-memorial/.

96. Jill Disis and Tim Evans, "Paula Cooper, Once Youngest Indiana Death Row
Inmate, Found Dead," *Indianapolis Star*, May 28, 2015, http://www.indystar
.com/story/news/crime/2015/05/27/paula-cooper-youngest-indiana-death-
row-inmate-found-dead/27971461/.

VI. EMERGENCY

1. Associated Press, "Flint's Finances in Better Shape; No More Emergency
Managers," *Yahoo! News*, April 29, 2015, http://news.yahoo.com/flints-finances-
better-shape-no-195902208.html;_ylt=AwrC1C13sENVCBMA7zDQtDMD;
_ylu=X3oDMTByOHZyb21tBGNvbG8DYmYxBHBvcwMxBHZ0aWQD
BHNlYwNzcg—.

2. "An even bigger struggle was shaping up at virtually the same time in Flint,
a GM company town, where 80 percent of the families were dependent on
that firm." David Halberstam, *The Reckoning* (New York: Open Road Media,
2012). Kindle edition.

3. "Yet it is no longer primarily a car firm. GM is rather a vast agglomeration of
financial assets and liabilities with a small car-making operation on the side. It
makes more money from financial services than from car manufacturing." See
Patrick Hosking, "The Business—Patrick Hosking Junks General Motors," *New
Statesman*, January 31, 2005, http://www.newstatesman.com/node/161394.

4. "But GM's grandest 'fuck you' to Flint was the closing of Fisher One—the
plant where the Sit-Down Strike began in 1936. On December 10, 1987, the
sixty-four-year-old plant produced its last automobile. The next day, over
three thousand shoprats were out of work. More than one remarked on the
symbolism of GM's shutting down the birthplace of the UAW. Vizard, the
autoworker-turned-labor-reporter, saw it as the endgame of GM's half-century
war with the union, which had been fought one strike, one grievance, at a
time." Edward McClelland, *Nothin' But Blue Skies: The Heyday, Hard Times,
and Hopes of America's Industrial Heartland* (New York: Bloomsbury Publishing,
2013). Kindle edition.

5. "*Fahrenheit 9/11* (2004): Recruiting the Poor Part II," online video, 2:00,
posted by AnyClip, October 28, 2011, http://www.metacafe.com/watch/
an-G6m9uJ442hbJmm/fahrenheit_9_11_2004_recruiting_the_poor_part
_ii/. (Clip excerpted from *Fahrenheit 9/11*, directed by Michael Moore (2004;
Culver City, CA: Sony Pictures Home Entertainment, 2004), DVD.)

6. "Today, GM employment has fallen to about 7,200 at eight facilities including
Flint Assembly, Flint Metal Center, Flint Engine Operations and Flint North
American Tooling Center. The automaker's Customer Care and Aftersales is
headquartered in Grand Blanc and it has two processing centers in Genesee

County." Melissa Burden and Michael Wayland, "GM to Invest $877M in Flint Truck Plant," *Detroit News*, August 4, 2015, http://www.detroitnews.com /story/business/autos/general-motors/2015/08/04/gm-invest-flint-truck-plant /31095645/.

7. "Flint, MI, Unemployment Rate Report," Homefacts.com, accessed April 14, 2016, http://www.homefacts.com/unemployment/Michigan/Genesee-County /Flint.html.

8. Burden and Wayland, "GM to Invest $877M"; Farhad Manjoo, "A Plan in Case Robots Take the Jobs: Give Everyone a Paycheck," *New York Times*, March 2, 2016, http://www.nytimes.com/2016/03/03/technology/plan-to-fight-robot-invasion-at-work-give-everyone-a-paycheck.html?action=click& contentCollection=us&module=NextInCollection&region=Footer&pgtype= article&version=spotlight&rref=collection%2Fspotlight%2Fconversation -starters.

9. Kristin Longley," State Panel Reviewing Flint's Finances Asks for Up to 30 More Days," *Michigan Live*, November 4, 2011, http://www.mlive.com/news/ flint/index.ssf/2011/11/state_panel_reviewing_flints_f.html.

10. Kristin Longley, "Emergency Manager: Flint's Financial Problems 'Massive,'" *Michigan Live*, January 12, 2012, http://www.mlive.com/news/flint/index.ssf /2012/01/emergency_manager_flints_finan.html.

11. Evan Osnos, "The Crisis in Flint Goes Deeper than the Water," *New Yorker*, January 20, 2016, http://www.newyorker.com/news/news-desk/ the-crisis-in-flint-goes-deeper-than-the-water.

12. Chris Lewis, "Does Michigan's Emergency-Manager Law Disenfranchise Black Citizens?" *Atlantic*, May 9, 2013, http://www.theatlantic.com/politics /archive/2013/05/does-michigans-emergency-manager-law-disenfranchise-black-citizens/275639/.

13. "With Detroit Under an Emergency Manager, Half of Michigan Blacks Will Have No Elected Local Government," *Eclectablog*, February 20, 2013, http:// www.eclectablog.com/2013/02/with-detroit-under-an-emergency-financial-manager-half-of-michigan-blacks-will-have-no-elected-local-government .html.

14. Ron Fonger, "Detroit Gives Notice: It's Terminating Water Contract Covering Flint, Genesee County in One Year," *Michigan Live*, April 19, 2013, http:// www.mlive.com/news/flint/index.ssf/2013/04/detroit_gives_notice_its _termi.html.

15. Monica Davey and Mary Williams Walsh, "Billions in Debt, Detroit Tumbles Into Insolvency," *New York Times*, July 18, 2013, http://www.nytimes.com /2013/07/19/us/detroit-files-for-bankruptcy.html?pagewanted=all&_r=0.

16. Josh Sanburn, "The Poisoning of an American City," *Time*, January 21, 2016, http://time.com/4188328/the-poisoning-of-an-american-city/.

17. "The future of Flint's water supply is in the hands of the state, and the man

appointed to fix the city's finances has advised breaking off ties with Detroit, its current water supplier." In Ron Fonger, "Flint Emergency Manager Endorses Water Pipeline, Final Decision Rests with State of Michigan," *Michigan Live*, March 29, 2013, http://www.mlive.com/news/flint/index.ssf/2013/03/flint_emergency_manager_endors.html.

18. "KWA officials have said they can build a new water pipeline to Lake Huron for $274 million and produce water far cheaper than continuing to buy from Detroit. Kurtz has said the city could save at least $4 million annually with the potential for even greater savings in the future." Ibid.

19. Jennifer Dixon, "How Flint's Water Crisis Unfolded," *Detroit Free Press*, accessed April 16, 2016, http://www.freep.com/pages/interactives/flint-water-crisis-timeline/.

20. Michael Torrice, "How Lead Ended Up in Flint's Tap Water," *Chemical and Engineering News*, February 11, 2016, http://cen.acs.org/articles/94/i7/Lead-Ended-Flints-Tap-Water.html.

21. Ron Fonger, "Ex-emergency Manager Says He's Not to Blame for Flint River Water Switch," *Michigan Live*, October 13, 2015, http://www.mlive.com/news/flint/index.ssf/2015/10/ex_emergency_manager_earley_sa.html.

22. "The Flint River contains chlorides (some of which likely come from road salt), but the water does not pose direct threats to fish, wildlife or people who use the river. Chlorides cause problems in drinking water mainly because they corrode metal in the pipes and plumbing fixtures that transport water into homes." "The Flint: A Good River with a Bad Reputation," Charles Stewart Mott Foundation, December 2, 2015, http://www.mott.org/news/news/2015/20151202-Flint-River-Article.

23. Torrice, "How Lead Ended Up."

24. Ron Fonger, "General Motors Shutting Off Flint River Water at Engine Plant Over Corrosion Worries," *Michigan Live*, October 13, 2014, http://www.mlive.com/news/flint/index.ssf/2014/10/general_motors_wont_use_flint.html.

25. Associated Press, "Flint Addressing Byproduct in Drinking Water," *Detroit News*, January 7, 2015, http://www.detroitnews.com/story/news/local/michigan/2015/01/07/flint-addressing-byproduct-drinking-water/21378731/.

26. "Events That Led to Flint's Water Crisis," *New York Times*, accessed April 16, 2016, http://www.nytimes.com/interactive/2016/01/21/us/flint-lead-water-timeline.html.

27. Julia Lurie, "Meet the Mom Who Helped Expose Flint's Toxic Water Nightmare," January 21, 2016, http://www.motherjones.com/politics/2016/01/mother-exposed-flint-lead-contamination-water-crisis.

28. "When Virginia Tech researchers tested the water in LeeAnne Walters's home in Flint, Mich., this past summer, one sample had lead levels that reached a staggering 13,200 parts per billion." In Torrice, "How Lead Ended Up."

29. Associated Press, "Doctors Urge Flint to Stop Using Water From Flint River,"

September 28, 2015, http://www.crainsdetroit.com/article/20150928/
NEWS01/150929872/doctors-urge-flint-to-stop-using-water-from-flint-river.

30. Kristi Tanner, "All Flint's Children Must Be Treated as Exposed to Lead,"
Detroit Free Press, January 16, 2016, http://www.freep.com/story/opinion
/contributors/raw-data/2016/01/16/map-8657-flints-youngest-children-
exposed-lead/78818888/.

31. Chad Livengood, "Flint Mayor: Water Fix Could Cost As Much As $1.5B,"
Detroit News, January 8, 2016, http://www.detroitnews.com/story/news
/politics/2016/01/07/flint-water/78404218/.

32. "Neuropsychological Effects of Lead Poisoning," Mount Washington Pedi-
atric Hospital, accessed April 16, 2016, http://www.mwph.org/programs/
lead-treatment/effects.

33. "About 20,000 properties among the city's 56,000 total are vacant or blighted, many
of them foreclosed for failure to pay property taxes." In Monica Davey, "As Aid
Floods Into Flint, a Fix Remains Far Off," *New York Times*, March 6, 2016, http://
www.nytimes.com/2016/03/06/us/as-aid-floods-into-flint-a-fix-remains-far-off
.html.

34. Dominic Adams, "Flint Tallies Nation's Highest Arson Rate—But Has Just
One Full-time Arson Investigator," *Michigan Live*, April 1, 2013, http://www
.mlive.com/news/flint/index.ssf/2013/04/flint_tallies_nations_highest.html.

35. Gary Ridley, "Arson: Blue-collar America Is Burning," *Michigan Live*, April
8, 2013, http://www.mlive.com/news/flint/index.ssf/2013/04/flint_not_the
_only_blue-collar.html.

36. Dominic Adams, "87-year-old Woman Raped, Robbed, Beaten While Bringing in Groceries," *Michigan Live*, October 15, 2012, http://www.mlive.com/
news/flint/index.ssf/2012/10/87-year-old_woman_raped_robbed.html.

37. Associated Press, "12-year-old Boy Victim of Fatal Shooting in Flint," *Detroit
Free Press*, March 14, 2015, http://www.freep.com/story/news/local/michigan
/2015/03/14/flint-boy-shooting-killed/24760101/.

38. David Harris, "Flint Most Violent City in the Nation for Third Year Running
in 2012, According to FBI Statistics," *Michigan Live*, June 4, 2013, http://www
.mlive.com/news/flint/index.ssf/2013/06/flint_most_violent_city_in_the
.html.

39. David Harris, "Flint No Longer Most Violent City in America, According to
New FBI Crime Stats," *Michigan Live*, February 19, 2014, http://www.mlive
.com/news/flint/index.ssf/2014/02/flint_loses_the_title_of_fbis.html.

40. Scott Paulson, "Most Dangerous Cities in the United States 2014:
FBI," *Examiner*, February 6, 2014, http://www.examiner.com/article/
most-dangerous-cities-2014-fbi.

41. "Crime in America 2015: Top 10 Most Dangerous Cities Under 200,000,"
Law Street, accessed April 16, 2016, http://lawstreetmedia.com/crime-
america-2015-top-10-dangerous-cities-200000/.

42. Steve Carmody, "Flint Schools Ponder Future of Unused Former Schools," Michigan Radio, September 1, 2015, http://michiganradio.org/post/ flint-schools-ponder-future-unused-former-schools.

43. Sarah Schuch, "Hugs, Tears and Goodbyes Punctuate Last Day for Three Closing Flint Schools," *Michigan Live*, June 11, 2015, http://www.mlive.com/ news/flint/index.ssf/2015/06/hugs_tears_and_good-byes_part.html.

44. Blake Thorne, "Flint Central High School Alumni Group Will Host Final Banquet," *Michigan Live*, May 16, 2012, http://www.mlive.com/news/flint/ index.ssf/2012/05/flint_central_high_school_alum_1.html.

45. Eric Dresden, "Kroger Closing Davison Road Store in Flint," *Michigan Live*, March 4, 2015, http://www.mlive.com/news/flint/index.ssf/2015/03/kroger _closing_davison_road_at.html.

46. Eric Dresden, "Closings of Pierson Road Meijer, Kroger Have Neighbors Concerned About Where They'll Get Food," *Michigan Live*, February 25, 2015, http://www.mlive.com/news/flint/index.ssf/2015/02/pierson_road _meijer_kroger_sup.html#incart_story_package.

47. Ron Fonger, "Kroger Says It's Closing Pierson Road Store in Flint," *Michigan Live*, July 8, 2014, http://www.mlive.com/news/flint/index.ssf/2014/07/ kroger_says_its_closing_pierso.html.

48. Susan Selasky, "Bus Program Helps Flint Residents Get Rides to Groceries," *Detroit Free Press*, February 4, 2016, http://www.freep.com/story/life/2016/02 /04/flint-water-crisis-bus-groceries/79809556/.

49. "Foods rich in calcium, vitamin C, and iron can help mitigate the effects of lead exposure. But many Flint residents don't have easy access to fresh fruits and vegetables." In Steve Carmody, "Mobile Food Banks to Deliver Fresh Produce to Flint Pantries," Michigan Radio, February 24, 2016, http:// michiganradio.org/post/mobile-food-banks-deliver-fresh-produce-flint- pantries#stream/0.

50. Sherry Fogle, "Food Deserts: Lack of Access to Food Stores Growing Concern Across S.C.," *Times and Democrat*, September 30, 2012, http://thetandd.com/ business/food-deserts-lack-of-access-to-food-stores-growing-concern/article _6f12f870-09be-11e2-910f-001a4bcf887a.html.

51. "South Bronx Supermarket Shortage Leaves Minorities Starved For Healthy Food," News One, accessed April 16, 2016, http://newsone.com/269697/ south-bronx-supermarket-shortage-keeps-healthy-food-away-from-blacks- and-latinos/.

52. Sabrina Tavernise, "Trying to Overcome the Stubborn Blight of Vacancies," *New York Times*, December 19, 2010, http://www.nytimes.com/2010/12/20/us /20youngstown.html?_r=1.

53. Hoag Levins, "A Photo History of RCA's Golden Years in Camden," HistoricCamdenCounty.com, March 2009, http://historiccamdencounty .com/ccnews138.shtml.

54. Chris Hedges, "City of Ruins," *Nation*, November 4, 2010, http://www.the nation.com/article/city-ruins/.

55. "Welcome to the Camden County MUA," Camden County Municipal Utilities Authority, September 24, 2010, http://www.ccmua.org/.

56. "Port of Camden," Ports America, accessed April 16, 2016, https://www .portsamerica.com/portofcamden-new-jersey.html.

57. "The collection of metal is weighed at the booth. This morning four men wait to see how much they will collect for the day's haul. Camden produces one million tons of scrap a year. Its huge shredding machines in the port can chop up automobiles and stoves into chunks the size of a baseball. Ships from Turkey, China, and India pull into the port, fill their holds with the scrap, and take it back to smelters. The scrap industry literally cannibalizes the city." In Chris Hedges and Joe Sacco, *Days of Destruction, Days of Revolt* (New York: Nation Books, 2014). Kindle edition.

58. "'We Don't Have Any Real Policing in Camden. They're Just Out Here to Pick Up the Bodies': Inside America's Most Dangerous City," *Daily Mail*, December 10, 2011, http://www.dailymail.co.uk/news/article-2072410/ Inside-Americas-dangerous-city-Camden-New-Jersey.html.

59. Greg Adomaitis, "Stopping Scrap Metal Theft Takes N.J. Assembly, Police, Purchaser Policies," *NJ.com*, February 7, 2015, http://www.nj.com/south/index. ssf/2015/02/eyes_on_nj_scrap_metal_theft_and_sales_include_ass.html.

60. Associated Press, "Elevated Lead Levels Found in Newark Schools' Drinking Water," *New York Times*, March 9, 2016, http://www.nytimes.com/2016/03/10/ nyregion/elevated-lead-levels-found-in-newark-schools-drinking-water.html.

61. Derick Waller, "Cleveland Children at Greatest Risk of Lead Poisoning in Ohio," Newsnet 5, January 29, 2016, http://www.newsnet5.com/news/ local-news/oh-cuyahoga/ cleveland-children-at-greatest-risk-of-lead-poisoning-in-ohio.

62. Yanan Wang, "Untold Cities Across America Have Higher Rates of Lead Poisoning than Flint," *Washington Post*, February 4, 2016, https:// www.washingtonpost.com/news/morning-mix/wp/2016/02/04/ untold-cities-across-america-have-higher-rates-of-lead-poisoning-than-flint/.

63. Dwight Ott and Melanie Burney, "High Lead Found in Camden District," *Philadelphia Inquirer*, August 11, 2002, http://articles.philly.com/2002-08-11/ news/25337441_1_bottled-water-drinking-water-school-buildings.

64. This point is underscored by Michael Eric Dyson, who examines the ways that the natural disaster of Hurricane Katrina was only the most prominent example of the exploitation and erasure of New Orleans's Black poor in *Come Hell or High Water: Hurricane Katrina and the Color of Disaster* (New York: Basic Civitas Books, 2006).

65. The term "Gilded Age," coined by Mark Twain, refers to the time period between 1870 and 1900, in which the United States witnessed rapid economic growth, industrialization, expansion of labor unions, and large amounts of

immigration. Of course, this era was also marked by gross wealth inequality and the maintenance of a racial apartheid state that denied Blacks access to the spoils of the moment of ostensible prosperity.

66. Jackson Lears, *Rebirth of a Nation: The Making of Modern America, 1877–1920* (New York: HarperCollins, 2009). Kindle edition.

67. Thomas Piketty, *Capital in the Twenty-First Century* (Cambridge, MA: Harvard University Press, 2014). Kindle edition.

68. Paul Krugman, *The Conscience of a Liberal* (New York: W. W. Norton & Company, 2009). Kindle edition.

69. Robert J. Gordon, *The Rise and Fall of American Growth: The U.S. Standard of Living Since the Civil War*, The Princeton Economic History of the Western World (Princeton, NJ: Princeton University Press, 2016). Kindle edition.

70. ". . . the heroism of the boys in blue (and gray) with their venal descendants in a 'Gilded Age.' The term was Mark Twain's and Charles Dudley Warner's, the title of their novel of 1873, and it came to characterize the epoch for many Americans, then and since." In Lears, *Rebirth of a Nation*, Kindle edition.

71. Matthew Josephson, *The Robber Barons* (New York: Mariner Books, 2015). Kindle edition.

72. Emma Roller, "Time to Talk Robots," op-ed, *New York Times*, January 5, 2016, http://www.nytimes.com/2016/01/05/opinion/campaign-stops/time-to-talk-robots.html.

73. Steven Rattner, "The Myth of Industrial Rebound," op-ed, *New York Times*, January 25, 2014, http://www.nytimes.com/2014/01/26/opinion/sunday/rattner-the-myth-of-industrial-rebound.html.

74. Ibid.

75. See Elise Gould and Heidi Shierholz, "The Compensation Penalty of 'Right to Work' Laws," *Economic Policy Institute Briefing Paper 299*, February 17, 2011, http://www.epi.org/publication/bp299/.

76. Monica Davey, "Limits on Unions Pass in Michigan, Once a Mainstay," *New York Times*, December 11, 2012, http://www.nytimes.com/2012/12/12/us/protesters-rally-over-michigan-union-limits-plan.html.

77. Elizabeth Hartfield, "Michigan Governor Signs Right to Work Bill Into Law," ABC News, December 11, 2012, http://abcnews.go.com/Politics/michigan-governor-signs-work-bill-law/story?id=17934332.

78. Sean Hackbarth, "Wisconsin Becomes 25th Right-to-Work State" *Above the Fold*, March 9, 2015, https://www.uschamber.com/above-the-fold/wisconsin-becomes-25th-right-work-state.

79. "West Virginia Becomes 26th Right-to-Work State," *National Law Review*, February 18, 2016, http://www.natlawreview.com/article/west-virginia-becomes-26th-right-to-work-state.

80. Linda Greenhouse, "A Chief Justice Without a Friend," op-ed, *New York*

Times, October 1, 2015, http://www.nytimes.com/2015/10/01/opinion/a-chief-justice-without-a-friend.html.

81. Matt A. V. Chaban, "An Altar to Donald Trump Swallows Up Public Space in Manhattan," *New York Times*, July 13, 2015, http://www.nytimes.com/2015/07/14/nyregion/an-altar-to-donald-trump-swallows-up-public-space-in-manhattan.html.

82. Quoted in Callum Borchers, "Donald Trump Hasn't Changed One Bit Since His First Media Feud in 1980," *Washington Post*, March 18, 2016, https://www.washingtonpost.com/news/the-fix/wp/2016/03/18/donald-trumps-first-media-controversy-is-a-really-great-story-just-a-really-fabulous-story/.

83. Chaban, "An Altar to Donald Trump."

84. Lisa W. Foderaro, "Privately Owned Park, Open to the Public, May Make Its Own Rules," *New York Times*, October 13, 2011, http://www.nytimes.com/2011/10/14/nyregion/zuccotti-park-is-privately-owned-but-open-to-the-public.html.

85. "J. Seward Johnson, 'Double Check,'" blog post, *Art Nerd New York*, October 25, 2010, http://artnerdnewyork.tumblr.com/post/1401544910/j-seward-johnson-double-check.

86. Nash Jenkins, "Marcy Borders, the Dust-Covered Woman in the Iconic 9/11 Photograph, Has Died of Cancer," *Time*, August 26, 2015, http://time.com/4010936/911-dust-woman-photograph-marcy-borders/.

87. Jenni Ryall, "Woman From Famous 9/11 'Dust Lady' Photograph Dies of Cancer," *Mashable*, August 26, 2015, http://mashable.com/2015/08/26/dust-lady-dies/#ySRMx.Egk5qT.

88. "AFP Photographers Recount 9/11: 'The Dust Lady' and the Man in the Lucky Suit," Facebook note, September 9, 2011, https://www.facebook.com/notes/afp-news-agency-agence-france-presse/afp-photographers-recount-911-the-dust-lady-and-the-man-in-the-lucky-suit/217467481640245.

89. Jonathan Lin, "9/11 'Dust Lady' Marcy Borders Dies after Battle with Stomach Cancer," *NJ.com*, August 25, 2015, http://www.nj.com/hudson/index.ssf/2015/08/911_dust_lady_marcy_borders_dies_after_battle_with.html.

90. Mattathias Schwartz, "Pre-Occupied," *New Yorker*, November 28, 2011, http://www.newyorker.com/magazine/2011/11/28/pre-occupied.

91. Ron Bieber, "Privatization Doesn't Work," *Detroit News*, March 9, 2016, http://www.detroitnews.com/story/opinion/2016/03/09/labor-voices-bieber-privatization/81499432/.

92. Henry Giroux, "Poisoned City: Flint and the Specter of Domestic Terrorism," *Truthout*, March 3, 2016, http://www.truth-out.org/news/item/35080-poisoned-city-flint-and-the-specter-of-domestic-terrorism.

Index